Red
Devils

Emilia, My Mother from Ukraine

Anatoly (Tony) Kandiew

Order this book online at www.trafford.com
or email orders@trafford.com

Most Trafford titles are also available at major online book retailers.

Print information available on the last page.

ISBN: 978-1-4907-4301-1 (sc)
ISBN: 978-1-4907-4302-8 (hc)

Library of Congress Control Number: 2014914045

Trafford rev. 01/21/2016

 www.trafford.com

North America & international
toll-free: 1 888 232 4444 (USA & Canada)
fax: 812 355 4082

CONTENTS

Dedication

This book is dedicated to my mother Emilia; who had the courage to resist Soviet tyranny, who had the determination to survive and save her children, who dedicated her energy to help humanity, for it was indeed a very difficult time.

This book is also dedicated to my wife Marinella; who encouraged me to write this book, who insisted I describe the real history, who was eager to understand the brainwashing of America, for the Truth Will Set America Free.

Many thanks to Paula Sullivan O'Brien, Ph.D.; who helped editing this book, who took an interest in this book, who made many wonderful comments, for it was a massive task.

Anatoly Kandiew

Introduction

This story was meant to be a "near autobiography" of a young boy age 5 to 12 during a horrible period of our time -- World War II and the direct aftermath. The events in the book were witnessed by me or are firsthand accounts of one form or another. However, some important characters in the book are not described; therefore, I have included them in the PROLOGUE.

In addition, many other events have not been described by me such as the "Candy Bombers'" and other events due to their political overtones. Let me explain.

Time line: June 24, 1948. When Sir Winston Churchill started the "Cold War" -- with his infamous 'Iron Curtain Speech' in 1946 -- Berlin was singled out to be economically "strangled" by the Soviets in retaliation. (It took them nearly two years to come up with a response.) They closed all access roads to Berlin and planned to starve the Berliners -- to teach the West a lesson. As always, Russia or their rulers know only one way to rule: by terror. This method they acquired from the Tartars, who ruled Moscow from 1240 to 1610. Ultimately, Catherine II conquered them in the Crimea in 1787.

But, America came to the rescue with an all-out airlift, flying in everything needed for the Berliner's survival: food, coal, medicine and so on. To the youngsters of Berlin, this was a 'miracle.' And it became practically a sacred duty to go to Tempelhof Airport and watch the American armada fly-in the supplies. American pilots spotted the boys and girls on their flight path and almost from the beginning the pilots started to drop little parachutes with a variety of candy, chewing gum and small chocolate bars in them. This was truly a miracle. I don't recall having seen a chocolate bar until then, never mind having one!

When the Berlin Airlift began in 1948, our gang (kids from our street) decided to make the pilgrimage to Tempelhof Airport, watch the candy bombers and collect their "dropping." When we arrived, there was a huge mob of kids. They had positioned themselves along the flight path and stood their ground. Sure enough each time a plane approached, it unloaded a heap of little parachutes all along their flight path. Thousands upon thousands (so it seemed) of little parachutes were slowly drifting to the ground, and the kids would break their cluster and dash toward a parachute. Amazingly, there were so many parachutes that each kid got at least one.

Still, for me it was an ordeal to go to Tempelhof, and I went only once. I would not tell my mother about it for fear that I would be grounded for a month or so. Basically, I was not allowed to stray too far from our residence. But, let me tell you -- the candy bombers were a big hit in Berlin...

Eventually, word got to the kids from East Berlin. They wrote letters to the "Candy Bombers" begging them to fly by in East Berlin. And, believe it or not, after some intense negotiations with the Soviets, the Americans were allowed to fly over the East Sector of Berlin and shower the kids with "bombs."

Very few people know about the lovable and heroic Candy Bombers. In my opinion this is very sad. They should be applauded, praised and advertised to the whole world. Let me assure you that to the Berliners, they will be remembered forever or at least as long as the city exists...

Time line: January 10, 1945. Berlin was overrun by Germans escaping the Soviet advance. The new wave of refugees told terrible tales of Soviet brutality. They were all hoping that Berlin would be the last stand of the Aryan race. If it was not, doom and gloom awaited the German people. First, every female from 6 to 66 would be raped and brutalized. Then the men would be castrated and brutalized. Then, all of them would be herded into cattle cars and dispatched to Kamchatka -- a remote corner in Siberia. There, the German nation would perish in the Soviet labor camps...

We knew that these rumors were not imaginary, the Soviets were tormenting the German minds of the atrocities they had committed in the Soviet Union. And now, payback time was closing in on them…

[As it turned out, Stalin changed his emphasis when Berlin was captured. His anger was redirected at the survivors of the former Soviet citizens and not the Germans. But who could predict Stalin's thinking?]

We decided to escape during this chaos from Berlin and go to Hamburg or Frankfurt or Nurnberg or Munich. We were more afraid of the 'red devils' than anyone else -- in Berlin.

A few days before, we prepared our suitcases and knapsacks. I had my Ranzen (backpack) and a small suitcase. My mother was about 8 months pregnant. She prepared a knapsack with emergency clothing: diapers, small blankets and some baby clothing. We decided not to give up our apartment for fear that we might not succeed. We locked up our apartment and sneaked out at night, undetected -- to the subway. The subway took us to the Autobahn, and there we hoped to hitch a truck which would take us to safety. I was not familiar with the subway that took us to the Autobahn, but George and my mother were. After a few changes, we ended up at the desired spot. We "parked" our baggage in one spot, and George took charge of us while my mother started searching for a truck.

After a while, she came back. She found a kind driver who was willing to take us to Hamburg. We took our baggage and piled into the truck. No sooner had we settled down when Grandma turned pale. Mother came to her rescue. The next thing I knew Grandma and mother, with her knapsack in one hand and Grandma in the other, climbed out of the truck and disappeared. A little while later, they were back. They climbed into the truck and sat down. A few minutes later, the story repeated itself. So out they went. Now the driver was getting annoyed. He came over to us and told us to get out since he had to leave and we were only holding him up. We got out. By then, mother and Grandma had returned. Mother was out of diapers while Grandma had the runs. So, we returned to our fortress…

Time line: May 4, 1945. The Soviets had surrounded Berlin and were taking over the suburbs house by house, street by street. We were in the inner center, surrounded by the river Spree. For us, the Soviets seemed still far away. My mother needed to see a friend of hers -- Elvira's mother.

They lived only a block away from us -- also in the inner circle. So, she took some things and was on her way. She came back hours later. When I asked her what happened, she explained, "As I reached their house I saw four soldiers lying on the ground right next to the building's entrance. I went over to them. They were Soviets and heavily wounded. Two were unconscious and two delirious. I rushed into the house, got two men and a heavy duty blanket, and then rushed back to the wounded soldiers. We took them into the apartment. Then I told Eva (Elvira's mother) to boil some water, and get four mattresses and linen. Then I cleaned the soldiers, performed first aid and bandaged them. When everything was done, I put Eva in charge and went home. That's why I am so late."

A few days later, the war was over. After we had been 'forcibly' registered, my mother had to see Eva again. She left, and after a long time she returned with a huge cart, dragged by two Soviet soldiers. They unloaded a "warehouse" full of merchandise: flour, sugar, potatoes by the sack, loads of bacon, butter and so much more. When they were done, they talked to my mother; and the next thing I heard was "piano." The two men disappeared with the cart and came back a little while later with a piano. They shlepped it to our apartment, talked to my mother and left. (The piano became my nemesis. Somehow Emilia wanted me to become a pianist -- to my dismay!)

Again I asked my mother what happened. She started: "You will not believe this. But, here it is: When I arrived at Eva's apartment there was a guard by her door. When I tried to get in, he asked for my papers and whom I was going to see. I told him my friend Eva. He took me inside, got Eva and asked, 'Is this she?' When Eva acknowledged, he turned to me and said, 'Come with me.' So, we left and I followed. He took me to an elegant building on the river Spree. It was a headquarters of sorts. We walked in and he announced, "Here she is!"

"Then I was led to a room. Inside was a commander -- I could not tell his rank -- but, he was smiling at me. "We were looking for you," he started. "I want to express my thanks for saving my soldiers. You've done a good job. How did you know how to make the cap of Monomach (a type of head bandage)?" he asked. I told him that I was from East Prussia, there I attended medical school and I was fluent in German and Russian. "Well," he continued "in that case I'll give you a cow, and a horse and wagon. I will load up the wagon for you with provisions, and then you can return home -- I'll even throw in a piano!"

"I did not know what to say. I had to extricate myself. So, I started: "I left many years ago. Now I have a family in Berlin, they would not appreciate the countryside after living in a big city. Thanks, but no thanks." It was amazing, he seemed to understand. He started:

"In that case, let me fill up a cart with the provisions you need and have my men take it over to your place. Good luck to you and again thank you for saving my men…"

****

Concordats

A concordat is the agreement between a country and the Papacy -- in perpetuity (forever). Today this seems to be insignificant but before World War II or more specifically, before the Nuremberg trials, the Pope was the most powerful person on earth.

Therefore, to understand European continental history, it is important to understand the underlying concordats. Once you understand the concordats, Western European history becomes nearly self-evident.

The first and most important concordat is the "German Concordat," in 800 AD between the Patriarch of Rome (Hadrian) and Charlemagne. The Patriarch promoted himself to Pope and leader of Christendom and promoted Charlemagne to be the Emperor of the Holy Roman Empire. The agreement was that Charlemagne and his descendants would protect the Pope and in return the descendants of Charlemagne were entitled to rule in Western Europe whenever the native dynasty died out -- also in perpetuity. In this way, by 1848, all of Western Europe was ruled by Germans. Even in England, the Germans ruled. (Who does not remember the antics of Harry the Nazi?). The only country escaping the German rule was Switzerland (It is said the Templars rule there).

Russia was ruled by Germans for a different reason. Peter the Great intended to take over the Holy Roman Empire. Leibnitz advised Peter to marry into the ruling German family – the Hohenstaufen. (And, starting with Catherine the Great, Germans ruled in Russia. And, every future Czar had to marry into the Hohenstaufen line. That is why Czar Nicholas II, Kaiser Wilhelm and King George V not only looked alike but looked nearly identical!)

However, just because a country was ruled by Germans does not mean they were sympathetic to the German cause: such as in World War I and World War II.

Occasionally, Papal will was not enforced: as for example with the reconquest of England and return to the Roman faith after Henry VIII broke away from Catholicism, despite the fact that the Papacy posted a bounty for England's reconquest and conversion. The bounty was 2 million Ducats. Naturally, some European rulers tried to collect it: Philip II, Napoleon and Hitler. But all failed.

Finally, the creation of the Holy Roman Empire was made in great haste, and all titles of the Roman Emperor were bestowed on the new Emperor, including the title of Pontifex Maximus. Julius Caesar was "Pontifex Maximus" as was every Roman Emperor thereafter. However, after some 200 years, the Pope decided that the title had to be taken away from the emperor (because it could be sold at a high price) -- and a battle ensued between the Pope and the Emperor called "investiture." And, the Pope won. Thus the German concordat dictates the rule in WesternEurope. Armed with that knowledge, European history is much easier to understand.

The next most important concordat is called the French concordat. It was made between Francis I and the Pope Ferdinand in Bologna in 1521. Francis I offered to pay an annual stipend to the Papacy in perpetuity in exchange for nominating French Bishops by the rulers of France, also in perpetuity.

This spawned French nationalism. This is why Napoleon could recruit Frenchmen and instill in them national pride. (At that time, nationalism was a non-existent entity. Families ruled in Europe: Habsburgs, Hohenstaufen, Hohenzollern and so on.)

****

The next most important concordat is called the Italian concordat between Benito Mussolini and the Pope in 1926.

Benito Mussolini found a solution to accommodate the Pope and the Italian state by creating the Vatican.

Napoleon partitioned Italy into regions which he could easily rule and manipulate. When Napoleon fell, Italian leaders realized that the days of city-states was over and a unified Italian state was needed. Thus, people like Cavour and Garibaldi started a national movement. But in the center of Italy was the Church-State run by the Pope. This state was simply taken over by the nationalists in 1865. Of course the Pope called on his protectors (The Habsburgs) to help him. They came to his aid but were defeated. So, now there was a Pope without a state! Thus, the Pope locked himself up in the Basilica and refused to serve Christendom. Mussolini solved the problem by creating the enclave called "The Vatican." It took many years before the many pieces of today's Italy were integrated into one nation. Venice and Lombardy were the last regions to be integrated.

To this day, a grateful nation keeps Mussolini descendants in political office. And, so the dealings of our forefathers go on and on…

****

Rapallo-land.

Rapallo is a small town in Italy. Starting in 1923 and until 1926, many treaties were negotiated and ratified there, in particular the treaty between Germany and the Soviet Union.

After Germany's defeat in World War I and the ensuing treaty of Versailles in 1919, Germany was not allowed to maintain a normal military (It was limited to 100,000 soldiers.), and Germany was forbidden to develop weapons of war: rifles, tanks, airplanes, U-boats and so on. Allied inspectors roamed throughout Germany, reported any and all violations and punished the perpetrators. Therefore, a viable alterative needed to be found -- far away from the prying eyes of the Allied inspectors. The German military began planning for a "REVANCHE" as early as 1922! They approached the Soviet Union, they found a receptive ear and met in Rapallo to discuss terms.

The Germans needed land far away from the Allied inspectors and, in exchange, they promised to share their technology. To keep everything "open" between them, they agreed to have their premises inspected by Soviet scientists and weapons specialists -- both in the area given to them in the Soviet Union and in Germany -- mainly to Porsche and his facilities. Thus, the plans were developed in secret in Germany by men like Porsche and implemented in the Soviet Union. The man in charge in the Soviet Union was Heinz Guderian. The principal area was near Kazan and a few other locations. Each area was fenced off and patrolled by Germans in Soviet uniforms. Whenever a German died accidentally, his remains were crated and shipped to Germany labeled "Defective Machine Parts."

Naturally the entire operation was top secret, and only a select few people knew about it. Thus from 1923 to 1933, the weapon development program was conducted by Germany in complete secrecy. When Hitler came to power in 1933, he was invited by Guderian for a "show and tell" demonstration near Kazan. This was the first demonstration of "Blitzkrieg", a coordinated attack of infantry, tanks and airforce. How was it possible? By short wave radio of course. Every commander had a short wave radio and could detail each attack for each unit.

Hitler was flabbergasted and was jumping for joy. By 1935, all Rapallo-land operations were moved to Germany and Hitler began his "REVANCHE."

How do I know this? My father was a member of the Soviet inspection team! How did he make it to that Team? By 1930 my father (Ivan Kornilovich Korniev) was the leading Soviet Chemist with over 100 patents to his name (the total was 107). And, he loved to go on the inspection tours because the inspectors were allotted western clothes: one overcoat, two suits, two pairs of shoes, two shirts, two belts, two pairs of socks and one hat of their choice…

Prologue

Here I will give a brief biography of the adults involved: Emilia my mother; Ivan my father; George my stepfather; and Anna, George's mother. Emma, my older sister by 7 years, and Masha, my stepsister who was about my age, are not described.

EMILIA.

Emilia was born with a "silver spoon" in her mouth. Her mother Anna was a successful art dealer; her father Gabriel was a very successful structural engineer who specialized in bridge building. Gabriel had two brothers: Max a bookkeeper/accountant and Leonhard a sausage maker. They were Germans who came to Russia/Ukraine to make their fortune -- by invitation of the Czarist government. Their original name was Grotte, and they came from the Wiesbaden area. When they arrived in the Ukraine, they took (with government permission) a good sounding Russian name.

Anna met Gabriel at a county fair and fell madly in love. When they married, her father gave Anna a dowry of 20,000 Rubles in gold. With that money, they bought a large estate outside of Kharkiev. The feature of the estate was a main house, a guest house, a huge apple orchard with "Antonov Apples" -- which paid the tax bill and was the primary source of income. Then there were four fields where they grew wheat, sunflowers and corn while the fourth field was "resting." And, of course, nearly one third was forest. In total the estate was about 5-6,000 acres.

The estate was well-known for its spring well. People came from afar to fill up with its waters. In front of the house was a huge oval where they grew all kinds of 'Canna-lilies.'

When Emilia was born on September 12, 1912, there was much jubilation. But within a few short years, Russia was drawn into a war that changed everything. Kulaks (property owners) were despised and persecuted. Their estates were plundered repeatedly, and the wells were poisoned (by killing an animal and throwing it into the well). Even when World War I was over (for Russia in 1917), the Ukraine was given to Germany by Russia as reparation for the war. In came the occupation troops, and the soldiers were shipped off to the Western Front. This lasted until 1919 when the war was over in the West. Then Russia plunged into a Civil War with Whites (Czarists) fighting Reds (Bolsheviks/Communists) until 1923.

The first sign of peace came to Ukraine in 1926 when all was partitioned and divided to suit the victors. But, then the tax collector demanded his share. The estate was assessed taxes for 1914 to 1926. The tax bill was more than the estate was worth.

Meanwhile Emilia went to school in 1917 (at age 5). But, there was a terrible shortage of teachers. So, instead of attending classes the assignments for each semester were posted, and each student could progress at his or her pace by submitting a paper or taking the required exams.

For Emilia this was wonderful because she could finish the 10-year course in 7 years. So, by the time she was 12, she had graduated from high school with distinction.   But, this posed a problem. She was too young to be accepted by a University even if she "fixed" her age. Adding a year or two might go undetected, but 4 years (at that age) was not possible.

At that time, the regime started a new program, to train young adults in agronomy in a "live-in-environment." The minimum age was 14. So, Emilia had her age "fixed" and was accepted in that school. It was a two-year program which included cooking, baking, planting, marinating and animal husbandry. Thus, by the time she was 14, she was a certified agronomist.

With her new records in hand, she applied to medical school in Odessa and was accepted. During recess or vacation, she would go see her mother in Kharkiev. By then, the estate was gone, and Anna lived in town. Gabriel was never home. As it turned out, he became a Communist and started a new family. Eventually, Anna found out and they got divorced. At that time divorce was easy. You sent in a postcard to the "Family Affair" office with your request for a divorce, and you were automatically divorced and received your notification by mail.

In her last semester, she went to see her mother when she met this dashing young man, Ivan, and fell in love with him. They got married, and she finished her medical school. My older sister, Emma was born on March 19, 1931 in Stalino.

Stalino was originally called Uzivka, or "(Howard) Hughes Town." It featured a large chemical plant where Ivan worked as Chief Chemist. Stalin changed it to Stalino.

In 1933, Ivan founded the Ukrainian Chemical Society as shown in the picture on the Internet. However, in 1935 he became violently sick when he inhaled noxious gases at work in the plant. After one month, he was terminated and all his privileges were suspended. Now Emilia took over, and with the aid of prominent specialists began his recovery. The main problem was they had no residence. (Their living quarters were confiscated since only working people were entitled to live properly in the workers "paradise!")

However, at that time, the government was building out the suburbs of Kiyiv (Kiev). So, Emilia gave Ivan their savings and told him to go to Kiyiv and find an apartment for them. Off went Ivan, and she did not hear a word from him. After a while, Emilia got worried. She packed up Emma, and together they went to Kiyiv. There, Ivan had family, and they quickly joined the search. Well, they found him with Max (her father's brother).

Ivan was looking all right but in the wrong places. Emilia settled in, got an apartment, signed up at Kiyiv University in Microbiology (The government planned to revitalize the river -Dnipro -- Dnieper when russified.), and volunteered to teach young adults, mostly orphans, the three r's: in her case, Russian History and Russian Literature. (It should be noted, it was illegal to teach anything Ukrainian in Ukraine and, if found out, a 10-year 'vacation' in Siberia was the reward!).

Emilia got an idea: why not participate in the "build-out?" The next day they were at the government office applying for two building lots, as both Emilia and Ivan qualified. They found a parcel that was just ideal: Two lots divided by a yar (ravine) with a small access path between both lots. Emilia knew exactly what she wanted. The front lot would have access to the road and be her garden while the back lot would be her staple-field to grow corn or sunflowers or wheat.

As part of the build-out she was entitled to a supply of raw timber. To turn raw timber into building material, she needed 'muscle power.' One evening class, she offered a job to load timber onto a truck. The entire class volunteered. The next day, she hired a truck and, with her students in tow, they went to the designated forester who gave her all the raw timber she could carry away -- enough to build 3 houses or more. Once the truck was loaded, they drove it to the mill and had the timber cut to specifications. Once it was cut, the truck was loaded again and the load brought to her building site. Within a few days, she had a huge pile of building material.

Next, she needed a contractor to build her house. She found one who was highly recommended. Next, she negotiated the cost. Well, the contractor preferred to be paid in finished building material. So, she got his specification for bricks, cement, cobblestone, shingles, tubing of all kinds and so on. In each case she ordered a little more than she was told. Thus, she built her house, and a big barn, and a fence and laid cobblestones between the house and the barn. Within less than a month, her house and her property was ready and fenced in. Then she began planting: six Antonov apple trees in the center, berry bushes along the fence and a 'cabbage patch' which grew all the kitchen essential herbs and greens. Opposite to the "cabbage patch" were the pigpens and geesepens. Then, she bought her pride: a huge St. Bernard. He was my best friend and protector – especially from the geese.

Once the buildings and their access were finished, she began practicing her knowledge of agronomy. She got about ten wooden barrels, had them cleaned and ordered the 'stuffing': a truck load of cabbage, green tomatoes, cucumbers and so much more. Then she hired women who cleaned and cut the vegetables and stuffed them into the barrels. Then Emilia prepared her concoction of marinades, specific for each product. The barrels were then stacked in her cellar.

By fall, Emilia was ready to do business. She advertised for sales women who would go regularly to the market. They would come, inspect her products and buy them. Thus, in no time at all, Emilia had a thriving business.

In addition to her "core business," she made sausages. They were a big hit with Ivan. But, she never made enough to take them to market. Ivan loved her marinated green tomatoes more than anything else.

Somehow she felt she created a spell over all Kandiew women: they would be the sole providers for their family. And, so far it has come to pass well into the 3rd generation of Kandiew women!

Ivan Kornilovich Korniew.

Ivan was born in 1902, the exact date was not known. But, for good measure he set his birthday to St. Ivan's day.

When World War I broke out, he was too young to join. When the war ended in the Ukraine in 1917, Ivan was 15. By then he had finished high school with distinction. But instead of going on to the University, he was eager to defend the Ukraine. When the war ended, Ukraine's trouble began. Bands of deserters and regular troops roamed the countryside. A Czech army was moving east to liberate the Czar. Rumanian, Hungarian and Bulgarian army units roamed in the Southwest, and so on.

The Ukrainian defense team came up with a strategy. They divided the Ukraine west of the Dnipro River into 50 kilometer squares (2500 square kilometers). And, each square was patrolled by a squad of 6 to 10 men and/or women on horseback. They would take on deserters but were forbidden to engage regular troops. Then they had to notify the defense team, and they would take the proper action. Ivan was attached to such a unit as he was an expert rider. In time, he became leader of his group. He often spoke of his exploits. In particular of his "Maxim machine gun," which he called his "Bayan," -- a musical instrument.

His term was up after 4 years. Then, he was admitted to Kiyiv University on a "fast-paced program" in Chemistry. By 1927, at the age of 25, he became an important Chemist because he was turning out one patent after another. By 1930, he was a household name in the Soviet Union, and that is when he met Emilia. In 1933, he founded the Ukrainian Chemical Society. But, in 1935 he inhaled noxious gases at the plant and got deathly sick. Now, Emilia stepped in to his rescue and began the long recovery to good heath. In the process, he lost his recognition, his apartment and other privileges. He was even 'deleted' from the "International Who's Who" for 1935 and subsequent years. In the workers "paradise" you work; and if you are maimed or wounded and unable to work, you are automatically excluded from that "paradise!"

Ivan's family was big and very colorful. They had a Hermit, a Witch, a Bluebeard and many more colorful characters in their family. One of his sisters was married to Grigori Zhukov, later to become Marshall Zhukov...

All this carried no weight in 1941 when the Germans surrouned Kiyiv. Nikita Khrushchev issued the order to have him murdered...

Anna, George's mother.

Anna was a beautiful women in her youth. Her date of birth is unknown to me. Best estimates are 1883 as the date she was born. At the age of about 17, she met and had an affair with Plehve junior, about 1900. Plehve junior was the son of V. Plehve the Minister of Interior in Czarist Russia -- a very high and powerful post (he was assassinated in 1904.)

Well, Anna got pregnant; and when Plehve junior found out, he split. So, there was Anna, not knowing what to do. Then she had an idea: why not confront his father? So, she dressed up in her finery and went to the big building in St. Petersburg. There she requested an audience with the minister on matters of "most urgent personal matters." She got her audience and presented her case. Plehve listened intently and then told her he would take care of the matter and told her never again to come to his office! He got her address and sent her on her way.

A few days later, a man showed up: Jakob Kandiew. He came with a proposal of marriage which she accepted. Jakob got a promotion, and Anna got herself a husband.

As it turned out, Jakob loved George. He could not do enough for him. And, after George finished high school, Jakob sent him to St. Petersburg to study Journalism -- George's favorite subject. However, as the Bolsheviks took over, they eradicated all 'lackeys' of the Czar and this included Jakob. When George found out, he became an ardent Anti-communist for the rest of his life.

George J. Kandiew.

George was born on September 21, 1902. His mother Anna loved him, and Jacob adored him. After he finished high school in 1919, he wanted to become a journalist. There was no better school of Journalism than in St. Petersburg. Jacob sent him there with no expenses spared. George settled in the center of town, sharing the room with another student. As soon as he settled in, the town became known as Leningrad. During all the commotion going on, his roommate decided to take a vacation in the Crimea. As soon as he left, the town was cordoned off. Nobody was allowed out, and nobody was allowed in.

Meanwhile, foreign diplomats, reporters and journalists tried to rent or buy a place in town. Prices were going through the roof. Every day George was offered staggering amounts of money to sell "his" apartment. And eventually he did. With his new found wealth, he had a great entourage of new friends. They moved into a hotel and were "living-it-up." In that group was a gorgeous Polish woman. She and George started an affair. She got pregnant with 'Masha.' Masha was born sometime in 1937 or 1938.

Eventually George's money ran out, and his entourage vanished. When the Polish woman found out that he was out of money, she left him with Masha and disappeared. So, here was George, alone with Masha. At the first opportunity he could, he left Leningrad and moved to his mother. There he found out that Jacob has been killed. He took his mother and Masha and moved to Kiyiv.

Once the Germans occupied Kiyiv in 1941, George volunteered to work for the Germans. There he met Emilia in the Uprava -- Kiyiv City-Government. By then, Emilia was Assistant to the Kuriniv District Mayor Dr. Bagazil.

(For the longest time George told everybody that his wife had died and he was left with Masha. It was only much later that he told the true story.)

CHAPTER 1

From Kiev to Berlin

Conscious awareness began today. In fact, it began this evening September 3, 1943 Kiev time. We were leaving our friends, our neighbors, and our possessions. We were escaping from the "Red Devils." We were escaping on the "last" train to "freedom." To Berlin. Actually, I don't know if it was the last train, my mother told me it was.

Somehow I knew from this day forward I had to grow up quickly. It was my responsibility to take care of my family. The shock of the recent past and the grim reality of the present seemed to demand this of me. I was not quite sure if I could measure up to this task. I was almost six years old.

My family consisted of mother, my sister and me. We carried all our possessions in knapsacks and suitcases. Nearly half of our cargo was food for survival on the journey. The remainder was clothing and some trinkets we just could not leave behind. The food was mostly cured bacon.

I still remember vividly how only a few days before, my mother had hired some men to kill our biggest pig. They did an awful job. The pig was squealing in pain as they butchered it in the barn. The squealing sound pierced our house, our neighborhood. The ordeal seemed to last forever. When the squealing stopped, I knew the ordeal was over.

The pig was cleaned in the barn. Its belly was slit open and the innards taken out. The carcass was brought into the house and cooked. Once the pig was cooked, it was 'laid-out' on our kitchen table then salted thoroughly. Slices, about four inches wide, were carved from the back to the belly. The fatty parts were sliced into slabs about six inches long. These slabs were salted again. Then, they were wrapped and packed into our suitcases and knapsacks. The rest of the meat was given to relatives and neighbors.

My mother was the head of our family. She was barely thirty one years old and with just cause both apprehensive and fearful of our future. She was abandoning not only our home, but the use of her education and language as well. In her newly chosen land, she and her family were outcasts. Without language her education was of little value.

Normally she was outgoing, friendly, and talkative, but the gravity of the situation made her stern and laconic. Normally she looked tall and slender, but on that day she looked stocky and plump, from the many layers of clothes she had on. Usually, she wore her almost black hair loose; that day she wore it in braids -- tied into a crown on top of her head. Her oval face was nearly chalk-white from the anguish and her thick, black, eyebrows only made her face paler. Despite the motley appearance, her deep blue eyes were dancing with anticipation. She had resigned herself to the coming ordeal, yet she was determined to succeed.

The last few days were hectic. Relatives and neighbors came over and tried to discourage my mother from leaving. They knew deep inside that this was the last time we would see each other. But, my mother was firm, "Do you think for one moment that I or my children have a future with the "Red Devils?" she would reply. "Oh, no…" she would continue, "not after what they did to my husband." Then, all arguments would stop. They would bless her, wish her good luck and help her pack, or give her advice, or the names and addresses of relatives and friends in the "West."

Western history books describe the first battle for Kiev as a rout of the Red Army. Technically it was. The army which was supposed to defend Kiev surrendered to the Germans. It surrendered practically without a fight. To the Ukrainian units, the Germans were liberators, and most soldiers preferred to fight with the Germans against Stalin.

This view, however, was not popular in the Soviet Union -- for it implied a preexisting anti-Communist sentiment. Therefore, it was more convenient to say that the army was defeated. This view was also not popular with Hitler, because it diminished the glory of the "invincible" German army. Since the Germans are considered to be good historians and their "facts" correspond to the Soviet "facts," it is only natural that it must be the truth. Thus, Stalin admitted a great defeat and Hitler claimed a great victory -- neither of which was true. The fact remains that the "official" history is false. Of the seven-hundred thousand defenders of Kiev, six-hundred and seventy thousand were "captured" and volunteered to fight Stalin!

Now at that time, military leaders in the Soviet Union were not at liberty to make unilateral decisions. It was more important that decisions were politically correct rather than militarily correct. Therefore, each military leader had a political advisor who could "over-rule" the military leader when a political objective was at stake. Of course, sometimes the political advisor was confronted with a "fait accompli," and proceeded to the next stage. The political advisor, was usually a member of the KGB, or a deputy of the state, or a commissar. That is, a well indoctrinated Communist. At that time, in the first battle for Kiev, Khrushchev was the political advisor for the defense of Kiev.

As the battle began to unfold, it became clear to Khrushchev that Kiev would fall. Since, at that stage of the battle, evacuation was not feasible, Khrushchev issued new directives while he still had the political power to do so. They were, "destroy the city and all individuals who could be of value to the Germans."

In military retreats bridges, railroad junctions, and munitions supplies are usually the first targets for destruction. To Khrushchev, however, monasteries, churches, museums, hospitals, and famous individuals were targeted first for elimination. They were politically more important, posing a threat to Communist survival. Accordingly, on August 19, 1941 his orders were executed. That morning, the city reverberated with many explosions set by Khrushchev and his commandos. That day the monastery of the Caves, St. Sophia Cathedral -- shrines dating back to the 9th century -- and many others were gutted.

By August 22, most public buildings were destroyed. He now turned to his second objective, the extermination of important individuals. Some accounts say about two hundred execution squads were formed. Each consisted of four loyal party members and each was armed with a submachine gun. These execution squads came from the ranks of loyal soldiers or partisans and were called commandos. They were sent out to hunt these individuals down and to kill them. Among these individuals was Ivan, Emilia's husband. On August 22, 1941, a commando found Ivan as he was crossing his wheat field. They mowed him down. They did not kill him, they just shot him repeatedly.

The sound of shots alarmed our neighbors. Many rushed to the scene. They found my father bleeding to death in the wheat field. The commando held the neighbors at bay. One of the neighbors left the murder scene and rushed to my mother who was at work. He told her what had happened. Frantically, Emilia rushed to the wheat field. By now, a multitude had assembled, but were still held at bay by the commando. The multitude, however, was getting unruly, shouting obscenities at the commando. When my mother arrived, the crowd parted and let her through. My father was still alive, but bleeding to death in agony. Ignoring the threats of the commando, she rushed to my father, screaming for a car or truck, to take him to the nearest hospital. One of the neighbors rushed out to get his truck, while my mother administered first aid. When he returned with his truck, my mother asked the neighbors to help her carry her husband. A few stepped forward, picked up my father and rushed him to the truck. Then, my mother and the driver raced to the nearest hospital. The doctors pronounced Ivan dead on arrival.

My mother returned home. She was sobbing. My sister Emma was in school, I was at home. The wife of a neighbor was with me; all she kept saying was, "Poor child -- why did this have to happen to you." My mother got her composure back. She came over to me. She took me by the hand and said, "Come with me."

Slowly they walked through their garden and into the wheat-field. She took me to the spot where my father was shot. She parted the wheat. A blood drenched patch was in front of us. The wheat was trampled to the ground while the pools of blood were still seeping into the black soil. "Do you see this?" she asked. I nodded my head. "Remember, for as long as you live," she continued, "your father was shot here by the 'Red Devils.'" I was silent, he did not comprehend the extent of her message. All I could say was, "Why?" She looked at me and started to weep again. "He was a good man, a scientist. He devoted his life to help other people. He was not a party member. He was not a nationalist. He minded his own business -- there was no reason for this." Now, both of us were sobbing. Then she continued, "These "Red Devils" have destroyed my family. My brother is still in Siberia. They have destroyed his family. And now, they have destroyed our family. When will these bastards stop!"

When Emma came home from school Emilia told her what had happened. Emma was almost hysterical. She grabbed a huge axe and was ready to go out and hunt down the commando. All she kept saying was, "I will find these bastards! I will kill these bastards!" And again, "I will find these bastards! I will kill these bastards!" She kept saying this over and over again. My mother looked at her and said, "Child, what do you think you are doing? You can barely lift that axe. How far do you think you will go? How will you find 'these bastards?' You don't think I have not thought of that? Everything went so quickly. They were strangers. They were not from these parts. Nobody recognized them."

A few days later the first Germans entered Kiev. By the end of September, Kiev was under German occupation. By October, the damage to the public buildings was repaired and much of the physical damage restored. But, the mental damage stayed on forever.

****

Each of us was assigned a load to carry for our journey. Since I was the youngest, I carried only a small knapsack. My sister Emma was about seven years older. She was assigned a knapsack and a small suitcase. My mother carried the most. A knapsack and two large suitcases. Our clothing was on us. We put on as much as we could. Two pairs of socks, two pairs of underwear, two pairs of pants, two or three shirts or blouses, one sweater, one jacket, an overcoat and a hat or cap. We were bundled up like mummies. In part, this was to protect us from the cold and in part this clothing had to last a long time. Whatever we could not wear was left behind or given away. In our luggage we each carried an extra pair of shoes.

We had very little time to plan our departure. One day Emilia came home from work, sat me down on a chair, called Emma, and told us we had to leave within the next three days. The "Red Devils" were very close, and we had no time to waste. That same day my mother hired the people to kill the pig. The next day George arrived. George was also fleeing to Berlin from the "Red Devils." He had come to help us hide our "valuables."

The same people who had butchered the pig earlier in the evening, had also dug a deep hole in the ground, about four feet wide, four feet long and at least six feet deep. My mother told them the dry well was not working properly, and she was going to put in a new one. By the end of the day, the hole was completed. Meanwhile, a truck had brought a load of sand, which was dumped near the hole. The earth from the hole had been spread evenly on a garden patch nearby.

When evening came, the rest of the mystery unfolded. My mother climbed into the hole as George carried two suitcases to it. He then lowered each suitcase into the hole. My mother placed the suitcases, then climbed back out. Then, they both shoveled sand into the hole. Then they would stop for a while and inspect, while my mother placed a few boards over the "buried treasure." Then, George would go back to the house for more suitcases. This continued until all suitcases were buried, and all the sand was used up. When they finished, my mother put a metal sieve over the hole. Then they returned to the house. My mother said, "Tomorrow the men will come and cement the top." The subject was closed. But, I remembered how a few days earlier, my mother had packed those suitcases with the strangest of items; glassware, linen, pictures and books. The strangest item of all was a gramophone. I never liked the sound of it. It squeaked and made strange noises. Yet, the adults seemed to find this object very amusing. They would put on records, play them -- laugh and giggle while this monster made strange sounds. They called it music, but to me this was noise. How could anyone be enamored by that contraption? Well, finally the monster got the "deep six."

Of course, now I can only be amused by the efforts to save the valuables this way. All the neighbors knew we were leaving. Surely, as soon as we turned the corner of our street, the whole neighborhood would dig up that hole and share in the booty. However, to this day, my mother believes, not all the "goodies" were unearthed!

We lived in a house outside of Kiev, in the Kuriniv district. Our home was a small farm. It had a main house with two guest rooms, a bedroom with a huge brick oven, a kitchen, an attic, and a cellar.

My favorite room was the bedroom. The bed was above the oven. The bed was about four feet above the floor and was always warm and cozy. The oven was in use most of the time. It was used to bake bread, cookies, and for large chores. We had a separate pot-bellied stove in the kitchen which my mother usually used in the summer but only to cook meals. Our center of activity in the house was the bedroom with the oven. Emma preferred to sleep in one of the guest-rooms. She usually slept with a "huge" axe. She started this habit shortly after we were robbed. She vowed to cut down any intruder with her axe. The kitchen and attic were not important to me, except that during the initial German occupation, we hid many young adults there, who were slated for deportation to Germany. They were mostly in their twenties, and were supposed to be going to Germany as "Ostarbeiter" (Eastern workers). They stayed in the attic for a very long time, about a year or so. But then, the situation began to change and they left. One of them, studied the routine in our house and, when he left, he came back with his friends and robbed us.

We had a beautiful St. Bernard who was my friend and protector during the day. At night, however, my sister Emma would chain him, so he would not roam around or chase the other animals. He was also kept chained while we were away. When the robbers came, the dog was chained and nobody was home. Then the robbers "stoned" the dog to death. They broke into the house and robbed us. Years later, my mother met one of the perpetrators. He begged for my mother's forgiveness and my mother forgave. At the time of the robbery my mother was heartbroken. By the time she met him again, the robbery was an insignificant event in our live, and did not matter at all.

The cellar was something else. I loved to go down to the cellar, taste the "goodies" and explore my father's wares. The goodies were casks of "fresh cabbage" (fresh sauerkraut), pickles, tomatoes, canned vegetables and fruits (in jars), and dried vegetables and fruits. It seemed as though we canned or dried practically everything!

My father was a chemist, a world class chemist with many patents, medals, and citations. His name was in the "International Who's Who" and one of his sisters was married to Marshal Zhukov. The other part of the cellar had all kinds of chemicals, machinery, and strange tools. I loved to examine these objects. I called the cellar "pobrik." I could never understand how anyone could be afraid of being locked in the cellar. My two most favorite spots in the house were the bedroom and the cellar. To this day I have the same preferences.

An unpaved road was the main artery from our community to the rest of the city. Our property had about two hundred feet frontage on that road. Then, it stretched "for a mile" from the road inward. Actually, there was a small part, about two hundred feet, which was our garden. Then came a ravine, which, on one side was at ground level with the main property while on the other side it fell into a huge ravine. The ravine was called a "yar." On the bottom of the "yar" was a tiny stream surrounded by quicksand. The bulk of our property was on the other side of the ravine. There, we grew wheat, corn, cabbage and many other vegetables.

On the property near the house, we grew strawberries, gooseberries, raspberries and fruit trees. A small patch was reserved for garden-vegetables: cucumbers, tomatoes, beans, parsley, onions, dill, garlic and lettuce.

The house and the barn were parallel to the road. The house was on one side and the barn on the other. Between them was an open but cobble-stoned area. Directly behind the house and the barn was our garden. This front parcel was fenced on three sides up to the ravine. In the front we had a large gate between the house and the barn. Beyond the ravine our property was wide open.

Aside from the St. Bernard, we also had a number of farm animals. A few pigs, a flock of geese, some chickens and a she-goat. The she goat was a champion milk producer. The goat was bought, specifically for me, by my father at a state fair. Allegedly, the goat could produce twenty liters of milk daily. But, the goat had a strange habit, she knew how to "milk herself," and she loved doing it. As a result, her milk production was hardly ever more than ten liters a day. We tried everything to break her of the habit. Things like unpleasant creams on her udder to discourage her sucking, but nothing worked. The only way to control her sucking was to walk her. This chore was assigned to my sister Emma. Emma did not resent this chore, as it gave her a chance to get away, and read books she was not supposed to. Emma was becoming an ardent Ukrainian and this was a crime during the Soviet regime.

Emma was a "tom-boy." She was not afraid of anyone. When she felt someone "infringed" on her "space," she would defend it ferociously. She even fought boys much older and much larger then she. To Emma, size was not a deterrent; she claimed -- determination was the deciding factor. Of course, she was much taller than I. I admired her strength and determination. Her features were a mix of my father's and mother's.

Her hair was dark and she preferred to wear it short. She was stocky with an almost round face. Black eyebrows and greenish-bluish eyes made her face unusual, yet inquisitive. She was a "book-worm" of sorts, but she was also a believer in ardent exercise.

One day Emma took the goat for a walk along the border of the ravine. She was reading one of her illicit books as the goat grazed along the ravine's edge. All of a sudden, the ground gave way under the goat, and down she went. The goat landed in a patch of quicksand and started to drown. When Emma saw the goat tumble down the ravine, she followed the goat. The goat needed to be saved, so Emma tried to pull the goat out of the quicksand, but to no avail. The harder Emma pulled on the goat, the more she got into it herself, until both were drowning in the quicksand.

I was in the garden when I faintly heard Emma's voice. I ran to the ravine and there was Emma trying to pull out the goat, while herself hopelessly caught in the quicksand. I ran to our neighbor for help. The neighbor and his son grabbed two boards, about four feet long, and dashed to the ravine, screaming at me to get more help. So, I ran to the next neighbor. He too grabbed a board and a rope and dashed to the ravine. Left without further instructions, I followed. There I saw how the men labored to save Emma. Emma in turn would not let go of the goat. In the end, both Emma and the goat were saved.

Needless to say, when my parents came home from work and were told of the incident, they went to the neighbors and thanked them. They offered them anything of value we possessed, but they refused to accept any gifts. We remain to this day in their debt.

My nemesis were the geese. Usually, we kept them in a small area in the garden near the barn. Occasionally, however, they would break out. Then, if I was in the garden, they would make a beeline for me. I was told not to be afraid of them. Then, I would try to chase them back into their enclosure. Usually, I succeeded. But, there was one gander who was not afraid of me at all. He would peck and attack me, until I would fall to the ground. Then, the remaining flock would join him and peck away at me. Of course, when my dog was around, this was not a problem. He would chase them into their pen. But, on occasion my dog was tied up or not around. Then my only salvation was to fall on the ground and scream as loud as I could to attract help. Usually, help was not too far away.

****

Now, only a few years ago events unfolded which changed my life forever. The Great War started in June of 1941. The greatest army ever assembled promised to establish a new order in Europe. The tyrant Stalin had finally met his match: Hitler and his "Wehrmacht" (armed forces). Of course, the Germans were only the spearhead for a massive force. The German invasion started with more than three million crack soldiers. Only the year before they had conquered France and a year before that, they had destroyed Poland. The German assault force was highly motorized and was ready to swing into any sector which provided an opening.

As a rule of thumb, each frontline soldier requires at least one in reserve, two in support, and six for manufacture and supply. This meant that an additional three million German soldiers were in reserve, six million in support and eighteen million in the German labor force. This was the foundation needed to supply this armada. Of course, in addition there were Italians, French (Vichy), Spanish, Dutch, Austrians, Croats, Slovenes, Bohemians, Moravians, Hungarians, Rumanians, Norwegians and Finns all ready and eager to join the German invasion. So too, the Germans counted on the Estonians, Latvians, and Lithuanians to join them once they were liberated from the Soviets. These other nationals were the bulk of the army. Another six million were frontline soldiers which could be counted on by Hitler. Who could possibly resist this onslaught?

The numbers were not that important, but the fact that "all of Europe" was part of this war of "liberation" is very important. The very code name for the invasion stated that is was a "Holy War:" Operation Barbarossa. (Barbarossa led a crusade to the Holy Land). At last, "civilized" Europe had recognized the brutality of Stalin, and had come to liberate all nationalities enslaved by the Soviets. In other words, a "Holy War" was launched against Communism. A war was started, to establish a new order; to destroy Communism once and for all.

This was also the sentiment in the Ukraine and in many other parts of the Soviet Union. In particular in 'White Russia' or Belorus, the Crimea, Armenia and Azerbaijan.

This sentiment was more than adequately justified. The previous war had inflicted about eighteen million casualties on Russia and its allies (1914 to 1917). The ensuing civil war inflicted about forty million casualties in Russia (1917 to 1923). Then the reign of Stalin decimated the population by another sixty million (1923 to 1941). Proportionately, the Ukraine suffered the most from Stalin's rule. Small farms were collectivized and chronic food shortages became common.

The artificial famine of 1931 to 1933 alone killed between six and nine million Ukrainian farmers. The exact numbers will only be tallied when the many mass graves are included in the count. More than twenty-five million Ukrainians were deported to Siberian labor camps, where most perished. On average, every family in the Ukraine had at least two members killed or deported by Stalin. Is it surprising then, that the "liberation" view was justified? Of course not. It was believed that no matter what the new order was, it could not possibly be as cruel as Stalin's reign of terror.

This sentiment was not uniform throughout the country, however. Some areas harbored devout Communists or were tightly run by them. To them, Hitler was the terror and the new order a facade to enslave them. Their argument was Poland and what Hitler did to the Poles. But, in the Ukraine, the Poles were despised because of their cruel rule when they tried to "colonize" the Ukraine in the name of the Roman Church and forced conversion to Catholicism. The Poles were the proverbial "conquistadors of the East" for the Holy Roman Empire from 1500 until 1772. Therefore, that argument found little support in the Ukraine.

In any event, when the war broke out, sentiment was divided, but mirrored the ethnic-national heritage. This sentiment was not understood by the Germans, nor understood by Hitler and even less understood in the West.

As the war unfolded, many battles were riddled with paradoxes. In some instances, whole armies surrendered to the Germans without firing a shot, asking to fight as German allies to liberate Russia, the Ukraine, the Crimea, Armenia, Azerbaijan and many other captive nations. Then, in other battles, the Soviet army units fought "literally" to the last man.

Brest-Litovsk is a good example. Here the Soviet army units fought literally to the last man. In Leningrad, the city would not surrender, holding the siege for 900 days until liberated by the Red Army! Only one in ten survived the siege of Leningrad. On the other hand, the most notorious case of the other extreme was that of General Vlasov and the Vlasov movement.

General Vlasov was in charge of Moscow's defense in 1941. He was put in charge of the 20th Army. This army was formed from volunteers, local militia, and anything Vlasov could "throw together." When the German armor arrived at Moscow and the battle began, Vlasov successfully defended the city. Then, he counter-attacked with his "rag-tag" army and drove the Germans back about 125 miles. This counter-attack destroyed the German morale. Visions of a Napoleonic retreat dashed through the German soldier's and officer's minds. The invincibility of the German forces was shattered. But, exhaustion and bad weather averted a total defeat and a panic-stricken rout. Thus, the Battle of Moscow was the first Allied victory -- not Stalingrad, not El Alamein and not Operation Torch.

Instead, "history" reports that "Siberian forces" were brought to the front and pushed the Germans back. Now the part that is true is that Vlasov was indeed the commander of a Siberian Army. Unfortunately, it was in China, about three-thousand miles away. The Siberian army was just good propaganda. It served to create the image of Communist loyalty and make "winter" appear "bigger than life." For surely, the Siberians knew how to cope with winter.

Vlasov was decorated and hailed for this feat. The Order of the "Red Banner," the Soviet Union's highest order, was bestowed on him. But, on June 12, 1942 Vlasov was captured by the Germans near Volkhov. By then, Vlasov was disillusioned with Communism and saw the Germans as liberators. And, he was not alone. By the end of 1942, nearly nine-hundred thousand former Soviet nationals were collaborating as "Hilfsarbeiters" (helpers), or Hiwis with the German Wehrmacht.

Vlasov, and many other notables, envisioned the creation of a "Russian Liberation Front," ROA, which planned to fight Stalin with the Germans, just like the many other nationals already integrated into the Wehrmacht, as autonomous and "equal" partners with the Germans. For this, Vlasov was hailed as a new "messiah," inspiring some ten million former Soviet citizens in the West and at least thirty million in the East. This became known as the Vlasov movement. By the end of 1942, more than one-million former Soviet nationals were ready to take up arms against Stalin and join the Vlasov movement. But, Hitler and his "Ostpolitik" (Eastern policy) focused on a different objective. In part, the Germans did not want to share in the "imminent glory of victory" and, in part, they did not trust Vlasov. Last but not least, this huge reservoir of humanity was meant to be enslaved, to serve the German "Herrenrasse" (master race). Only in late 1944, was Vlasov and his army -- by then still nearly nine-hundred thousand strong -- were allowed to operate against the Soviet forces near Frankfurt on the Oder. By then, it did not matter. The war was lost and Vlasov was just another pawn. When the war ended, Vlasov tried to surrender to the Americans.

He tried to surrender to General Patton at Pilsen, then to General Patch and so on. But, General Eisenhower would not accept Vlasov's surrender, even though Vlasov and his soldiers had fought in German uniform and as regular German units. Vlasov ended up dismissing his soldiers, who then were hunted down, shot, or repatriated forcibly to the Soviet Union. The West refused to "deal" with the problem of Soviet collaborators in order not to offend Stalin. So, Vlasov was turned over to the Soviet Allies. The next day, they took both Vlasov and his adjutant to Moscow where they were hanged in Red Square.

Conservative estimates suggest that, about seven million former Soviet citizens were repatriated forcibly from: Germany, France, Italy, Denmark, Norway, Sweden and the USA. At that time, many of whom were citizens of these countries. [See, "Operation Keelhaul," by Julius Epstein].

To Stalin, human life meant nothing! The population was purged from time to time for "good measure." The party was purged from time to time for "good measure." His ethnic Georgia was purged from time to time for "good measure." He was even insensitive to his own family. Thus, Stalin is the proverbial "beast" of the Bible. Stalin's son was captured by the Germans just before the German debacle at Stalingrad. Hitler tried to exchange prisoners with Stalin. Hitler offered Stalin's son for Field Marshal Paulus. Stalin declined the exchange.

Another common tactic of Stalin was, not to evacuate cities during a battle. This was done on purpose. Stalin's reasoning was simple: Soldiers fight better for a live city. This tactic was used in Leningrad, Kiev, Moscow, Stalingrad, Rostov and many others. Of course, the result on the civilian population was devastating. Civilian casualties frequently outnumbered military casualties by factors of ten to one and more. Stalin felt no remorse over this decimation of humanity.

Even to the Germans this view was foreign. They could not reconcile how, on one hand, Russians were fighting to the last man, and in other instances they surrendered when the German army was in sight. The many victories of the Germans in the first year of their campaign in Russia, were shrouded in these paradoxes. A huge number of Russian prisoners were taken. Surely, Stalin had to run out of reserves. Both took steps to stop this human flood. Stalin issued an edict: "Every Soviet national captured by the Germans was a 'traitor' to the Motherland." Hitler countered with: "Not one step back for the Fatherland!"

The German high command elected to use the most advantageous interpretation for this paradox: The Wehrmacht was so powerful and so superior, that any opposition vanished or was vanquished. Very little credit was ever afforded to the other European forces collaborating with the Germans. So, the first Allied victory -- the Battle of Moscow in 1941 -- goes unmentioned in the annals of World War II. The Germans call the defeat a setback, attributed to the winter, with a continuation still to come. The Soviets cannot praise a traitor (Vlasov) and praise the Siberians who had no part in that battle. (Army Group North lost 95% of its armor at Moscow).

The German invasion into the Soviet Union was divided into three major army groups to improve mobility and cover an initial front of more than one thousand miles. That is, many armies operated under one supreme command as one unit in their sector. The three were: Army Group North with von Leeb, Army Group Center with von Bock and, Army Group South with von Rundstedt. Each army group was supported by Panzer (tank) Groups and an air fleet (Luftwaffe).

Army Group North had two armies. They were led by von Manstein and von Reinhardt. It also had one Panzer Group led by Keller and one air fleet. Their primary objective was to liberate the Baltic states. They were then to join up with the Finns for the impending attack on Leningrad and Moscow. When the offensive began, von Leeb quickly pierced through the Soviet resistance, but Leningrad would not capitulate and could not be taken. Von Leeb left part of his army to annihilate Leningrad. In rapid moves Army Group North approached Moscow. Only the defense of Moscow by Vlasov prevented its fall in 1941.

Army Group Center was meant to be both the main punch and the most mobile force. This was true because the industrial supply line in the Soviet Union was anchored around the Brest-Litovsk, Kiev, and Smolensk triangle. It had to be the most mobile in order to be able to join forces with Army Group North, or South, depending on the fortunes of the war. It had two armies and two Panzer Groups. One Panzer Group was led by Guderian; the other by Hoth. The supporting air fleet was commanded by Kesselring. The advance moved relatively slowly. It encountered a lot of resistance at Brest-Litovsk and, by winter they advanced only to a town called Kursk, far from their primary objective.

Of course, the ultimate objective in the first year was to "shorten" the front. At the time of the invasion, the front spanned from the Baltic Sea to the Rumanian border, or about one thousand miles. In order to shrink this front effectively, the "imaginary" line of Archangel to Astrakhan had to be secured. This new "front" would reduce the effective front to about two hundred and fifty miles. Then, the Ural Mountain range and the Caspian Sea would provide a natural defense perimeter. While ninety percent of the Soviet Union lies beyond that line, the bulk of the economy and heavy industry lies in front of it. If Hitler could capture the European part of the Soviet Union, he could deal with the remaining part at his leisure. The Ural Mountains and the Caspian Sea would provide a natural defense for the future development of the war. Of course, this German main objective was never achieved. Instead, just the opposite situation developed. Instead of reducing the front, the front actually increased to nearly two thousand miles by 1942!

Army Group South started with three armies, including the infamous Sixth Army led by Paulus. It had one Panzer Group led by von Kleist and one air fleet. Army Group South found many willing collaborators along its way. Wholesale armies surrendered to the Germans without a battle. On paper, their advance matched step for step that of Army Group North, the Rumanian armies joining Army Group South almost on the invasion date. The first battle of Kiev is usually described as a rout of the Red Army in that sector. It was. The Ukrainians looked to the Germans as liberators and surrendered without a fight. [See, "Unternehmen Barbarossa," Paul Carell]

The Germans entered Kiev officially, on September 20, 1941 and paraded through the streets on September 21, 1941. The resident population received the German soldiers as liberators, showering them with flowers. Archival films are plentiful, depicting these events. Finally, the yoke of Communism and Stalin was broken, or so the Ukrainians thought. However, as the front-line soldiers moved on, administrators and enforcers moved in. Many of the administrators were Croats, Slovenes and other ethnic groups which saw the Ukrainians as a danger to their own privileged status in the Reich (Empire). These administrators were more than willing to obey every directive of the Nazis.

Then, Army Group South continued its march towards Rostov, intending to capture Georgia, Azerbaijan and Baku. In 1942, Rostov fell to the Germans and the entire center for heavy industry was now in German hands. But, the appearance of glory is often closely followed by "hubris." Hitler's first fatal mistake was to split Army Group South from its Panzers. Two German armies and two Rumanian armies moved past Rostov and into Stalingrad, while Kleist and his Panzers, moved towards Rostov and the ultimate goal of Baku. Again, while Georgia was taken,

Kleist never reached Baku. His Panzers were of little value in the hilly terrain. Meanwhile, Paulus, with his two German armies and the two Rumanian armies walked straight into their mass grave -- into Stalingrad.

Initially, Ukrainians were more than willing to collaborate with the Germans. Many went voluntarily to Germany to help out in the German war effort. Many voluntarily joined the German army and so on. But gradually, the German brutality abated this euphoria. Often, the population was rounded up in the streets and in the markets. Victims were screened for "Aryan" traits. Then, the prisoners were mistreated according to their racial origin. Jews and Gypsies were imprisoned immediately. Their possessions were confiscated. Slavs with Aryan features or of German stock were promoted to "Volksdeutsche" (of German stock). Everybody else was just another "Untermensch" (Subhuman).

Humanity was grouped into a caste system. On top of that order were the Aryans or "true Germans or Austrians and lesser Aryans, such as the Italians, French, Spanish, Dutch and the English. Then, came the inferior races but with Aryan characteristics, the Japanese and, in Europe, the Finns, Hungarians, Latvians, Lithuanians, Estonians, Moravians, and Bohemians, were claimed to be of "mongolic warrior" stock. The lowest Aryan characteristics were nations once ruled by the Aryans who had traces of, or "diluted" Aryan blood. These were: Croats, Slovenes and "Volksdeutsche" in general. The rest of humanity was simply called an "Untermensch," the lowest of which was the Jew.

Of course, this classification was not only wrong but highly inconsistent. For example, Poland, which is of Slavic stock, was ruled by the Germans. King Casimir had invited the Germans to rule the Poles, around 1040. Many Germans then settled in Poland and intermarried. They even changed their alphabet to conform with that of the Germans. They became Catholic in 966 rather than Orthodox, and the Poles were used in the East as the "conquistadors" for the Holy Roman Empire. Yet they failed to conquer the Slavs. For this reason, Hitler was determined to "erase" all Poles from the face of the earth. During the war, Poland was the only country, which had its name changed to "General-Gouvernement."

Now historians have pinpointed three major migration centers. We are not sure when and why these migrations took place, but the three centers were Aryan, Mongolic and Turkic in nature. The Aryan center is believed to be found in today's Northern Iraq, Northern Persia, Afghanistan, and Northern Pakistan. From here, the Aryans swept through Europe, Asia Minor, and India.

The "first" suspected migration from this Aryan center were the Hellenes, who conquered today's Greece and the shores of Asia Minor. The Greeks then colonized Italy, North Africa, Spain, and the shores of the Black Sea. However, the Bible mentions that Abraham came from Ur. Therefore, it stands to reason that prior to the Hellenic migrations other migrations occurred also: Etruscan, Celt and so on. Since Ur is in today's Iraq, it stands to reason that this migration was also Aryan.

Of course this makes the Jews the original Aryans and there we are, predating the Greeks, the Germans, and the Slavs. The second suspected migration, from the Aryan center, were the Teutonic tribes or the Germans. They moved through central Europe and settled from the Dnieper to the Pyrenees. The Roman Empire waged war against these tribes, subjugating some of them. The third suspected migration from this center were the Slavs. They pushed the prior German tribes further west and compacted them. Some even moved through Europe and settled in North Africa (Alani).

For example: Originally, the Burgundians had settled on the Baltic shore. The Slavic migration pushed them into today's France. The Ostrogoths and the Visigoths were all part of this Slavic migration. The Visigoths and Ostrogoths combined, conquered Rome, and settled in Italy. Does this make today's Italy Slavic? Perhaps, but this does make Jews, Greeks, Germans and Russians all of the same stock.

In addition, the Aryans also migrated into India and established an Empire there. This establishes India to be also of Aryan stock. Finally the Aryans moved into Persia, Iraq and Jordan. This makes Persia, Iraq and Jordan are also Aryan. Therefore, an Aryan subdivision is just not possible within the many ethnic groups Hitler tried to separate. That is, once the "stigma" of the language is overcome, a member of one ethnic group can easily pass for another member within this family of nations. What remains are certain physical differences and the difference in color.

Wedged between the second and third Aryan migration was the first recorded Mongolic migration into Europe, the Huns. Attila decimated the German tribes and set up kingdoms in Europe. The Finns, Latvians, Lithuanians and Estonians are said to be remnants of this migration. (The Hungarians were a later migration). Even in the great German saga, "Die

Nibelungen," the foes of Siegfried are destroyed at the court of Etzel (in Hungary). However, over the years the Hungarians intermingled with Germans and Slavs and very little remained of their Mongolic traits. Thus, central Europe was Aryan and contained a few Mongolic traits.

The Tartars were the third recorded Mongolic migration. The Tartars destroyed the great Rus Empire and its center Kiev, in 1240. While the Ukrainians were fighting the Tartars, the Prince of Moscow submitted himself to the Tartar Kahn's rule in 1243 becoming his vassal -- Alexander Nevsky. For the next two-hundred years, the Muscovites paid tribute to the Tartar Khan. They served him and expanded their rule at the expense of the Ukrainians and other Slavs. For their loyal service to the Khan, the Prince of Moscow (Alexander Nevsky) was permitted to take the title, "Of all of Rus(sia)." This "title" was kept by the rulers of Moscow after the Tartars were defeated in 1380 by Dimitri Donskoi. Then the Tartars merged with the Muscovites into a new nation once the Khanate of Kazan and Astrachan were defeated by Ivan the Terrible. In 1792, the Crimean Tartars were conquered by Catherine II. Gradually, the great Ukrainian Kingdom was destroyed by the Tartars and the Muscovites. The great cities of Suzdal and Novgorod were conquered and integrated into the Duchy of Muscovy. The only sanctuary for the other Slavs from the Tartars and Muscovites was to flee into the swamps and deep forests abundant in that region. Gradually, a new Slavic population shift occurred in the Ukrainian area of today's Zaporozhje. Shortly thereafter the "Zaporozhian Sitch" emerged as a new power which was independent of both Moscow and the Tartars. This became the homeland of the Cossacks.

Eventually the Tartars were defeated by the Muscovites and the Duchy of Muscovy became Russia (Peter I called it Rossia, as it is called today by the natives). Voltaire was hired to write the desired history for Moscow. He called it Russe, hence Russia. The new rulers of Russia and Moscow needed a new title. Therefore, an old Slavic title was resurrected, Czar. Therefore, from 1505 on the rulers of Moscow and Russia called themselves Czars and the first Russian monarchy was created. By 1700 Peter the Great or Peter I, had subjugated most of the Slavic tribes along with many parts of Siberia, calling himself an Emperor. Thus, in the formation and evolution of nations, the Russian nation is relatively new on the European theatre. For that reason, the history of Russia consists of three stages: 1) The Princes of Moscow who were vassals of the Khan,

1243 until 1505; 2) the period of Russian Monarchy from 1505 until 1700 under whom the Slavs were further subjugated; and finally, 3) the Russian Empire from 1700 until 1917. (The Romanovs ruled from 1613 to 1917).

Now every nation needs and requires a saga, a heroic past. This is necessary, in order to create a "bigger than life" picture of a nation and to match Western European tradition and lore. (A "me too" attitude). How could Russia create this tradition? Simple, take it from the Ukrainians and claim it to be their own. But, whenever this thievery occurs, the thief must persecute the victim. Did not the Christians appropriate the Torah from the Jews and persecute them thereafter? The systematic persecution of the Jews begins after the translation of the Bible. After the Vulgate translation. [Before that time, Christians were considered to be only a sect of the Jews]. In the same way the systematic persecution of the Ukrainians begins with the theft of the Ukrainian heritage by the Russians.

The stage has now been set. First, History is rewritten, then ancient documents vanish and finally, fraudulent documents are brought forward to support a new thesis. Finally, a very well known foreigner is hired to write your history -- Voltaire. The Ukraine was the "bread-basket" of Europe from the days of Herodotus and the Scythians until 1931 when Stalin collectivized the farms. Then, abruptly from 1931 on, the Ukraine could not feed itself!

Starting with Czar Peter I, and not ending until the fall of Communism, every European power has tried to control and to dominate the Ukraine: Greece, Rome, Germany, Austria, Turkey, Poland and Lithuania. Even England and France tried to control this fertile land. Some three-hundred-fifty years ago, a Hetman (leader of the Cossacks) decided that the best alternative of all was to seek an alliance with Russia (or Sweden or Turkey).

This treaty against other invaders is the only alliance which binds Russia and the Ukraine. From that day on, however, whether Russia was ruled by a Czar or a Communist leader, the Ukrainian intelligentsia was persecuted and systematically annihilated. After World War I, the Ukraine had an opportunity to become a free nation and declared its independence. So, what happened? First, the Austrians came and carved out the Western Ukraine for their rule. Then, the Germans wanted a piece. Then, Poland wanted a piece, and finally Russia wanted the Eastern half. Ukrainian Communists saw their salvation in Communism -- Kulish and others. How well did the Ukraine do under Communism?

Intellectuals were persecuted with the same fervor under Communism as under the Czars. They were banished to Siberia, hunted down and shot, tortured, and maimed. The Ukrainian language was raped by the Russians and the Ukrainian history was "russified." The single largest nuclear accident occurred in the Ukraine. The crop and buried debris are still killing the population from radiation.

Does it not stand to reason that the East was a "melting pot" of the many migrations? Historians cannot agree on this point, but this explanation of the migration center is just as plausible as any other. This then, makes the migrations also of Aryan or partially Aryan origin. The last Turkic migration was into today's Turkey and quickly expanded into the Balkans.

At one time Vienna was nearly taken by the Turkic invaders.(1683) Then, they turned south, conquered Greece, Asia Minor, the Middle East and North Africa. The end result was the huge Ottoman Empire which lasted through World War I. When the Ottoman Empire was dismantled and dismembered to suit the victor's colonial ambitions, many small and impotent nations were created on purpose. The richest of these nations were integrated into the British Commonwealth. Thus, Caesar's motto, "Divide and conquer," is alive and well.

Hitler's racial class structure did not allow for differentiation by color. This is understandable for in Europe, prior to the time of WW II, there were no people of color, and the few that were of color, served their nation with great distinction. For example -- Pushkin, a great Russian poet, was the descendent of a Negro slave.

Aside from a few singular cases, we could also look at generalizations. Modern study of human evolution suggests that the "original" man evolved in Africa. From Africa, he migrated into Asia and the great migration centers. From the migration centers, they disbursed throughout Europe and Asia in massive and cataclysmic waves. From Asia, humanity settled the Pacific Islands and the American continent. How did Egypt originate? Is it not possible that the initial migration from Africa established these kingdoms along the way -- just like the later migrations did?

Egypt is the source of western culture and civilization. The Greek culture is based on the Egyptian culture. The root of humanity begins in

Africa. Does it not stand to reason that humanity has the same origin? Why should we ever create caste systems to dehumanize mankind? Clearly, there is only one answer, to serve a selfish and egotistical purpose and, to hide one's own inadequacy.

Of course, as the Germans settled in Kiev, their first objective was to classify the population according to the new German caste system and to assign jobs. The new order was showing its teeth. "Das Arbeitsamt" (the State Employment Office) was operating. By September 26, 1941, they had reclassified the population with Teutonic efficiency in Kiev.

We were lucky. Somewhere in my mother's past was a German ancestor. This made us automatically "Volksdeutsche." Since the death of my father had caused a lot of anti-Communist feelings in our district, many neighbors and friends encouraged my mother to take an "official" position in the city administration, which she did. She became the Assistant Mayor in the Kuriniv district. She reported directly to the Mayor of that district, Dr. Bagazil.

As the second wave of German soldiers and administrators came to Kiev, new directives came from Berlin. Essentially they covered three points:

1) Seize or recruit able-bodied workers for factory work in Germany.
2) Make plans to reform the farms and make the Ukraine provide raw materials and food for Germany.
3) Bring all valuables to Germany.

Within weeks the railroad station was rebuilt and endless trains brought war material to Kiev: Tanks, trucks, artillery pieces, shells and motorbikes. The trains were then re-loaded, this time with human cargo, to work in the German factories. They were loaded with dismantled factories, food stuffs, and with the art treasures of the Ukraine.

At first, many volunteered to go to Germany to work. But, increasingly, there were fewer and fewer volunteers. Now the Germans had to resort to force. Raids were conducted on the streets, in the markets, and in the homes. Humanity was herded up, classified, and disbursed. "You -- work on the farm. You -- are privileged to go to Germany. You -- work in a factory. And, you -- die."

Still, compared with the Communist regime, the first winter was tolerable by most accounts and an expected famine was averted. At least the Germans seemed gentler in their cruelty. Killings were few, when compared with the Soviets, and only saboteurs were openly shot. During a war, this was almost acceptable. The work assignments were usually sensible. The rationing of food and clothing was disliked, but begrudgingly tolerated. Only the repatriation of workers bothered most people.

This is why, each time my mother found out that someone she knew was slated to be repatriated, she would get a message to them and find a home for them where they could hide. Soon our attic was full of young adults. As resistance to repatriation grew, German brutality grew also. Thus, a vicious cycle started. As German brutality increased, so did the resistance. By the spring of 1942, partisans began to emerge and by the end of 1942, partisan units had started to engage German soldiers. By 1943, the once euphoric reception of the Germans had turned into bitter hatred and open rebellion.

Then, in the spring of 1943, the repatriation policy stopped. Be it that Kiev was sufficiently depleted, or be it that a new region was targeted for repatriation, it was not explained. In any event, in the spring of 1943, the danger had passed and the young adults left their hideouts. So, one day our attic tenants left also.

Of course, after the debacle of Stalingrad, the tide turned against the Axis powers. Paulus and his Sixth Army surrendered, two Rumanian armies were annihilated, one Hungarian army was destroyed and von Kleist with his Panzer Group barely escaped the trap. Stalingrad became a mass grave for German, Rumanian and Hungarian "hubris." Approximately one quarter of the German Wehrmacht was destroyed at Stalingrad, and another quarter was so badly mauled that they became useless in the ensuing campaigns. Fresh recruits needed to be brought in and the new salient needed to be plugged. Von Rundstedt resigned, Brautisch (the overall commander of the Wehrmacht) resigned and Hitler assumed complete command of the Russian front.

Late 1942 saw Hitler appoint von Manstein to the Supreme Command of the Kursk salient. Von Manstein was the best strategist so far in the Russian campaign. He understood the deployment of armor and he was most successful with the Soviet tactics. Stalin appointed Zhukov as Supreme Commander on the Soviet side. Both sides knew that one way or another, the bulge at Kursk needed to be resolved. During the winter of 1942 and through the spring of 1943, panzers, artillery, and soldiers were amassed for the battle.

The key to the battle was the density of the artillery, and Zhukov made sure his was superior. As the battle unfolded, the German Panzers were literally annihilated; the Luftwaffe was decimated; and by June, Kursk became the greatest rout of German armor in Russia. Combined, some five-thousand Panzers were destroyed, nearly two-thousand airplanes were destroyed, and almost half a million German soldiers were captured.

It is said that, after the Battle of Kursk, the German Wehrmacht was exhausted and was unable to launch another offensive on the Russian front. Therefore, in a technical sense, World War II ended after the Battle of Kursk. What remained were mopup operations to rid the country of the invader and to plan the conquest of Germany and Berlin.

This intelligence was delivered to Hitler in the autumn of 1943. Hitler raged and refused to face reality. He removed von Manstein in disgrace. He moved Guderian to the Western front and sought new generals who could cheer him up instead. By 1944, the situation was so desperate that the German military decided to assassinate Hitler and make peace at any cost.

Unfortunately, Hitler survived the assassination attempt. He rounded up the generals involved and allowed them to commit suicide -- so that national honor could be preserved. What was curious in 1944 to the masses was, that a great number of German generals were killed in combat, all at the same time, and from different sectors of the front. Unsuspecting Germans lamented their great misfortune, at such a difficult time.

So, what started in Kiev as a rout of the Red Army ended with a rout of the German Wehrmacht. Neither of these is true. In the first battle for Kiev, the Ukrainians looked to the Germans as liberators and did not fight them. In the second battle for Kiev, the forces left to defend Kiev were decimated, exhausted and tired of this endless and hopeless war. But, the two dictators believed that they had evened the score on a chalkboard, with yet another reckoning to come. Did humanity and its suffering mean anything to them? Of course not! The individuals and their lives were not even important enough in the juxtaposition of dummy forces on a mock war battlefield.

****

The train we were assigned to was a supply train. The train had just unloaded fresh recruits, some dilapidated armor, mounds of mail, and cartons of supplies. It was restocked with, wheat, corn, vegetables, iron ore, lumber, roofing nails and was headed back to Berlin. About a thousand families were allowed to find room on that train, wherever they could -- provided they had the papers allowing them to leave. These families were also escaping from the "Red Devils." We were in this crowd. George was travelling with us. George had his mother and his daughter with him. My mother turned to me and said, "Say hello to Masha." I turned to Masha and said, "Hello."

All closed cars were restricted for supplies only. The supply was much more important than humanity. The humanity assembled to escape could only use open rail cars. The train was long and had many open cars. We found a car which carried roofing nails. It was a flatbed car with low railings on all sides. The nails were loose and formed one massive heap. My mother lifted me over the railing and said, "Stay there." George lifted Masha and dropped her next to me. Then, George's mother, my sister, my mother and George climbed into the flatbed car. They came to us, they put down a blanket and we sat down. When I looked around, I could see many people wedged between the nails and the railing of the car. All huddled together in family groups. Some covered themselves with blankets and some just held on to each other. We just sat there. I thought to myself, "This is exciting! Finally, I can go on a real train ride, and to Berlin of all places."

CHAPTER 2

Proskurov

We sat on the train for what seemed an eternity. The nails were piercing my clothes. I had the distinct feeling that if this wait continued much longer I would swell up in welts and die. I turned to my mother and winced, "I don't like to sit on the nails. They hurt." My mother reached out to me, took me in her lap, and began gently singing a Ukrainian lullaby:

> "Sleep my youngster, sleep my darling, bayushky bayou. In your crib shines the moon of silver from above to you. Sleep my youngster, sleep on further, bayushky bayou."

After the first verse I was sound asleep.

The next thing I remembered was a jolt. I woke up hearing everybody cursing at the nails. Everybody in our car had experienced the same prickling of the nails as I had. Now that the train had started to move, the initial shock of the motion literally "nailed" everybody. They cursed the "Red Devils" for making such inferior nails:

> "These bloody Reds can't even make rounded nails."

-- and --

"Sons of bitches, the points are sharp as needles as if they knew they would torture our asses until the end!"

-- and --

"If these nails were made in Germany, they would be gentle as a feather and tough like diamonds. But no, we have to sit on this garbage."

Everybody hurriedly put more padding on the nails to make the ride more comfortable. Soon, the train started moving faster and faster. And, finally we were at full speed.

We travelled by night because by now, after the Battle of Kursk, the Soviets held complete air superiority. The Soviets strafed anything that moved: Trains, trucks, cars, motorcycles, even horses and buggies. It was just too dangerous to travel during the day. The night gave us some cover from a potential air attack.

Meanwhile, as we left the outskirts of Kiev, we could see brilliant fireworks. Rockets were going bzzzz…, bzzzz…, bzzzz… and, in between them, a flash of lighting and booom…; then another sequence of bzzzz…, bzzzz…, bzzzz… and another flash of lightening and booom… and this continued all night.

I turned to my mother and said, "Look at the fireworks, mama." She turned to me and said, "Son, these are not fireworks. The Red Devils are bombarding our hometown. For every flash you see, another human life is extinguished." I turned sad. I started counting the flashes. Pretty soon, I was at the end of my number repertoire, but the flashes continued. Only now they were fainter. And, with each passing moment, they became fainter and fainter. The only time we lost sight of the spectacle was when we went through a tunnel or entered a dense forest. But, as soon as we were in the open again, the spectacle continued. After a while, it became routine; and I paid no attention to it at all.

The air was crisp and cold. The speed of the train only accentuated the cold. It became bitter cold. Despite all the clothing we had on, despite all the preparations we had made, we were not properly clothed for the ride. We started to snuggle up to preserve body heat. Masha and I were in the center, the adults were close together shielding us from the wind. I fell asleep again.

I woke up because the motion stopped. Our train had come to a halt. I looked up and saw only the faces of the adults: George, my mother and George's mother. Emma was not in sight. I jumped up and looked for Emma.

"Where is Emma?" I asked my mother.

"Oh, she had to go to the toilet," my mother replied.

I looked around, but there was no toilet in sight.

"So, where is Emma?" I asked again.

"Oh, that girl, she jumped off the train and disappeared in the woods. I told her not to go far, but she is probably a mile away. I hope the train does not start moving," my mother lamented.

The train was not going anywhere. We were "parked" in a stretch of dense forest which obscured the train from the air. It was dawn, and the locomotive was turned off. Here, we would sit out the day for travelling by day was sheer suicide. An official "conductor" walked down the tracks and said softly every fifty steps or so, "Disembark until evening, but no fires."

Everybody began to disembark. We left most of our luggage on the train. George took the blankets, and my mother took her knapsack. We strolled a few paces into the woods and made ourselves comfortable. My mother opened her knapsack. She produced a knife and doled out bread and bacon to everybody in our group. To this day, I think this was one of the best meals I have ever eaten.

After our meal, we rested for a while. Then things became boring. The adults just sat around and talked. They discussed how soon they would return to their homes and old jobs. To them, the Germans were not "licked." Only a temporary setback made us leave our homes. George's mother even suggested that maybe the German victory was already complete, and we could return to Kiev tonight.

However, George replied, "Remember the bzzzz... sound?... Those were Katjushas (portable missile launchers). And, the boom sound?... Those where the shells of the T34 (medium tank). The German armor we did not hear at all." After a while, he continued, "But, then again,... the Germans use lighter shells,... so we probably did not hear them because their sound does not carry so far," he said pensively.

George was a contrarian. He liked to defend "the other point of view." He was educated in St. Petersburg. To him, St. Petersburg was the intellectual center of the "universe." He claimed it had the best

University for Mathematics, Physics, Medicine, Chemistry, Biology, History and Journalism. He was very proud of being a Journalist from St. Petersburg. Born in 1902, he was too young for military service during WW I. However, the reason and progress of the War turned him against the Czar. To him, the senseless slaughter of badly-equipped Russian soldiers was a clear sign of the Czar's incompetence and insensitivity to the people. During the Revolution, his father was murdered by the Bolsheviks. He turned into an ardent anti-Communist and moved to Kiev with his mother. According to him, Kiev was the only other respectable place for intellectuals. He married, and his wife soon had a daughter. In one of Stalin's mass roundups, his wife was caught and murdered (which was a cover story). Thus, Stalin's reign of terror only confirmed George's earlier convictions. When the Germans entered Kiev, he volunteered to work for them. My mother met George in early 1943, and he became our friend.

For a Slav, he was very tall and wiry, about six feet two inches tall. Because of his height and lack of military training, his posture was very bad. He tended to "bend down," when he was standing, appearing much shorter than he was. A large hooked nose, a massive pipe in his mouth, and one hand on the pipe dominated his appearance. Only then, one would notice his dark hair, bushy eyebrows, and oval face. His eyes, however, were restless. They "danced" when he talked. I often had the impression that he did not like to focus on anything or anybody for very long.

Many of his views expressed his disappointment and disenchantment with governmental "systems." He felt that education was only another form of indoctrination by the system for economic enslavement. Universities taught nothing practical. They taught nothing which created wealth and financial independence. They produced only better "coolies" for their industrial complex. By the time a subject was taught, it was obsolete for practical use. A good butcher or baker had a much better future for survival than an intellectual. The intellectual community was "incestuous." They only copied from each other, complimented each other, and regurgitated plagiarisms of one form or another to each other. A true intellectual had to spend some time in prison to raise his or her consciousness. But, that was too high a price to pay for potential fame. Thus, George resigned himself to being just another intellectual, despising manual work and lamenting his lot.

In contrast, his mother was very short and appeared frail. While she was in her mid sixties, she was everything but frail. She was strong-willed and determined. Yet she had a way of getting her way in a mild and calm manner. She never raised her voice. Her long white hair demanded respect, and she got it from everybody in our party. She appeared confused and disoriented on the train ride only because she resisted leaving her home in every possible way, seeking reassurances from all that this was the only alternative left.

I decided to get acquainted with Masha. I walked over to her and looked at her piercingly from head to toe. She was rather cute. Maybe a bit older than I was, but close enough to my age.

"How old are you?" I asked.

She looked at me sternly and replied, "Seven, but next month I will be eight."

"Do you want to play tag?" I asked.

She jumped up and yelled, "Ok, you're it," and she took off. I tried to follow her, but my clothes would not permit it. I felt I was in a sack, tied up to my neck with a load of potatoes on my back. I was bundled like a mummy, and my limbs would not move in my clothes. Playing tag was a bad idea. Somehow I had to "finesse" this situation:

"Not today," I yelled after her. "Some other time," I continued.

She seemed disappointed and she came back slowly. All I could hear her say was a faint, "Slow-poke," and she sat down pretending to listen to the adults. Emma was in a world all by herself. She had a book and was reading intensely. So, I just walked around, kicking at some sand and leaves to pass the boredom.

The day proved uneventful. By dusk, the conductor came around and waved the "all aboard" sign. We scurried back to the train and assumed our prior positions. Somehow the nails seemed sharper and colder than from the night before. Soon the train was back in motion. I fell asleep almost instantly. The routine was not bad I thought. Surely, by tomorrow, we would be in Berlin.

Again, I woke up because the train jerked and came to a stop. I looked up, and it was pitch black outside. Even the stars were not visible. Curious, I thought, why did we stop? But, very soon my eyes adjusted, and I could see faintly in the dark.

Our conductor came running down the train, yelling, "The partisans demolished the rails ahead of us. Get off the train!" Apparently, there was real danger because the conductor was frantic as he ran down the train. We disembarked and huddled together as if we could make the train move again or fix the rails. The conductor waved to us to get closer. We assembled near him, and he began his explanation:

"The rails ahead have been blown up. Most likely there are mines on the track. You have two choices:

1) About three miles down the track is the town of Proskurov. You can make it there before daybreak. Most likely the partisans are gone. They usually strike and disappear.

-- or --

2) You can stay here and wait for help. Surely, help is on the way. If not, within twenty minutes, we will be missed at the railroad junction in Proskurov. Then, a team will be sent to look for us. However, it may take them the rest of the night to fix the rails. So, the choice is yours. Walk or wait."

My mother and George exchanged quick looks, and the message appeared to be clear to them. We were walking to Proskurov. If the train could not be moved by dawn, it was a sitting duck.

Every war can be dissected into two major components: A strategy and a tactic. Western mentality has one perception what strategy and tactics are. Eastern mentality has a completely different perception.

In its broadest sense, the strategy is the objective of the war. The ultimate objective, of course, is victory and the spoils to the victor. The strategy is the means by which the objective is achieved. So, if the strategy of this war was to defeat the Soviet Union, the Axis powers were derelict in their duty.

Western strategy hinged on one basic premise: Demonstrate the superiority and skill of the forces; then, intimidate the opposing military, and settle for a "mutually" acceptable peace. By the eighteenth century, this was epitomized by "maneuvers." It was not uncommon to "engage" in a "battle" without any significant casualties. This was called "civilized" warfare.

Until the end of World War II, "soldiering" or being a soldier, was the noblest "profession" a man could aspire to. The only other acceptable profession was the "Priesthood." Merchants, artisans and poets were "second class" citizens when compared with "soldiers" and the titles they earned. Titles, land and a pension were mainly earned through soldiering.

Kings generally ruled over a "homogeneous" ethnic group. But kingdoms were "awarded" by the Emperor either for particular merit or by succession. A ruling king was often not of the same ethnic stock as the population. For example, The House of Hannover, who were Germans, became the rulers of England in 1714 when Queen Anne died. But, at the same time, the King of England continued to be also the Duke of Hanover. That is, the King of England was the ruler of two diverse ethnic groups, the Germans in Hannover and the English. This dual rule was sanctioned by the emperor at that time. From the Emperor's point of view, England was again brought back into the fold of the Holy Roman Empire. (Henry VIII had broken away from the Empire). Thus, what the Spanish Armada could not accomplish by military might was accomplished by Leibniz by way of lineage to the throne of England. Of course, only much later would England become a major antagonist of the Holy Roman Empire. Again, however, this new role for England was not foreseen at that time.

Therefore, the army of an emperor could consist of many diverse ethnic groups -- and more often than not it did. In each case, however, these ethnic groups were usually loyal subjects of the Emperor. Since soldiering was usually very profitable, the profit motive needed to be de-emphasized in the soldier's profession. Therefore, we differentiate the "loyal" servants from the hired "beasts." Loyal servants accept soldiering as part of their duty to their sovereign, while mercenaries serve for their own greed. In this way, we polarize when using a new word: Mercenaries. We imply this distinction between soldiers and mercenaries. As if rape, pillage and plunder makes a lot of difference whether it is performed in the name of a king, dictator, elected official or for personal gratification in a war. Yet, to this day, we tend to make this subtle distinction.

Of course, this subtle distinction between soldiers and mercenaries can be exploited for greater political advantage whether it is founded or not. In fact, the English propaganda has vilified the German nation since the days of the Revolutionary War of 1776 in America in order to suit their greater ambitions in North America. Before Napoleon, national awareness was virtually non-existent in Europe. This was so because the Holy Roman Empire ruled many diverse "nations." It ruled over people with many diverse languages, and it ruled many diverse ethnic groups. In fact, the Holy Roman Empire could be called the original "melting pot" in Europe: Arabs, Germans, Mongols, Moors, Slavs, Turks and many other ethnic groups were ruled by the Emperor. Therefore, officers in the Imperial Army had no national loyalty. What mattered was the rank they served and what promotions were available to them. So, diverse nationals served even more diverse nations.

Today we consider the pre-Napoleonic military formations to be archaic. To avoid desertion, soldiers formed a dense square which was loosely surrounded by officers. We call these formations a "carree." When a real battle ensued, the officers were decimated first. This was economically more productive for the Emperor for the officers earned a lot more than the enlisted men. And since the Emperor was habitually behind in pay to his soldiers, his larger liabilities were disposed of first.

When Napoleon came to power, he "revolutionized" this concept. The "carree" was disbanded and replaced with a "squad." A squad was the smallest fighting unit headed by an officer. Multiple squads formed a battalion and multiple battalions formed a division. Multiple divisions formed an army, and multiple armies formed an army group. The precise ratios varied depending on the peace or war situation which prevailed or the particular preferences of a nation. Eventually, all modern armies adopted this structure. However, the key was that a true and direct hierarchy was established. So, when Napoleon encountered the "old" style formations in Europe, he was able to decimate them with ease. That is, the "old" style formations carried only one half or one third of the potential punch as the Napoleonic formations.

Eastern strategy was different. While Russia conformed to the "old style" formations to suit the western leaders, the inherent tactic in a war was completely different. The first mission was to survive the opponent's onslaught. Then, hit him were it hurts until the opponent exhausts himself. That is, it is essentially a strategy of survival. Without this "innate" strategy of survival, the Slavic nations would have perished a long time ago. Attila the Hun defeated the Slavs; in the end, he was destroyed by them. The Tartars defeated the Ukrainian Kingdom, but they were eventually destroyed and driven out of Europe. Peter I defeated the Cossacks, yet the Ukrainians survived. Napoleon captured Moscow only for his army to be annihilated at the Niemen. Hitler claimed victory and invincibility only for his armies to be decimated. Stalin terrorized the Ukraine only for his Empire to disintegrate.

The first recorded incident of a massive invasion is described by Herodotus. Darius, the King of Persia, decided to punish the Scythians, the ancestors of the Ukrainians, for their insolence. Darius raised a massive army and invaded the Scythian homeland (the present day Ukraine). The Scythians abandoned their homes and towns and evaded a battle for the longest time. Then, after they had lured the army of Darius into a deep forest which was surrounded by swamps, they attacked at night and destroyed the greater part of his army. Darius retreated in panic. As he retreated, his army was nearly decimated. Had it not been for the Thracians, who guarded the bridge-head across the river Danube for Darius and remained loyal to him during the campaign, the victory would have been a complete rout. (As reported by Herodotus.)

The Scythians were overcome by the Sarmatians; and the Sarmatians, by the Alani. Ancient burial sites suggest that they intermingled rather than destroying each another. The Alani were defeated by Attila the Hun. They combined with the Goths, swept through Europe, and eventually settled in North Africa. Then, the Antae moved in and combined with the remaining Alani, Goths and Sarmatians.

Collectively we call these people the Ostrogoths and Visigoths or Goths. The Ostogoths included the Sarmatians, Alani and Suevi or Suebe. The Visigoths included the Vikings and the Vandals. At one time, the Ostrogoths and Visigoths ruled a huge Empire in Europe and North Africa. It spanned from the Caspian Sea through Central Europe and into Southern France and Spain. In North Africa, they reigned in today's Morocco, Algeria and Tunisia. Earlier historians refer to them by their specific tribal names. Later historians call them collectively the Visigoths. For example, the Suevi settled in Northwest Spain. The Alani settled in North Africa. The Ostrogoths were invited by Emperor Zeno to settle in Italy to prevent a Germanic invasion. They settled in Italy and intermingled with the population. Their King became the Roman Emperor (Thoedoric.)

Their Kings preferred to be called "Judges" rather than Kings. The title of a Judge implied "wisdom," rather than military leadership. They ruled this vast Empire from about 400 to 750. Then the Germanic tribes began to dominate France; and the Franks in particular. Then the Visigoths were systematically destroyed. The main reason they were destroyed was because of their difference in Christian belief. They were Arian Christians while the Franks were Catholic. While the Arian belief was Christian, it advocated that Christ was "human" and was not of the same "substance" as the "Father" or the "Holy Ghost." This pitted the Germanic tribes into a "holy war" against the Visigoths.

The next major invasion was the invasion of the Tartars. At that time, the Ukraine was a major power. Its only rival was the Byzantine Empire. Kiev was a match for Rome and Constantinople. In fact, Constantinople was invaded and defeated by the Ukrainians -- to abolish the annual tribute paid to Constantinople. In 911, a peace was made, and to seal the peace, a Byzantine princess became the wife of the Ukrainian King Volodymir.

The Tartars attacked Kiev and decimated the inhabitants. Western tactics proved fatal for the Ukraine. However, the population escaped into the woods and swamps of the land. For nearly two hundred years, the cities and citizenry paid tribute to the Tartar Khan. Yet, each time the Tartars came in large numbers, the citizenry would abandon the cities and flee into the woods and the swamps. The Tartars would sack and burn the cities, but finally they would leave. Then, the population would come back and rebuild the cities. Eventually, the Tartars were defeated by Dimitri Donskoi and, much later, driven out of Eastern Europe.

Then came the German knights. They had just successfully conquered Poland, and with Polish help they came to conquer the Slavs. At first, the knights were unstoppable. Every army was mauled but managed to retreat. Then, Vitus (from Lituania) lured them into the swamps at Tannenberg and destroyed the knights and their allies. This defeat "insulted" the German honor and an "equalizer" needed to be found to even the "score," to restore German honor. In World War I, Samsonov's army was defeated by a Frenchman in German service (Francois) hundreds of miles away from Tannenberg. Of course, the credit could not go to a Frenchman. The credits went to von Hindenburg and Ludendorff (who were on the western front at that time). The fact, that the battle was not even close to Tannenberg did not matter. It was close enough to equalize national honor.

Then came Napoleon. Napoleon came for victory's sake. Only a few years before, in 1806, Napoleon and the Czar "partitioned" Europe. They met at Tilsit in the middle of the River Niemen on a barge in "no man's land." They divided Europe and made an alliance (the Treaty of Tilsit). The map of Europe was reduced to four nations: France, Russia, England and Turkey (The Ottoman Empire). France was to the west, Russia to the east of the Niemen; England and the Ottoman Empire were "tolerated" by default. This treaty was signed while Napoleon waged the "Continental Blockade" against England.

Then, for no apparent reason, Napoleon invaded his Russian ally. The nations of Europe came with Napoleon: Germans (from all states), Spaniards, Italians (from all states), Austrians, Bohemians, Moravians, Hungarians, Croats, Slovenes, Rumanians and the Poles. The most fervent were the Poles. While some three-hundred thousand Frenchmen formed the spearhead, the bulk of the "Grand Army" were foreigners.

An opportunity presented itself to "cleanse" their national disgrace with a "holy war" on Russia. How could one lose? The greatest conqueror of all time had set his eyes on Russia. How could one miss this opportunity to join his bandwagon?

When Kutuzov was assigned the job of defeating Napoleon, his first and primary mission was to survive -- how to direct a defensive which would liberate Russia from this horde. The loss of one city or a hundred cities did not matter to Kutuzov. Kutuzov had to "thin out" the invader first. He had to find the invader's Achilles heel. The only thing Kutuzov knew was that time and space were on his side, not numbers, not tactics, just time and space. War was not a game of chess, but a game of "go." But, "that" game of go was convertible into a game of chess at any moment.

And now the partisans. The partisans were the most natural form of tactics for the Slavs. The Cossacks "wrote" the book on partisan tactics. This tactic proved invaluable for two thousand years. Why should it fail this time? A few tanks, a few armored vehicles? Entropy would take care of the tanks and armor. Time and space were on the side of the partisans. They could strike at will and wound the invader -- one wound, two wounds and so on. Eventually, the invader would bleed to death from the many superficial wounds.

We took our luggage off the train, strapped on our knapsack and started to walk along the railroad tracks. At first, it seemed like a lot of fun. At last, I could break in the new shoes I had on. A few families started walking with us along the tracks. The majority stayed with the train. We started to walk and we walked and we walked...

After a while, I thought what an endless journey. Emma was wrestling with her suitcase. Then, she dropped it in disgust, ran to the nearest tree and broke off a good-sized branch. She put her suitcase on the branch and started to pull on the branch. This was fine for a while, but from time to time, the suitcase would slip off the branch, and she had to put it back in place. Her idea caught on. Soon, almost everybody with suitcases was using the same trick.

In retrospect, the walk was not that bad. I complained a lot because my shoes began to hurt, and I was perspiring throughout. Earlier, on the train, I must have caught a cold, and now the cold was rapidly getting worse. The fact that I was perspiring made the situation even worse because I would open my coat until I was cold. Then, I would close it to warm up. Meanwhile, the adults were preoccupied carrying the baggage, while I acted as I pleased.

We moved in a single file. In front was "Grandma." Behind her was my mother; then came George, then Masha and then me. And in the rear was Emma. We walked for about one hundred yards. Then, we stopped for a short while. My mother would inspect for "damage" control. Then, we would start up again and then stop again. And, this continued all night. The train was no longer in sight. Help was not in sight, and there was no sign of the partisans. However, soon we could see the silhouette of a town. There, at last, Proskurov was in sight! Only a few yards further, there was a sharp bend in the tracks. When we turned the corner, we could see trucks crossing the railroad tracks a short distance away. A road! Why didn't anybody think of that? A road frequently parallels a railroad track. We were too exhausted to think further. We arrived at the road and my mother yelled at a driver, "Which way is Proskurov?"

"My way," the driver shouted back. "If you want, I'll give you all a lift," he continued.

Oh, did we want a lift. This driver was a god-send. My mother yelled back, "Yes, please give us a lift." The driver pulled over, packed us into the truck and said, "Where to?"

"To the train station," my mother replied.

The driver took us to the train station alright. But, there was hardly anything left of it. It must have been just recently mined or bombed. The rails were all twisted up. The platform was destroyed, and the roof was bullet ridden. We disembarked anyway.

My mother went to the station master, and he assured us that by evening the trains would be running again on schedule. My mother returned with the good news. But it was not to be. Not that September evening -- Berlin had to wait.

I was coughing and running a fever. My face was red, and I was shivering. My mother looked at me, and I heard only one word: "Pneumonia." My mother bundled me up, told Emma to take care of me, and she disappeared. After a while she came back and said to George, "Tola must go to a hospital. We have to stay here. You can see we cannot continue. If you wish, you continue with your mother and Masha. I will meet you in Berlin."

George looked at her and said, "What nonsense, naturally we will stay with you until he is well, and then we will continue on together."

That night, I was admitted to the hospital. Actually, I felt quite fine except for the hot and cold flashes which were running through my body. My bones hurt, and I started to cough blood. In the hospital, I was getting all the attention one could possibly ask for. The nurses kept running in and out of my room. All kept saying, "Look at this beautiful Aryan. Blonde hair, blue eyes and such a cute boy."

During the day, Emma would visit me and encourage me with a few laconic words, "How is my brother today? Fine, that's fine. Get well soon," and she would vanish, her duty fulfilled. My mother was with me all the time. I don't know how she managed it, but apparently she found a good job, good quarters, and had plenty of time in the hospital for me, too. Masha and "grandma" came occasionally; George, never.

As events unravelled later on, here is what happened. As soon as my mother placed me in the hospital, she went to the local Arbeitsamt. There she showed her travel orders and requested an extension since I was in the hospital with pneumonia. She was sent to the local "Gebietskommissiorat," (regional administration). The commandant was a major in the Wehrmacht. That day, the major had wounded himself cleaning his gun. Normally, this was not a serious matter. But, due to the panic of the all-out retreat on the Russian front, however, soldiers were maiming themselves to evade being sent there. Consequently, Hitler had issued a new directive which in part said the following: "Anyone inflicting a wound on himself was a coward, an evader of duties to the fatherland, and was to be treated as a deserter, or shot on the spot."

This put the major in a precarious position. If he went to the hospital, he would be reported for a self-inflicted gun shot wound. The Gestapo was sure to investigate his case, and the chances were very high that he could be tried and possibly executed for a self-inflicted wound -- to set an example. Now, enter this "Volksdeutsche," with medical training, a degree in bio-chemistry and pharmacology, and a specialist in agronomy! The major offered her a job as an agronomist on the spot, provided she would also tend to his slight wound. Naturally, my mother accepted the offer. Quarters were assigned to her and her immediate family. This included "grandmother," George and Masha.

The major proved to be a real "Mensch" (human being). A good and kind-hearted man. He always found us extra provisions, he cared for our family, and he was kind and civilized with us. He gave us a list of relatives and friends in Berlin and in other parts of Germany. He insisted we turn to these people for help and assistance if we ever needed it. He took a liking to me. He had lost a son on the Russian front, and I reminded him of his son.

After a while, the situation became somewhat uneasy for my mother. His kindness was overwhelming. For all practical purposes, he started to court my mother. Therefore, my mother decided to marry George and untie this Gordian Knot.

I was released from the hospital within a few weeks. Now technically, we could continue the journey at any time, but we had found a safe haven, and it was difficult to leave paradise. The reality was that the front came closer every day. By December 1, the front was only twenty miles away. It was high time to seek refuge in Berlin. On December 3, we were scheduled to depart. This time, not on a freight train full of nails, but on a regular passenger train with seats, and a toilet to boot.

Again, the train travelled mostly at night. On only a few occasions did our train-men take a chance and travel by day. Eventually, we reached Cottbus. On the previous night, Cottbus had literally been erased from the map. A massive Allied air raid destroyed the city and all its major communications links. Thus, just before Cottbus, our train journey came to an end. Trucks ferried us to the other side of Cottbus, where another train was supposed to await us to continue our journey. At the appointed stop, the trucks were waiting for us. Unceremoniously, all passengers were herded into the trucks and ferried through Cottbus.

Destruction of this magnitude I had never seen before, nor since. The city was razed to the ground. Not one building was standing within my peripheral vision. The destruction was complete. A few survivors were on the streets. They were trying to clean up the debris and gather up the dead. Dead corpses were lined up along the street waiting for the mortuary truck. In the air was the foul smell of destruction. My mother tried to cover my nose and eyes with a handkerchief. I resisted and watched our passage through this once lively town. The living were trying to make the roads passable. The few civilians seemed to be in a daze. The soldiers seemed to be in shock. The civilians walked like zombies. They walked the streets in confusion and were trying to pick up a few bricks here and there to clear the road and to re-arrange the dead. Intermittently, motorized checkpoints would check our travel orders and destination. The soldiers were grim.

Apparently, the soldiers had never seen anything like this either. Our trucks were whisked through all the checkpoints, and we arrived at the designated railroad station. I remember how everybody had tears in their eyes. Yet, their faces were grim and stern. The torture and suffering we had just seen could only exist in a sick mind. It could not be real -- yet, here it was, we had just witnessed it.

We arrived at the rail junction and the expected train was not there. A mass of people stood along-side a long platforms waiting for trains which never arrived. We were directed to one platform and told our train would arrive shortly. Shortly, in those days, meant sometimes between today and next week.

Meanwhile, the great food my mother had prepared for our journey had already been consumed. Since we were travelling on a "posh" train, we expected to be in Berlin the same day. But, here it was evening, and the snacks we brought with us were eaten already, and we had only covered about half the distance to Berlin.

Of course, my mother had some supplies. A large bar of butter -- real butter mind you and a bag of sugar. She improvised immediately. The butter came out. The sugar came out, and a spoon came out. She carved out little butter balls, sprinkled them with sugar and we had a meal. I could eat only three or four such butter balls. I almost started to vomit after the last one. There had to be another answer. How could one possibly get some bread, I thought.

In those days, only water could be had at the train station. Everything else was rationed, and we had no ration cards. So, while the others were feasting, I started to walk slowly up the platform. At last, I spotted what I needed. I spotted a group of four or five soldiers cutting up a loaf of bread. I came closer and closer to them. I did not dare to look them in the eyes. But, steadily I was inching closer and closer. My eyes were fixed on the bread. I had no idea what to do next, but before there is a next, the objective must be found. Finally, one of the soldiers spotted me. He grinned at me and said, "Nu, Hans willst du ein stuck Brot?"

I had no idea what he said. German was foreign to me at that time. He had asked me if I wanted a piece of bread. All I did was stare at the bread. I was devouring the bread he held in his hand, with my mind. The soldier sensed that I wanted more than a piece. He grinned again and said, "Nu, Hans hier ist das Brot," and he handed me the remainder of the loaf. I took the bread, cracked a smile and uttered one of the few German words I knew, "Danke." I turned and made a bee-line to my mother. All I could hear in back of me was, "Der Hans ist ein schones Kind."

I arrived at my mother's not a moment too soon. Practically everybody was ready to throw up from the concoction my mother was doling out. I gave her the bread. She looked at me and said, "How did you get this bread?" I turned and pointed to the soldiers. They waved from the distance, and my mother bowed with gratitude and waved back. Now, we could continue with the real meal. The loaf of bread proved ample food for all of us. Grandma looked at me and uttered, "God protects children and drunks."

Our train came, we boarded, and it finally appeared we were destined to make it to Berlin, non-stop -- at least to my recollection. The train "zoomed" to the city. My mother tells me that after we boarded, I fell sound asleep and did not wake up until we were in Berlin.

CHAPTER 3

Berlin 1943 to 1944

Finally we had arrived. I was anxious to find out what freedom was all about. This was the city which epitomized freedom and safety to us. We took our luggage and exited the train.

My first impression was awe and inspiration. A huge hall like structure spanned endlessly as far as the eye could see. Trains were everywhere. Dozens of trains were constantly coming and going. I could clearly hear the announcer, but I could not understand a word. Wow, I thought to myself, I am going to like this place.

When all of us got out of the train my mother assembled everybody and told them, "This is a big place. Stay together and don't get lost. But, if you get lost, go to the station master and stay there," and she pointed in the direction of a huge building. A porter came. We loaded up our baggage and followed the porter. The porter took us through the main building to a waiting taxi. He unloaded our baggage into the taxi, and my mother paid him.

We were ready to pile into the taxi when we heard, "Halt!" And, shortly thereafter, "Papiere." A tall, good-looking policeman was standing right behind us with his hand stretched out. My mother gave him her travel orders. Calmly, almost deliberately, he started to examine her papers.

"Hm…, Volksdeutsche," I heard him say. The policeman now started to look us over. First my mother, then me, then Emma. Apparently, we had passed his inspection. Then, he turned to George and said, "Papiere."

George had his travel orders ready and handed them to him. Again, he examined the papers calmly and deliberately. "Hm…, Ostland?" I heard him say. Now he started to look over George, grandmother and Masha. There was clearly something he did not like. He walked around the taxi. He looked around, as if he was counting the number of taxies in front of the train station. Then, he looked at our luggage and back to us again. I could sense that he did not know what to do with us. He looked at me, and I gave him a broad smile. He smiled back and started to walk around the taxi again.

He stopped in front of us and said, "Gut,… In Ordnung."

Apparently we passed his inspection. We piled into the taxi, and the driver asked, "Wohin?" My mother gave the direction, "Reichsministerium." The driver started the taxi and drove away.

Apparently, as we later found out, taxis were generally reserved for "solid" Aryans. My mother passed the inspection only because of her travel orders. George was an "Untermensch," and his usage of the taxi was actually forbidden. But, his travel orders requested him to report to the "Reichsministerium," to assume the post of editor-in-chief. The policeman was in a dilemma. On the one hand, George and his family members were forbidden to take a taxi. While, on the other, his "job title" was sufficiently important to use a taxi. The fact that my mother was married to George seemed to make no difference.

I was glued to the window. The street we were on was wide, paved, clean, and full of small shops. I have been to the market in Kiev many times. There, many small stands expose their wares. From fruits to vegetables, from clothes to tools, from farm animals to feed, all were in the open. You could see the merchandise, you could touch it and select it. That is, when there was merchandise.

Here it was different. The shops had glass windows. Each store seemed like a small fortress, and all seemed to be well stocked. Each store seemed larger than the last, and all had beautiful displays in their windows. I had made up my mind. If this was freedom, then I liked it.

We arrived at our destination. My mother and George went inside while we waited in the taxi. After about ten minutes, my mother came out and told the driver, "Antonauer-strasse 22." The driver started the taxi and drove us to the new destination. These were the living quarters assigned to us.

The new quarters were practically in the very center of Berlin. About four hundred yards southeast of us was the Brandenburg Gate. About four hundred yards southwest of us was the Victory Statue (Siegessaule). About one hundred yards west of us was the "Hansa Platz."

And, practically next to us, only a short block away, was the "Tiergarten," a wonderful park in the center of Berlin with a zoo. One short block from us, was the "subway" (S-Bahn) station "Believue." Actually, our section of the city was called "Alt-Moabiet."

The building we were assigned to was wonderful. It was massive, well-kept and "spick and span." It was a six story walkup. Our apartment was on the second floor. The apartment was very large. But, the apartment was cold -- it had no oven with a bed over it. However, it did have many rooms: A kitchen, two bedrooms, a family room and a toilet. Grandma, George and my mother had one room. Emma, Masha and I shared the other. The toilet had a contraption I had never seen before. They called it a "water closet." A bowl on the bottom, a water tank on top and a chain to be pulled wherever one was finished with one's business. Ingenious, but wasteful of water, I thought.

While the women were inspecting the apartment, I stood at the window and kept looking into the street. I noticed many kids about my age. After all, I thought freedom had many interesting tradeoffs. Instead of being on a farm, one had to live with many people. Instead of sleeping in a nice warm bed, one had to sleep on a cold cot, or an iron bed. What other tradeoffs needed to be made?

The women started to clean the apartment. Every room was swept and washed, and the furniture in the apartment was dusted and cleaned. By now, I was starved. The women were dashing back and forth with their chores. I was clearly in the way. I figured I could sneak out for a while and meet some of the kids on the street. So, slowly I made my way to the door, down the stairs and into the street. Then, I just stood there, in front of the house, waiting to meet some kids. But, nobody came to meet me

Adults were strolling by. Even kids in uniforms walked by. But nobody paid any attention to me. They just walked by me as though I were not there. After a while, I decided to go back to the apartment. And, I did.

The pace in the city was not rushed, but calm and deliberate. The war seemed to be going on somewhere else. The war seemed not to effect the city at all. At first, I did not notice any ruins or even damaged buildings. The reality of war seemed to be well concealed.

Soon George arrived, and he brought with him all kinds of food: sausages, bread, butter, rolls, flour, fruits, vegetables and tea. George loved to drink tea, and he prepared it in a very special way. While my mother was preparing the meal, George made his tea. Each sequence in the tea-making process had to be perfect. Otherwise, so he claimed, the tea was ruined.

First, a large pot of water needed to be boiled. That pot needed to have an opening wide enough to hold another small pot. Then, about two heaping spoonful's of tea were sprinkled into the bottom of a small pot.

Hot water was poured into the small pot until the small pot was about half full with hot water. Then, the small pot was placed into the opening of the large pot, and the tea was "steamed" for a while. After ten to fifteen minutes, the tea was ready.

Now the second part was just as important as the first part. To serve the tea, a "straight" glass was needed. A strainer was put on top of the glass and a small amount of the tea concentrate was poured into the glass. Then, hot water was added from the large pot. And, the tea was ready.

Of course the principle was based on a "Samovar." But, because Samovars were difficult to get in most parts of the world, this was the closest approximation to the process. George came originally from St. Petersburg. There, Samovars were very popular. But, in the Ukraine or in Germany, a Samovar was a novelty of sorts and was not easy to find. Of course, the other problem was the "straight" glass. George had an obsession about that. When the glass was not straight, it was just no good. And, most glasses were not meant to hold piping hot water. So, most glasses burst on him, and he was forever complaining about the quality of the glasses.

Be that as it may, dinner was ready, the tea was ready and we sat down for our meal. About midway through our meal, we heard a siren. George jumped up, closed all the windows and pulled the heavy shades down. We continued to eat. We were still eating, when we heard a lot of noises outside on the staircase. Somebody knocked on our door. My mother went to the door, and there was an elderly woman all dressed up for a survival expedition. Her clothes were bulging. She obviously had layers of clothes on. She held a pillow in one hand and a flashlight in the other. Strapped on her back was a knapsack.

"Let's go," she said. "You don't want to be caught in a raid. Do you?"

We got up, put our clothes on, put out the lights and joined the crowd. The easiest way was just to follow the crowd, and we did. But, when we got outside, there were columns of people moving silently and quietly in many different directions. One column was moving toward the Tiergarten. Another column was moving almost the opposite way, towards the Believue subway station. And, another column was moving in a third direction. My mother ran up to the lady and asked her, "Where are we going?"

"Well, I normally go to the Tiergarten-bunker. The big Zoo bunker is reserved for Aryans. It is impregnable. Some go to the subway. Actually, you could also go into the basement below, or any basement that is reinforced. But that is very dangerous!"

My mother fell back to us and said, "We are going to the Tiergarten-bunker," as we continued our walk quietly in the column we were in. Actually, it was a nice, short walk. Within a minute or so from the time of the siren, we were at the bunker.

The bunker had six entrances, and columns of people seemed to be "swallowed" up by these entrances. The original single file seemed to split into six arteries all by itself. Each artery led to one entrance. It was a bit eerie, but very orderly and efficient. When a section was filled up, the door was closed and the artery vanished. Somehow, each bunker seemed to swallow up all those willing to enter. There seemed to be an infinite amount of room in each bunker. Actually, the bunkers were quite small: only the humanity it swallowed was packed very densely.

The bunker was actually a trench, dug in a zig-zag fashion. The trench was about eight feet deep in the ground and about six feet wide. On the sides of the trench were concrete slabs. Each slab was about three feet wide, six feet long and one foot thick. Each slab was of reinforced concrete. The top was also made of concrete slabs, which rested on the two vertical slabs below. A mound of topsoil covered the erector-set-like concrete slab construction. And grass grew from the mound of topsoil, so the bunker was not readily visible in the park. Only the entrances beckoned to the world below.

Along the walls, inside the bunker, were fixed benches.

They were about eighteen inches wide and hugged the wall of the bunker on each side. This left approximately thirty-two inches of walking space between the benches. Two doors controlled one section.

This particular bunker was three separate but connected bunkers. Each individual bunker was separated by concrete slabs.

As we approached the bunker, it was pitch black outside. The whole city was blanketed in darkness. No sooner were we ready to enter, when a second alarm sounded. All of a sudden, searchlights lit up all over the sky, and we could hear, "Tak-tak-tak… tak-tak-tak… tak-tak-tak…" from the flack guns firing at the bombers.

There were guides by the door and they were urging the stragglers to get in faster. All we could hear was, "Schnell, schnell, schnell… geht rein." We entered the bunker and got seated. There was plenty of room inside. From inside the bunker we could only hear, "Boom, boom, boom…" as the bombs were dropping.

The humanity inside was completely silent. All praying in their own way, that no harm would come to their property or loved ones.

The raid lasted about half an hour; then, another siren. Almost in unison, the crowd would get up, breathe a sigh of relief, and simultaneously mumble: "Entwarnung." The ordeal for the night was over. Humanity could leave the bunker and pretend that nothing had happened.

The mood going home was cheerful, almost gay. Why not? Humanity survived another day. How about tomorrow? Well, tomorrow was too far away. Humanity had to live this day. Humanity felt it earned this next day of life. Tomorrow's ordeal would begin again at dusk, or later, or maybe not at all.

We came back to our apartment, and everything was just as we left it. Only the food got cold. But, the tea was still hot. Grandmother made tea for everybody and gave us some cookies. I had enough for one day; I went to bed.

Next morning I got up early, but my mother and George were already gone. They had gone to work. My mother was a journalist, and George was the editor-in-chief for a journal called "Satirikon," an anti-Communist journal. They worked for "Vinetta," the Russian propaganda arm of the "Reichsministerium." Ultimately, that whole department reported to Goebbels.

Their pay was very good, about 1500 Reichsmark each. At the start of the War, in 1941, one Reichsmark was worth about half a dollar. The problem was that the money was almost useless. Basic products and merchandise were obtainable only through ration cards. There was no "secondary" market or black market. Money alone bought very little. Moreover, a ration card without money was also useless. So, somewhere, there had to be a black market. We never tried to find out. The penalty was just too severe -- instant execution.

The ration cards were structured according to Aryan heritage, skill, position, and so on. I believe there were at least twelve varieties of ration cards. They allowed for a fixed quantity of bread, butter, meat and so on. They were issued each month anew. However, instead of buying bread, one could buy flour and the base quantity almost doubled. Instead of buying meat one could buy sausages and the base quantity doubled again. Instead of butter, one could buy margarine or lard and the base quantity quadrupled. Certain vegetables and nuts were available without ration cards -- the kind the Germans did not eat or were not fond of: for example, Garlic. We loved garlic. Garlic could be bought without ration cards. Potatoes, onions, beets and cabbage could be bought without ration cards also. In the fruit category, apples were most plentiful. Occasionally pears, plums and cherries were also available without ration cards. For us this was heaven.

The butter was very bad at that time. But, the lard was very good. So, we bought usually lard instead of butter. Garlic was plentiful. So, an end-piece of dark bread, spread with lard and rubbed with a whole kernel of garlic on the crust became my favorite food. It was nutritious, healthy and filling.

Our staple food was "Borscht." A large pot would last our family two or three days. It required one whole and firm cabbage, six potatoes, four carrots, two tomatoes (when available) or tomato paste, two medium beets for coloring and a few bones with some meat on them.

The meat was boiled in a large pot until the meat was nearly cooked. Then the cabbage was thinly sliced, along with the peeled potatoes, carrots and beets. This vegetable concoction was then steam fried until it was nearly done. Then, the vegetables were dumped into the pot with the boiling meat.

Ten minutes later the Borscht was ready. The key to a good Borscht is that the vegetables are not overcooked, the meat is well done, and the potatoes are cooked. The meat is usually beef or veal or even chicken. Sometimes, we made Borscht without meat. Then, we substituted beans or mushrooms. But the mushrooms have to be "real" mushrooms (white). In German they are called "Steinpilze."

Clothing, shoes, bedding, linens and so on were also rationed. Again, all of it could be exchanged for fabric at some ridiculous factor; for example, one table cloth for twenty yards of fabric. So, my grandmother sharpened her sewing skills. We bought a used sewing machine, and we were in business.

Soon, each of us had an extensive wardrobe, and our "Schrank" (a free standing clothes closet) was bursting at the seams. We had more food, more clothing, and more money than we ever had in the best of times in the Soviet Union.

In addition, many products were available in "Ersatz" (artificial) form without ration coupons: powdered milk, ice cream, "Schlag" (whipped cream), and coffee and so on. And, last but not least, there was plenty of work for all age groups and all skills. That was the role of the "Arbeitsamt." Unemployment was non-existent. In that sense, the regime was a "worker's" paradise.

Of course, Stalin, Mussolini and Hitler realized that unemployment is the cause of discontent. Therefore, a job needed to be created for every member of its citizenry. This priority is the government's responsibility to its citizenry and earned it their broad support. Ultimately, each citizen needs to support his family and himself. When the government resorts to direct subsidy of its citizenry, except in special short time situations, that un-earned support is ultimately resented and breeds discontent. The reason un-earned support is resented is that indirectly, a caste system is created, which can be readily identified, stereotyped and persecuted.

Finally, Stalin, Mussolini and Hitler realized that propaganda carried much more weight than facts. To lend credence to a thesis in propaganda, the arts, sports and channeled cultural pursuits became their focus. That is, practically any propaganda campaign could be carried out successfully when the arts and sports supported the thesis. Therefore, a lot of emphasis was placed on "win the Olympics," "having the best soccer team," "having the best ballet," "having the best opera," "having the best chess player," and so on.

Supremacy or superiority in a sport or art form implied superiority in other fields. While we know that one need not imply the other, skeptics are easily converted with real examples. So, in wartime Germany of 1943, the arts and sports flourished. But, they were "channeled." They were channeled to affirm the intent of the Reich. Secondary heroes were prominently displayed and advertized. It was a matter of national pride to know the German medal winners of the 1936 Olympics. Also, a superficial tally of the medal winners showed clearly that Germany was "superior" to all nations in the world. The standard argument was simple: assign a weight of five for a gold medal, a weight of three for a silver medal, and a weight of one for bronze. Then, compute the combined weight. Take the population count, in millions, and divide it into the combined weight. The resultant ratio was used as a nation's "fitness ratio." Then, for the 1936 Olympics, Germany had the best fitness ratio.

How could Jessy Owens be explained? Easy, the same way von Clausewitz explains Napoleon's defeat in Russia: an accident (Borodino), a freak event (failure to prepare for winter), external forces intervened (winter) and so on. Almost any "rational" explanation will do. The norm is twisted into an exception, and the exception becomes the norm. Why can this be so readily done? Prior actions support the thesis. Prior victories proved beyond a doubt that Napoleon was superior. What was the singular factor that was different?

The inability to defeat the Russians at Borodino? No, -- Napoleon did not win every battle before. But, he found a way to extricate himself in a losing situation.

The distance? No, -- Napoleon conquered all of Europe. FromSpain to Prussia, from Italy to Flanders. A combined distance much larger than to Borodino or Moscow. His invasion route was roughly five hundred miles from the border of his Empire toMoscow. Therefore, the only "rational" explanation became the winter. And, we are quick to concur. Why? It is because then the solution is simple. His defeat can be explained in simple terms, and his prior victories are reconciled. The fact that it is false does not matter. It is plausible; therefore it is readily acceptable.

So, here it was -- the end of 1943. The war had lasted three summers. Why was the winter still the dominant factor in the war? If winter was so cruel and inhospitable to Germans, maybe the "Lebensraum" (living space) was not suited to being German? Maybe the Teutonic blood was just too thin to survive the Russian winter? Why not leave that icy desert to the Slavs that live there now?

But this presents a paradox. The winter is the propaganda which veils incompetence. The major defeat at Kursk was in the summer of 1943. Leningrad held the siege for three consecutive summers. The second battle for Kiev was in the summer and early fall. Brest-Litovsk happened in the summer. True, it was taken, but at what price! Stalingrad was just another Brest-Litovsk, except the element of surprise was on the German side in Brest Litovsk and on the Soviet side at Stalingrad.

At Stalingrad, the Germans committed hubris. Kleist and his panzers were diverted to Baku. With Kleist's panzers, Stalingrad would have been taken before the winter. Again, so what? Another "Stalingrad" would have awaited them at another place. Sooner or later, the Axis armada had to exhaust itself. Sooner or later, the supply lines had to collapse. The war in Russia could not be supplied from Berlin. Other supply centers were needed, and Germany refused to establish them. This is the hubris I am talking about. This is the major error committed in the war, not the winter!

How does this compare to Napoleon's debacle? Actually, Napoleon's plan was much better. Only the execution was worse. His plan was to strike with all his might at the center. Capture the capital, which was only 500 miles away, and victory was assured. Napoleon's plan mandated the establishment of major supply centers along the route to Moscow. Napoleon labored under the simplistic impression that when the capital was taken, the enemy was defeated.

Therefore, his thrust was at Moscow. However, the key to Napoleon's plan was Smolensk. Smolensk was to be the defensive perimeter and supply center for the massive army. Borodino was a surprise for Napoleon, and as the battle unfolded, Napoleon lost his nerve.

When Ney broke the Russian flank, Ney requested "The Guard" to inflict the mortal blow. When the messenger arrived and Napoleon read the message, he turned to the messenger and said, "What non-sense! I will not risk my "Guard" two thousand leagues from Paris!" (But, he was only 400 miles from the border).

Of course, the Russians had similar opportunities. Kutuzov (the Russian commander in-chief) had suffered a humiliating defeat at Austerlitz just a few years before. After Austerlitz, his fear of Napoleon was real and deep-rooted. Kutuzov did not want to engage Napoleon. He wanted to confine him, to limit his conquest. Kutuzov was forced to fight Napoleon at Borodino; and when the opportunity presented itself, he was more than willing to leave the battlefield.

At the height of the battle, Platov, a Cossack general, broke through the French flank. He sent a messenger to Kutuzov requesting the reserves to destroy the French. Kutuzov kept nearly one third of the army in reserve. Kutuzov's reply was practically identical, "What non-sense! I cannot risk the safety of the army and the defense of mother Russia!" (He was not defending Moscow but Mother Russia).

When Napoleon entered Moscow, the Russian army encamped only a few miles away at Malo Yaroslavets, thereby daring Napoleon to attack. Now, it was Napoleon's turn to be afraid of attacking a well-fortified and re-built Russian army. This Russian army harassed the French. Moscow was not safe because she was not defensible. Eventually, a full scale attack would destroy the French, making the withdrawal inevitable.

Why did not the French army prepare itself for the winter? Moscow was a big city. There were plenty of supplies there to refit two armies of the size of Napoleon's in winter clothes. The reason was simple. The retreat was meant to be to Smolensk. There, the garrison was well stocked with supplies, food, clothing and ammunition. Smolensk was less than two-hundred and fifty miles away. This is why the army left Moscow unprepared for the winter. Only a ten-day's march away lurked safety.

Why did Napoleon retreat along the same way he came? Was not his path depleted of all food and supplies? The army retreated along the same path for precisely the same reason as before. Smolensk was the sanctuary for the French, and the Kaluga road was the shortest path to it! But, when the retreating army of Napoleon reached Smolensk, the discipline and fighting spirit of the French was broken. The retreating army raided the supplies, plundered the garrison and anarchy set in. Napoleon did nothing to restore the discipline and order of his army.

Once Smolensk was ravished, the army became a horde of undisciplined mercenaries. Their energy turned inward. On to the next garrison (Vilna); and then, on to the next (Kovno). Each garrison was plundered and destroyed by its own soldiers. The garrisons fell like dominoes. It became clear that sanctuary was on the other side of the river Niemen. So, not soldiers, but packs of marauding hordes pressed on to the Niemen.

All Kutuzov could do was guide and confine the marauding horde along the path they came. Their retreat was natural. Their direction was predetermined by the garrisons they had established before. Kutuzov's dilemma was that there was no army to defeat. This once mighty army, the pride of France, was devouring itself. But, soon it was apparent to Kutuzov that this endless horde was racing to the Niemen. The crossings at the Niemen could be clearly defined (Kovno). So, all Kutuzov had to do was decimate the remnants of the once mighty army at the Niemen. Less than two percent of the French and her allied soldiers made it across the Niemen successfully. (5,000 French soldiers returned out of 300,000. The allied figures were not recorded but had similar casualties. The total army was 750,000 by some accounts.)

These facts destroy the myth and mystiques of the "Grand Army." How could one reconcile their prior glory with their actions on the Kaluga road? A simple and plausible solution needed to be found: The Russian winter. The Russian winter is a perfect solution, a solution worthy of a Greek tragedy. A freak event? Divine intervention had prevented the glorious army from achieving its mission? The honor and greatness of the army is preserved; national honor is preserved; and, -- we are fed propaganda!

By December 1943, the German army was in a similar predicament. It was close to a Napoleonic rout. The crack troops of the German Wehrmacht were destroyed. Only pockets of German resistance remained. To prevent the apparent and inevitable collapse of the German army, Hitler sent directives to all garrisons to, "Fight to the last man."

By now, the garrisons and pockets of resistance were doomed anyway. They were doomed if they stayed and fought; and they were doomed if they retreated. To Hitler and his high command, it was clear that a retreat would quickly disintegrate into a hysterical and marauding horde. Visions of the Napoleonic rout pre-occupied both Hitler and his staff. Wagner's "Die Gotterdammerung," was all too real. The pendulum had swung, and doom was now inevitable. This is why and when the German high command recommended that Hitler sue for peace at any price.

The German high command had visions that at least the German territories could be saved and the hopelessly abandoned army units could be extricated. But, Hitler's sick mind had another vision. He felt he waged a "holy war" against Communism. The "Lebensraum" motive took on a secondary role. To him, the impending allied invasion could only be the salvation he was hoping for.

Hitler thought Communism was a real threat, not only to fascism, but also to capitalism. So, he felt he could sue for peace in the West, and then convince the western forces to join him in his "holy war" in the east.

In the beginning of 1944, this propaganda shift became apparent. The propaganda against the Slavs, the Jews, and the Gypsies became vicious. The propaganda against the West became full of sick humor. Hitler started to "court" the British in his own sick way.

> "I could have destroyed the British at Dunkirk, but I spared them for a greater mission."
>
> -- and --
>
> "I could have leveled England, but I spared them for a nobler task."

Hitler was not so kind to the Americans. To him theAmericans were a "race of mongrels, led by a deranged cripple." To Hitler, this "race of mongrels" was "brainwashed" by the English and had no mind of its own. In fact, the more the English exploited the Americans, the more the Americans seemed to cherish the British.

The "lend-lease" arrangement was a sure sign that Roosevelt was "itching" to join the war. Only Congress prevented him from doing so. After the Japanese attack on Pearl Harbor, the standard argument was this:

"Did not Roosevelt strip the island of Hawaii of its defenses to make sure the Japanese attack would succeed and America be drawn into the war? Only a deranged cripple could commit such a heinous deed on his citizenry, to join the British in this futile war."

After the invasion of Normandy, a new slogan emerged. The Americans and Canadians suffered the greatest losses at the beachheads in Normandy. The British encountered only superficial resistance. Did it not stand to reason, since the British conducted the overall intelligence activity, that the Americans and the Canadians were used by the British as "cannon fodder?" This led to a new slogan.

"The mongrels are used as cannon fodder, and they like it!"

This sentiment was not only prevalent in Germany, but as the western front became a reality, German counter offensives were deliberately directed at the "mongrels." Consequently, the Americans and Canadians suffered high casualties while the British paraded along the shore. Montgomery avoided all confrontations with the Wehrmacht; f o r example, The Battle of the Ardennes was directed directly and specifically at the Americans. It was directed directly at Bastogne with intentions on Antwerp. When the siege of Bastogne began, the closest and most efficient armor was under Montgomery's command near Mons. Yet,

Patton was sent from Nancy through "impossible" terrain to relieve the siege of Bastogne. (Mons to Bastogne is about 70 flat miles; Nancy to Bastogne, about 85 miles through the Alps, in the winter, in the snow, on serpentine and treacherous roads).

So, the "bloodiest" beachheads were assigned by the English to the Americans and Canadians at Normandy. And, during the only offensive on the western front, the English were "picnicking" on the coast while Patton cris-crossed the Alps to save Bastogne. Of course, De Gaulle quickly followed the tactics of the English. The Americans fought the battle for Paris yet "mocked" French troops walked into Paris victoriously! History reports that: Paris was liberated by the "Free French" under De Gaulle. So, it was clear to the Germans that the Americans had no "national" ambition. The Americans had no territorial ambition. Americans were used by the English and the French as their obedient but dumb gladiators, fulfilling Webster's definition of mercenary to the letter (aka: Bubus Americanus).

****

Today I was determined to find a few friends. Grandma had made breakfast for us. Emma, Masha, and I were eating at the table. Grandma started the conversation:

"Very soon now, all of you have to learn German. And, you have to learn it fast and well. Soon, you will go to German school and you cannot embarrass us. Remember, if you do, they will punish not only you, but Emilia, George and me as well."

I paid no attention. "What kind of punishment could they inflict anyhow?" I thought to myself. "Was it not more important to find friends?" I was determined to find friends. Today I was going to make a few new friends. Well, maybe just one.

I put on a jacket and ran downstairs. Across the street were a few boys. Some my age, some older and one was much older, maybe thirteen or fourteen. I stood there and just looked at them. I noticed they all wore uniforms. The oldest boy noticed me and whispered something to a boy, slightly bigger than I. That boy started crossing the street and approached me. He came close and started talking. I listened but did not understand a word of what he said. I just shrugged my shoulders.

The next thing I knew, I saw "stars." The kid had just landed a "proverbial" right hook on my chin. When the kid "unloaded," the whole group dashed across the street and the little ones began attacking me. My first reaction was that this was much worse than the geese at home.

By the third or fourth punch I was on the ground. When I tried to get up, another right hook would send me back to the ground. An older kid had assumed a "guardian" position. Each time I would try to get up, a well-directed punch would send me back to the ground. So, I lay there for a moment; then I made a dash for the smallest kid. I got to him and landed a few punches of my own. But, it was futile. The older kids grabbed me and a few well directed punches sent me to the ground again.

By now, a few women came to my help. They were screaming and yelling. The group of kids took off and ran down the street. A few women ran after them. They caught two of the younger ones. The others got away. So, here I was -- with four or five women trying to comfort me.

They wiped off the blood from my face, but they could not stop my nose from bleeding. One of the women just turned me on my back and said, "Lieg still!" I just lay there, blood oozing into my mouth. I was not crying I would not give them the satisfaction of knowing I was hurting.

They brought the two kids to me and the women started to yell and scream at them. Eventually, one of the kids reached out his hand to me, and I accepted his "peace offer." His name was Heinrich.

By now the nose bleeding had stopped. I got up and went back to the apartment. Heck, I thought, there had to be a better way to make friends.

At home my grandmother was all upset. She was upset at me, for "starting" a fight. She was upset that I had black and blue marks on my face. But, she cleaned my face and made a remedy for my bruises.

When my mother came home from work, I got another litany. I was told that right or wrong, the next time she found out that I was in a fight, she would personally give me such a lashing I would never forget. Then, the inevitable raid siren sounded and the incident was forgotten. When we returned from the bunker, my mother tucked we in and said, "Tomorrow Elvira will come and teach you German." The case was closed.

Slowly, I began to become more aware of my surroundings and neighbors. My first observation was that Berlin was devoid of young men. Males from sixteen to sixty were "very rare" in Berlin at that time. Infrequently would a young male walk down the street, at least in our neighborhood. And then, he was seldom alone. Two, three or more females were usually literally hanging and clinging on to him.

A male cult was developing. Women would drop their inhibitions and modesty. They would openly stare at such "forlorn creatures." They would approach them, and start a conversation about anything: The war, politics, sports, and for a date. This was done in a very "matter of fact" way. With no inhibitions and with no scruples. Thus, the male ego reigned supreme. Male presence became sufficient to warrant admiration. Tall, short, thin and thick -- all males were wooed and admired at that time. Did humanity lose its perspective, or did nature intend it to be that way?

As far as western civilization is concerned, this phenomenon seemed to be the intent of nature for the primary duty of a male was to make war. "Soldiering" was a respected profession. In fact, it was the only profession, except for priesthood, where a male could make his mark for himself and for society. Thus, western Europe always found a way to decimate the adult male population. Therefore, a married female would stay faithful and loyal to her husband until she was absolutely sure he had died.

Thus, in the Odyssey, Penelope was faithful to Ulysses until there was no doubt in her mind of his death. Only after twenty years of waiting, did she reluctantly agree to marry somebody else. Even then, that somebody else had to be at least a close facsimile of Ulysses. The suitors had to submit to a test of strength with the armor of Ulysses. But a once-married female saw her chances dwindle in this field of eligible males. Therefore, if and when suitors presented themselves, they were kept "handy" just for that eventuality. Thus, Penelope entertained her suitors for ten years.

Starting with the Greeks and ending with Hitler, Europe was always at war. A local war, a "holy" war, or just another war. In between was the Hundred Year War, the Thirty Year War and the Seven Year War; and many wars too numerous to mention.

However, a holy war of the magnitude Hitler embarked on posed a population paradox. On one hand, the adult male populations were far removed from the female population. On the other hand, the "government" needed new recruits to replace the casualties in the field of battle. So the female population was urged to "procreate," but the question was "With whom?"

The female "procreation" part of the paradox Hitler had resolved successfully with his "Mother's Day" propaganda campaign. It was the "duty" of a female to "produce" at least four sons. This duty was openly rewarded with public pomp and fanfare. Medals were awarded and special ration cards were issued on those occasions. These women were celebrated as "complete" Aryan women. All women who "produced" anything less had to try harder or were just "unworthy" Aryans. Thus, the "milieu" was set. Women had to "procreate," and this duty to procreate became the responsibility of women.

The problem was that of how to resolve the male part of this paradox. Hitler came up with a fiendish solution.

Any Aryan male was a suitable partner at any time, regardless of his marital status! Thus, when adult males were sent home on leave, it was their mission and duty to father at least four children before they returned to active duty.

In fact, a new norm was established, to help out the bashful and the weak in spirit: Orgiastic festivals were staged to "procreate" the Aryan race. There, males and females danced themselves into a frenzy and procreated the Aryan race. These orgiastic festivals were not the exception but were the order of the day by 1944. Thus, the German female became the most submissive female in the world.

Elvira arrived punctually the next morning. Elvira was about sixteen years old and had completed her primary education in Germany. Her family were Russian emigrees from the first emigration, from the revolutionary period, when "whites" were fighting the "reds," (1918-1922). She was slender, tall and well rounded for her age. Dark brown hair fell loosely to her back. Her face was slim and matched her body well. Her eyes were sparkling with exuberance. I could not tell if her assignment made her happy, or she was always so enthusiastic. But, from the very start she took a liking to me. I could sense it immediately. I could feel her eyes looking me over and over again. Her eyes were large and soft brown. Dark natural eyebrows accentuated her somewhat pale face. Her lips were sensuous. Not too thin and not too thick, just right. Her mouth was very small and protruded out of her face. She seemed to "pucker" when she talked. Elvira paid practically no attention to Emma and Masha.

Elvira came over to me, put her arm around me in a very familiar yet gentle way and spurted, "Well, let's get on with it. Let's learn some German." Her Russian was "phony." She mimicked the lisp of the

Russian aristocracy. But, her German was very good. No lisp, no accent -- just like the German we heard all around us on the street.

She started with the German alphabet. She drew each letter both in its "Latin" form, then in its corresponding "German" form. She did this for both capital and lower case form. For each letter she gave us the correct Russian sound. She made us repeat each sound. First, individually, and then altogether. We did this "endlessly."

Then, she started with "keywords." Monosyllable keywords she called them. She insisted that these words were essential by themselves. These words would not "give us away" as Slavs. They were mostly verbs and some key nouns without their article. She insisted we "stay away" from the articles until we had a better grasp of the German language for the wrong "gender" of the article was the first sign of a Slav. For many nouns, the gender in Russian and German is different.

Her method was effective, at least on me. By the end of the day, I felt I was becoming a "real" German. All the while, she kept caressing me, hugging me and, flirting with me. She took every opportunity to hug me when I did something right and to fondle me when I did something wrong. I loved her attention. Oh, if I could only grow up real quick and make passionate love to this wonderful creature, I thought to myself.

Elvira gave us assignments for the next day. We were to write and speak the words out loud, at least twenty times; write and pronounce each letter in the alphabet, at least ten times. Next day she would come with textbooks for us. When Elvira left, she gave me a big hug and I could feel her firm beasts. Oh, what a woman, I thought! How could I possibly grow up faster and be with this woman?

Emma and Masha were not impressed with her performance. All Emma kept saying was: "What a flirt. Oh goodness, what a flirt." And, I kept saying to myself: "I definitely like flirts!"

I could understand why Emma was not impressed with Elvira's teaching method. For one, Emma already had "extensive" schooling, while I had spent only, a few days in the "Kindergarten" in Kiev. I did not like it at all. We were made to play very silly games and "real life on the farm" was just so much more exciting. I became so "unruly" that my mother had to take me home and keep me on the farm, and that is just what I wanted. On the farm was my dog and my she-goat. Even the geese and pigs were more exciting than "Kindergarten."

The educational system was different in the Soviet Union than in Germany. In the Soviet Union, children start at the age of seven and attend school for ten years. After ten years, they receive a diploma if they successfully complete their work. The diploma is called the "ten years course." Emma had finished half of that course, and Masha had finished one year. Obviously, they were exposed to "inferior teaching methods" so I thought. After the ten years course, students could matriculate at a university.

In Germany, the system was different. At six, all children had to attend public school. At age ten or eleven, depending on the ability of the student, one could take an entrance exam to a Gymnasium or Oberrealschule. If the student passed, the student was schooled for the "sciences" in the Oberrealschule or for law or medicine in the Gymnasium. That schooling continued for nine years in peace or for eight years during war at the respective "high schools."

Those that failed the entrance exam had to continue in the public school. There, they completed the "elementary" nine years and then spent two years in "apprenticeship," learning a trade.

Occasionally, permission was granted to take the exam at age ten and, then again, at age eleven when the exam was failed the first time. Usually, the teachers discouraged taking the exam the second time. Once a student failed that exam, one was marked for life -- able to perform only "low level work."

That was not the worst part. Suppose one passed the exam and failed the second or third year of the "high school." Then, back to public school was a personal disgrace, and an apprenticeship was usually not possible.

So, at a very tender age, a critical decision was placed on an unsuspecting student. Of course, when the family had "means," the child was transferred to a private school. Usually, the school was in Switzerland, and the student continued his or her education privately. However, the bulk of the students ended up in "limbo," without a higher education and without a trade.

To fail any one year was relatively easy for, each year, there were from ten to twelve subjects to be covered. Failure in any one of the six major subjects meant repeating the whole year, every subject. For example, Albert Einstein failed a language and was dismissed from his "high school." Albert Einstein was fortunate that his parents had the means to send him to Switzerland, and he was able to complete his education there.

The graduates of these "high schools" in Germany, are highly admired. The degree is called the "Abitur." Only one percent complete the nine years without failure. When a male approaches his Abitur, he becomes part of the most eligible and the most desirable set of bachelors. For each German was convinced only "renaissance men" are produced by this system.

Actually, quite the contrary is true. The system produces "jacks of all trades," and many masters are cast into "limbo." Many specialists in the "high technology" fields are former failures of that system Albert Einstein being my finest example.

By 1944, two major emigrations from Russia and the Soviet Union intermingled in Berlin and throughout the rest of Germany. While the Czarist regime was oppressive, it was not downright brutal. For serious or political crimes, offenders were usually "banished" for a period of time. Stalin, Lenin and Rasputin were banished repeatedly. Generally, only the most hardened criminals were executed.

When the Revolution started, the "whites," or the supporters of the Czar, fought a losing battle. The initial wave of emigrants occurred then. They consisted of Czarist functionaries and the nobility, later followed by prisoners of war and Galicians from the Western Ukraine. During the brief Austrian occupation, they swarmed into the west.

While Kerensky, the provisional leader of the Russian government, tried to continue the war against Germany, Lenin was prepared to sue for peace at "any price." Lenin knew that Germany was finished in World War I, and any peace would be re-negotiated later on anyway. History has proven Lenin right, at least on that point. While Lenin pressed on with his "peace" propaganda, Trotsky was training a new army to give the Bolsheviks more "muscle." At this most critical time, the "Reds or Bolsheviks" were outgunned and outnumbered by about ten to one by their enemies. Nine foreign and "White" armies tried to contain the spread of Communism and carve out a piece of the vast Russian territories for themselves. The Americans, the English, the Poles, the Czechs and a multitude of "White armies" from Siberia to the Ukraine vowed to destroy the Bolsheviks. However, the newly-formed army of Trotsky annihilated the nine opposing armies one by one. The last two armies, led by Denikin and Wrangel ended up operating in the southern Ukraine. The Red Army literally pushed them into the Black Sea. Before annihilation, the British and the French sent relief. They "evacuated" the besieged "White" armies and their families. Most evacuees were re-located into Serbia, Bosnia, Greece and Macedonia. From there, these refugees made their way to Italy, France, Belgium, Germany and the USA.

Some say that the success of the Red Army was their propaganda slogan "The Land to the People." This slogan had a direct and personal appeal. Meanwhile, the slogan of the "Whites" was "For the Czar and Mother Russia." This slogan was washed out. The reasons were as follows:

1) The Czarist regime was oppressive and to most peasants this slogan had little or no appeal. Serfdom was introduced by the Czarina Catherine II in 1772 in the Eastern Ukraine and abolished in 1861 by Alexander II. But serfdom was still vivid in many minds. (Poland had introduced serfdom around 1500 and maintained it throughout their rule in the Western Ukraine. The Polish nobles were the "conquistadors of the East" and vassals of the Emperor of the Holy Roman Empire).

2) The Czarina was of German ancestry. During the war with Germany she was sending "care packages" to her relatives in Germany. To the majority of the population, this bordered on "treason."

3) The Czarina was the "dominant" figure in the government. Many key posts were staffed by Germans, the Chief of the War Ministry, in particular -- Sturmer.

4) Rasputin, a defrocked monk, controlled the Czarina and the government.

5) The Czar's brother proved to be inept and totally incompetent as a military leader.

6) Often, Russian soldiers were sent into battle without a rifle or with only a few shells for their dilapidated contraption (rifle).

7) The Czar was "dumping" badly trained and poorly equipped recruits at the German front to relieve the French and English! Millions of Russians were used as cannon fodder to help the French!

That war, World War I, made no sense what-so-ever! Not that any war made sense, but this war was insane. This insanity was visible everywhere: From inept and incompetent leadership to acute and chronic shortages. A former foe, who only recently waged a holy war against

Russia, required bottomless sacrifices. It was clear to the lowest peasant that madness had overcome the Czar.

On the other hand, the slogan of the "Reds" and their propaganda made perfect sense: Stop the war and distribute the land to the people.

The second "Russian" emigration occurred during World War II. For the most part, Slavs were repatriated into Germany as "Ostarbeiter" or eastern slave laborers. However, large population segments moved voluntarily to Germany to support the German war effort against the Communists. Once the population had a "taste" of Communism, any other government was "heaven."

Volksdeutsche and collaborators formed this last group. Many Germans had settled in Russia and intermarried. The offspring with even the "slightest" trace of German lineage was sufficient to be classified as Volksdeutche. Thus, the two emigrations mistrusted each other and generally avoided each other. My mother's father was a German -- Gabriel Grotte. Therefore, we became Volksdeutsche.

Elvira arrived as scheduled. She had the promised books with her. I dashed over to her and gave her a big hug. Gently, she ran her fingers through my hair. Then she pulled my head away a little bit and said: "Do you know, you have such beautiful blonde hair? Do you?" Then she bent down towards me and continued: "...and such beautiful blue eyes!"

We settled down for our lessons. I mimicked Elvira enthusiastically in the pronunciation. The lessons were no chores at all. I loved her way of teaching. But, most of all, I loved her attention for me.

Within a few weeks it became clear, that my pronunciation was far superior to Emma's and Masha's. I caught every nuance, every inclination of the sound. Emma and Masha were still struggling with the nuances of the sounds. Emma of course read the first book from cover to cover the first day. Her vocabulary was larger than mine, and she could read faster and better than I could. But, her pronunciation was not perfect. Emma was getting very upset. She was upset at herself for not being able to "hear" the sound variations.

She would pace up and down the room and read out loud from a book. But, her pronunciation was not "perfect." Soon, Emma was getting her own books. She was now pacing up and down the room and reading out loud all the time. But, here and there she would mispronounce a word, and I would make fun of her.

Also, the gender of nouns posed a problem to both Emma and Masha. They kept saying that the gender was illogical and non sensical. For example, "What fool would call the moon male?" she would say. Then, she would explain and rationalize, using Greek mythology and Roman mythology and so on. She kept resisting reality, and she made it difficult for herself. I had no problem with the gender. I accepted the definition, and the rest came naturally.

Meanwhile, the raids got to be longer and longer. We kept spending more and more time in the bunker. Then, Berlin began being raided during the day. Then, day-raids became the norm. There was less and less time to go to the bunker, so very often we would just run into our cellar and wait out the raid.

Slowly Berlin was showing signs of destruction. Buildings were burning or smoldering. Ruins were visible everywhere. The once pretty and clean streets were now littered with rubble.

Occasionally, Elvira would not show up. This would happen after a long night raid or an early day raid. Then, I would seize that opportunity and run down to the street. I would look around and see how our street was being systematically bombed into ashes. The greatest damage was near the subway. We were at the other end; and as one moved away from the subway, the damage decreased slightly.

I had the distinct feeling that our building was "ready" to go any day now. Our building was hit often. Practically after every raid, a few "phosphor" bombs would hit our building, but clean-up crews, mostly women and old men would be there on the spot to fix the damage.

One day, as I was on the street just looking around, I saw Heinrich. He was walking quickly towards me. He looked "spiffy" in his light-brown shirt, black tie and black pants. I was wondering why he was not cold. I had a coat on. It was rather chilly outside even though it was a bright day and the sun was shining. I had not seen Heinrich since our last encounter.

Heinrich came up to me and asked, "Do you want to go with me to a parade?" Of course I wanted to go to a parade, but first I had to tell grandma, and she would not let me. Those were the instructions, I was sure of that. So, I asked, "Where is the parade." He looked at me and said, "Oh, just down the block on the Ku-dam." I had no idea where the Ku-dam was, but his "just down the block" qualifier assured me that it was very close by. So, I agreed.

We walked to the end of our street to the circular intersection, then down an artery from the circle. Heinrich knew his way around Berlin. I was impressed. A short way down the block, we saw a crowd. We reached the crowd, but Heinrich continued on. He turned to me and said, "Let's get a nice spot," as he pressed on. Finally he stopped. Nonchalantly he pushed his way to the front, to the curb of the street. I stayed right behind him. We reached the curb. We had a good view of the street. But, the street was empty. I looked at Heinrich. I did not say a word. Heinrich sensed my curiosity, he said, "Soon, any moment now."

We just stood there and waited. I thought this was rather boring. In back of us were the adults. Mostly women and a few old men. Across, on the other side of the street, were also mostly women, old men and a few kids on the curb. Then, it dawned on me: There was grim silence all around us. Something was not right. I was at parades before. The parades I had gone to were happy, people were talking; there was noise in the air. Here, everybody just stood in grim silence.

Then, out of a side street, I could see a soldier on a horse turning onto the street we were on. Behind the soldier, about twenty paces behind him, a strange group of people dragged themselves after the soldier. Behind them, about twenty paces behind them, was another soldier on a horse. This procession moved very slowly and deliberately down our street. I tried to make out this procession.

The lead soldier on the horse was in a guard uniform. A metal breast plate hung a few inches from his chin. His uniform was studded with medals. The rest of the procession was blocked by the rider. But, the rider was an old man, much older than George, I thought. The horse was malnourished -- its ribs were showing each time the horse took a step forward. I had a distinct feeling that both rider and horse were both ready to collapse all by themselves. Yet, in slow motion, the rider and horse, and this lot of humanity moved steadily forward.

Then, the rest of the procession became visible. They were badly malnourished men and women. The men wore long black coats and black hats. The hats were strange, they sat loosely on their heads. The women wore thick black dresses. They also wore a large wrap or large scarf. Some had their heads wrapped and the rest of their scarves were draped around their shoulders. Some had their scarves wrapped around their necks. Everybody in that procession carried a "potty" in one had while the other hand was free. They all wore a yellow band with the Star of David on their left arm. And they all wore the star of David on their coats or dresses. They all looked to the ground. Not one looked at us. I thought I would get sick! I felt that only a stray glance at me from that crowd would start me sobbing. Even in the worst of times in the Ukraine, I had not seen anything like this. The crowd was grim and determined. Not a sound was heard as this flock of humanity passed by us.

As soon as the procession passed, the crowd disbanded. I only looked at Heinrich I could not speak. He turned to me and started, "Did you see those potties? Do you know,… they actually eat out of them!" I still could not speak.

Slowly we made our way home. Along the way home, I was thinking about this "parade." I could not get the picture out of my mind. One question kept nagging me. Finally, I asked Heinrich, "What did these people do?"

He turned to me and said, "Don't you know? They started the war. My father was killed in the war. I hate them."

I knew that Heinrich was wrong. My father had told me that Germany had started the war. Practically every slogan in Germany was flaunting that Germany had started the war and was proud to continue it.

In the evening, when my mother came home from work, I told her what happened. She was very upset with me. She started her litany first," I told you never to go beyond the sight of our house. I told you not to play with the HJ (Hitler Youth). What do I have to do to make you understand this?" She looked at me again and continued, "In war many people suffer. We suffered more than our share. What do you want me to do?" I just stood there and kept looking at her. She knew that her anger or explanation did not satisfy me. Then she sat me on the bed. She sat next to me and she started again, "Oh my son, my son… Promise me not to, tell anyone." I looked at her and said, "I promise."

"Well, every morning when George and I go to work, we pass a fenced area. At first, it was empty, and we wondered why this area was fenced in. It was only a small park. But then, they surrounded it with barbed wire and put large pieces of sheet metal in front of it. One day, I couldn't resist it. I found a seam in the sheet metal with a tiny hole. Do you know what I saw?" and she looked at me. I shook my head. And, she continued, "People. I saw women, children and men all herded together. They looked like skeletons. I made George look through that hole. And he did. Do you know what we did?" I shook my head again. And, she continued, "We went to the bakery and bought a whole bag of rolls. We used up almost a month's supply on my card. We took this bag to the same spot. Then, I banged on the metal, and I could see how they came close to us. Then, George heaved that bag of rolls over the fence, and it landed right in front of them. They could not see us, but they knew we were there. They threw us kisses and took the bread." She paused for a while, she could see that I was pleased.

Then she continued, "And, do you know what we do every morning when we go to work?" I shook my head in anticipation. "Every morning we buy rolls, and every morning George heaves those rolls over the fence. They already know when we are coming. They just stand there, waiting for us." I thought for a while and I asked, "Why don't you use my ration card also?"

My mother looked at me with a sad smile and continued, "Son, we have used every ration card we have. Yours, Emma's, Masha's and Grandma's. We used up our bread rations in ten days." I thought for a while and asked, "But how come we have bread all month long? I didn't notice any shortages?" My mother smiled at me again and continued, "Son, it's very simple. We trade. We trade a little butter for bread, a little meat for bread. In the end, we have just enough, and these poor souls have something to eat." Now I was satisfied.

In some small, insignificant way, we helped humanity. I had one more question, "Mama,… are they all Jews?" She looked at me and smiled faintly, "Son, I don't know if they are Jews. All I know is that they are people. And these people are starving to death. And I am doing everything I can to help them."

Then, she looked at me sternly and said: "Remember, you promised… not a word to anyone. Otherwise, all of us will end up behind that wall!" Then she hugged me. I had a feeling she was glad to have talked to me. Then, she pulled me away, looked me straight in the eyes and said cheerfully, "Tomorrow we are leaving for Plauen."

CHAPTER 4

Plauen

My mother and George had received new travel orders. My mother was sent to Plauen to attend a "drawing and sketching" course, and George was sent to Forstlausitz. So, like it or not, our family was split up. This was the situation despite the fact that she was pregnant and we were expecting the new addition to our family by February or March of 1945. My mother, Emma and I went to Plauen; and George, Grandma, and Masha went to Forstlausitz.

We were assigned the most luxurious quarters in Plauen. A retired leather industrialist, Max was willing to provide quarters in his own home, provided there was a male child in the family. Quarters were normally pre-arranged for work-related assignments. The individual providing the quarters could specify the terms, such as, the number of children, their age, their sex, pets or no pets, and so on. The "provider" of the quarters was normally sent a brief "resume" and pictures of the family.

Max had four sons. By 1944, all four sons had been killed on the Russian front. One at Stalingrad, one at Leningrad and the other two in the Battle at Kursk. Max had no other children. His wife had died only a short time ago, and he lived in this "mansion" of a house with his sister Elsee.

Plauen is about one hundred and fifty miles south-south-west of Berlin. Plauen had no strategic value and consequently had been spared from the allied air raids. Plauen was a sleepy town at the foot of the "Erzgebirge," a small mountain range.

Max came to meet us at the train station. Max was short, stocky and jovial. He recognized us right away and made a bee-line for us, as soon as we got off the train. He greeted my mother, my sister, and then he focused his attention on me. I could see it. He liked me right away. He gave me a broad smile and said: "So,… you are Tola." He stretched out his hand to me, and I pressed his hand very firmly. He seemed to like my grip. He continued," We are going to get along just fine."

A porter loaded up our luggage and wheeled it down to the end of the platform. A huge, four-door Mercedes convertible was waiting for us. The top was down. It was a bright and sunny day. Max opened the back door for my mother and Emma. Then, he took me to the front passenger side. He opened the door for me, and I climbed into the car. Max got in and started to drive. It was obvious that Max loved to drive this car. Max drove it gently, but deliberately, through town and to his mansion.

At the mansion, Elsee was outside at the entrance, waiting for us. Max pulled up right to the front entrance and parked the car. Max got out and opened the door for my mother. He came around the car and opened the door for Emma. Then, he opened the door for me. I got out. Max took my hand, and hand-in-hand we walked towards Elsee. Elsee hugged my mother, Emma and me.

I could not believe it. Here we came for "simple" quarters, and we were received like family. The attention was overwhelming. Max was very pleased, but Elsee was overjoyed. Max had a maid and a cook. They were both his age or a little bit older. Our luggage was "taken care of." And, each of us was given our own private room on the second floor of the house. Each room had a private toilet. We were given ten minutes to "freshen up."

I had no idea what that meant. We were then to meet downstairs in the dining room. All I remember was going to the bathroom, washing my hands and face, and counting ten times to sixty. I had no intention of embarrassing my mother or be a nuisance to Max and Elsee. Still, when I came downstairs, I was the first. Max and Elsee were genuinely excited. They sat me on a leather sofa and started asking me about the trip, about Berlin, about the air-raids, and so on. Elsee was very bubbly. She would ask a question; and as soon as I would answer, she was ready with another. Max just sat there and kept smiling at me.

Soon my mother, then Emma, came down. They had changed clothes. "Aha," I said to myself, "…that's what they mean when they say freshen up." I had only taken off my coat and had on the same clothes as on the trip. After some more chit-chat, the cook came and announced that dinner was ready. Max got up and gently motioned everybody into the dining room.

The dining room was large. It was larger than my bedroom. It had a large open entrance on one end. On the other end were two swinging doors for the kitchen, and a massive "china closet" gazed down at us. Actually, the main entrance had two hidden sliding doors. The swinging doors were in the wall side of the room.

On the left side of the room was a huge rounded bay window. The window was of stained glass in yellow, beige, and light brown hues. In the center of the stained glass window was the figure of a man, working on pieces of skins with a pile of leather on one side. On the opposite side of the window was the main wall. It was studded with trophies, pictures, and stuffed deer heads.

A massive chandelier was bulging with cut crystal. The table was covered with an embroidered tablecloth. But, the table was full of silverware, glasses and plates, even though only a section of the table was set. There were plates upon plates, and then small plates on the side. I had never seen anything like that before in my life. I was afraid to sit at the table. What if I break something, I thought, and they throw me out!

These were not plates or dishes we were accustomed to using. These were "fancy" pieces with pictures on them. They were "carved" and "gilded" and elaborate. So, I figured the better part of valor was to observe what the others were doing. I decided to focus my attention on Max and do whatever he was doing. Max was elected to be my role model.

But, to my chagrin, Max seated me next to him. Max sat at the head of the table. On one side of Max was my mother, on the other was I. Next to me was Emma, and across from Emma was Elsee. I had only a peripheral view of Max. So, I picked Elsee as my new role model. She sat diagonally across from me, and it was easier for me to watch her. Inconspicuously, I watched Elsee. She took a napkin out of a glass in front of her, opened it up; and it "vanished" below the table. That was easy I saw the napkin in front of me, and I pulled it out of the glass. Then, I opened it ceremoniously and "plopped" it on my lap.

The cook came and poured water into one of the glasses in front of us. The cook started always with Max. Then he would serve the adults on the other side, then Emma and me. Then, the cook would serve Max again. In effect, Max approved every item before it was served to everybody else. Presumably, if anything was not in order, Max would tell the cook.

Then, the cook disappeared and came out with a large ceramic bowl. He opened the lid, and the aroma drifted down the table. I became weak. The bowl was filled with delicious mushroom soup. I could smell it, and my mouth was watering. I was so hungry. All of a sudden, I felt I could devour everything. I had to control myself I kept saying to myself.

When I looked back at Elsee, she had a slice of dark bread on one of the small plates next to the stacked big plates. Next to her bread was a cube of butter. "How did it get there?" I asked myself. I raised my head a little bit to look around as Max was passing a basket with slices of bread and rolls to me. I took a dark slice of bread and passed the basket to Emma. No sooner had I passed the bread to Emma, when Max passed me the butter on a small ceramic plate. On the plate was also a small knife.

I had not seen so much butter in one place for a long time. I glanced at Max's plate, but there was no butter on his plate. Then, I glanced at my mother's plate and noticed that she had a smaller slice than Elsee. So, meticulously, I carved a slice about the size of my mother's and put it on my small plate.

Meanwhile, the cook was serving the soup. Among all the utensils on the table -- three knives on one side, three forks on the other side and two spoons beyond the stacked large plates for each setting -- it was very difficult to determine which utensil to use for a particular activity. I glanced at Elsee, and I noticed that she was using the smallest knife to spread the butter on the slice of bread. So, I found the smallest knife and spread "my" butter on "my" piece of dark bread. As soon as I finished, I took a bite. Oh, how wonderful it tasted!

Then I searched for the large spoon. At first, I could not find it. On one side of the stacked plates were different-sizeed forks, and on the other different-sized knives. And, beyond the stacked plates was just a tiny teaspoon. Surely that was the wrong utensil. I looked around and could see that everybody was using a "big" spoon. I looked again, and there it was.

Because my head was barely above the table, the stacked plates had concealed the spoon from my view. I retrieved the spoon and started eating the soup. In retrospect, all I can say is that the soup was not delicious, -- it was divine.

When we finished with the soup, I was full and I thought this was the end of the meal. The cook came and picked up the soup plate and the large spoon. But, nobody was getting up. I kept looking at Elsee, then at Max. I could see that they had no intention of getting up. So, I decided to sit there just like everybody else. Max was talking with my mother.

This is when I realized how bad her German was. She knew the words, but she mispronounced them and very often used the wrong article. My mother was a "dead" giveaway. All her mistakes were clearly Slavic. ELsee talked with Emma. Emma's German was much better but it was still obviously Slavic. Emma's pronunciation was not correct. It was not obviously Slavic, but it was not correct. I knew that my German was the best. From time to time Max would glance at me and smile, and I would smile back.

Then the cook came again. He carried a large glass bowl. From that bowl, he served a cucumber salad into a small dish next to the remaining large plate. The cook disappeared and came back again. This time, he carried a huge but covered ceramic tray. He put the tray next to Max and opened the lid. There was a huge roasted goose!

The goose was surrounded with roasted potatoes, apples, sauerkraut, and many other "frivolous" things. The aroma sent goose bumps down my throat! Max nodded to the cook, and the cook proceeded to carve the goose. Then, the cook served everybody. He would ask each of us "which" type of meat. Then, he would serve the meat, add a few roasted potatoes, a baked apple, some sauerkraut, and stuffing. I looked at my portion and drooled.

There was only one problem. Too many utensils were still on the table. How did one attack this sumptuous meal? I could see how my mother was at a loss. So, I watched Elsee. I noticed how Elsee took the largest fork into her left hand and the largest knife into her right hand, and proceeded to cut the meat into a bite-sized piece and eat it. Then she would put some sauerkraut on her fork and eat it also. But, she never switched the utensils. Then, I took a glance at Max and he did the same thing. He never switched the knife and fork. My mother, on the other hand, kept switching the knife and fork during the meal. I decided to imitate Max and Elsee. The meal was "out of this world."

When we finished the second meal, I was stuffed and ready to burst at the seams. Surely this was the end of this scrumptious dinner. Well, the cook came, cleaned off the used plates, utensils, and the bread plate. But, then he came back again, brushed off the eating areas into a tray, and re-arranged some dishes. For the adults, he placed a small plate and a small dish with a cup in front of them. But, for Emma and me he placed only a small plate. Then, the cook turned to Emma and said, "Milch?" I could see how Emma nodded, so I nodded also. The cook disappeared and brought two large glasses of milk -- one for Emma and one for me.

Wow, real milk was in front of me. No matter how full I was I had to drink it, and I did. Then, the cook came back with a pot of coffee and a tray with cookies, fruits, and cheese.

I was amazed and dumbfounded. Did these people know there was a war going on? Maybe, I thought for a moment, the war was just in the "other" parts of world and they were not affected by it at all. Here we were feasting while the rest of humanity was destitute and starving.

By now I was tired, full, and content. The only thing I was good for was to go to sleep, which I did. This kind of feast was not the order of the day. But, it was their "typical" Sunday meal. Meals during the week, were "less formal" and less elaborate. But, to us, the worst meal during the week was better than our Sunday meals in Berlin. I did miss my mother's Borscht and her baked goodies. By the third day, Max and Elsee insisted that we call them Uncle Max and Aunt Elsee.

Our daily routine was simple. In the morning, my mother would go to her school and return very late in the evening. Emma would come down in the morning, have breakfast and go to school. Emma would come back in the late afternoon. My mother had pre-arranged tutors for both Emma and me, but Uncle Max volunteered to be our tutor. He asked my mother to cancel her arrangements and to leave both Emma and me in his care. My mother agreed to leave me with Uncle Max, but my mother insisted that Emma needed tutoring and two kids would be just too much for him. I must say Uncle Max and Aunt Elsee were genuinely disappointed with my mother's decision. But, I was very happy that my mother entrusted me with him. So, Uncle Max established a schedule which occupied us all day long until my mother came home from work. He was very systematic. He was prepared and had all the necessary books in his library.

We would start with a small breakfast. A glass of milk and a bun with marmalade and butter for me, coffee and a bun for Uncle Max. Then, he would take me into his study and teach me German, arithmetic, geography and history. German and arithmetic were very "dry," and we would do that first. Geography and history were very "alive" and we would do that last. Actually, geography was a "game" and history was "story telling."

Uncle Max liked to teach geography in a "real" way, as a game. He had a large globe of the world which turned around its north-south axis. The globe could also be positioned on an east-west axis. The game was to position the globe in a "random" manner, then to rotate the globe and stop it with one finger randomly. Wherever your finger stopped the globe you were required to name the country, its capital, a mountain range, and a major river without "cheating." The globe was not political but topographical. When the finger landed on a body of water, the characteristics of that body of water had to be named. I relished that game and, in no time at all, got very proficient at it.

To Uncle Max, history was the history of wars. To him, the outcomes of great wars hinged on "key" military or political leaders. And, according to him, the "fruits" of a great war had to be lasting. That is, to extend beyond the conqueror's lifetime. Therefore, to Uncle Max, the greatest military leaders were: Alexander the Great, Julius Caesar, "Karl der Grosse" (Charlemagne), "Friedrich der Grosse" (Frederick the Great), Peter the Great, and Bismarck. To him, Hannibal and Napoleon were failures. He called them "flashes of greatness." To him, "flashes of greatness" were like "fool's gold." They were the great deceptions of history. The great deceptions of history consumed themselves. Uncle Max did not like to talk about Hitler. Be it that he lost his sons, or be it that he felt it was another great deception, I never found out. He felt that it was "premature" to place Hitler among the great military leaders. So, each day, he would tell me the story of one leader, and then I had to read up on the story. He had an endless set of biographies in his library.

I remember how one day I asked "what started this war." He thought for a moment and said, "The Treaty of Versailles. Of course," he repeated, "… the Treaty of Versailles." That was the extent of his explanation.

Then, we would break for lunch -- a small sandwich and a glass of milk for me, a cup of coffee and a sandwich for him. After lunch, Uncle Max and I would take a short walk in his garden. It was there he would casually "test" me on the morning's lessons. He would do this in an inconspicuous way -- with the flowers in the garden, the trees, and the walkway and so on. He always applied the lessons to nature or our surroundings.

After the walk, we would go on an actual "excursion." Sometimes, we would go to his factory. There, he would explain the process, the equipment, and the mechanical parts. Then, he would mention the great inventors or great thinkers of all time. To him, Euclid, Archimedes, Euler, and Gauss were all the great thinkers one ever needed to know about. And, he would explain how these thinkers solved a problem. Again, to him, a great thinker was one who solved a problem, not one who posed one, or split hairs about it. I relished his way of teaching.

Sometimes Uncle Max would take me for a ride in his Mercedes. He would drive slowly through the mountain roads of the "Erzgebirge." We would stop at a lookout point, and he would describe the landscape, the town or "whatever" was in sight or of particular interest. I remember how once he explained the vegetation on the mountain, how it "thinned out" as it tried to grow towards the mountain peaks. He loved nature. Often we would stop and examine the flowers along the way. Then, he would explain the parts of a flower and so on. We often returned home intoxicated from the flower fragrances.

Our excursions were never long. One hour, sometimes even less. But, his excursions always had a purpose, a direction. Usually, it was directed towards our next day's lesson.

We were always home before Emma came back from her tutor. Then, if there was enough time, Uncle Max would talk about discipline and manners.

To Uncle Max, discipline came first and was the most fundamental aspect of civilization. To him, discipline could only be learned by being a soldier for a while. He subdivided manners into "eating" manners and "social" manners. To Uncle Max, eating showed the level of civilized social behavior. That is, table manners were important, needed to be learned, and adhered to. Then, he would demonstrate to me the table manners he felt were in order. The worst thing one could do was to slurp the soup. That, to Uncle Max, was downright barbarian. I remember, when he told me that, my mind raced to our first dinner and I kept asking myself, "Did I slurp?" I then reassured myself that I had not.

Social manners included "salutation" and dancing. To him, it was imperative that young males "clicked" their heels, even with a handshake. Without the clicking of heels, a salutation was just not complete. So, Uncle Max showed me how to click my heels. At that moment, I was still wearing my shoes from Berlin, and my click would just not come out as sharp as his. He looked at my shoes and said, "They are awful. Of course you can't click your heels." He measured my shoes, and the next day, I had two pairs of new shoes. Sure enough, his shoes made clicking very easy.

Dancing was also very important. He felt that any male who could not dance the "Marsch" (foxtrot for closeness to marching) was a useless social creature for the Marsch was the most natural dance step for a male. All "those other" dance steps were too feminine. So, Uncle Max would put a good Marsch on his gramophone and teach me the Marsch. I was amazed how easy it was to learn dancing.

Uncle Max showered us with gifts. He had a present for my mother, for Emma, and me every day. But, somehow I always ended up with twice as much as both of them put together. At first, my mother was embarrassed and refused all gifts. But, he had a way to rationalize the need and purpose of each gift. Eventually, my mother caved in, and I think this made her very uneasy.

He changed our entire wardrobe. Little by little, day by day, he brought new things. Pretty soon our closets were bursting at the seams.

Two items were of particular interest to me. School children in Germany carried their books to school in a "Ranzen." A Ranzen is a backpack, which was strapped to the back, similar to a knapsack, except that it was sturdy and firm. Uncle Max had a handmade Ranzen made for me in his factory of the sturdiest leather possible. That Ranzen, while light and comfortable, was sturdier than the Zoo-bunker in Berlin. It would be the envy of everyone for years to come.

And, Uncle Max got me a miniature rifle. This is when my mother tried to draw the line, but he explained that a rifle was only a necessary tool to teach discipline. Eventually, my mother gave in. I got to keep the rifle, and Uncle Max showed me the "drill" maneuvers, which I had to learn. I loved it. Soon, I was parading in his garden, with Uncle Max as the "drill sergeant," and I was executing each maneuver in a truly "Prussian" way. He was proud of me, and I was very proud of myself. Only my mother was counting the days when we could leave paradise.

By August 1944, my mother's course was completed, and we had to make plans to return to Berlin. Uncle Max begged my mother not to return. He assured her that he could change the order by adopting our family, including George and his family members. My mother was very flattered, but could not accept -- the Soviet front was now less than one hundred miles away. Falling into Soviet hands meant certain death for her, if not all of us. Surely, so she hoped, Berlin was a safer place. In principle, Uncle Max agreed; but then he begged my mother to leave me with him. He assured her that he would adopt me and take care of me. That my mother, Emma, George, Grandma and Masha would be welcome to come back anytime, and join us. My mother would not budge. My mother felt that "nobody" would or could, take better care of her children than she. She was not going to leave Emma or me behind. For better or worse, my mother was determined to keep our family together.

I remember how, on that fateful evening, we sat together and wept together. Uncle Max would find a rational argument, and my mother would find a stronger one. We kept crying and hugging each other.

We knew we would not see each other again. A freak chance had brought us together, and the inevitability of the hour was now tearing us apart.

Next morning, Uncle Max and Aunt Elsee took us to the train station. The inevitable was resolved; and stoically, we had to live with our decision. We hugged one last time; then boarded the train. All I could hear from Uncle Max was, "Don't forget to write to Uncle Max and Aunt Elsee...." And our train rolled out of Plauen.

I remember crying on the train for a long time. "Why could we not stay in this sanctuary? "What was my mother's real reason for leaving," I asked myself? When I calmed down, I began to question her. I asked, "Mama, why did we leave? Please tell me."

She hugged me and started: "Uncle Max and Aunt Else are the kindest people I have ever met. They were sincere. They wanted us to stay. It was difficult for me to make the decision, but I did. I had two reasons: safety and survival."

I was stunned. Did we not leave paradise on earth? Was this not the ultimate safety? Forget about survival. If living in luxury meant survival, then I would choose luxury every time. I looked at her in disbelief. Her explanation made no sense to me whatsoever. Then, I just looked at her and said, "Yah, yah… sure, sure." She knew she had to explain much more, and she continued, "Do you think it was safe to stay in Plauen?" she asked. I just sat there. She continued: "Wait till the 'Red Devils' get there and show them what starvation is all about. Then, every neighbor in that town will turn us in. They will turn us in for one slice of bread!" She paused, and then she almost said to herself. "We must go to a large city. There, is anonymity in great numbers. Everybody will have their hands full, trying to survive from day to day. There will be no energy left to squeal on us."

Then, she looked at me again and asked, "Do you think Uncle Max knows how to survive?" "Now, that was a ridiculous question to ask," I thought, "He had a factory, a Mercedes and a beautiful home. Did he know how to survive!" I wished I could survive like him. She looked at me again and said, "Uncle Max has everything, yet he has nothing!" How could this be? Was she playing words with me? I looked in disbelief. She knew I did not believe her. So, she went on, "Uncle Max has everything for his comfort: A house, a car, a factory, and a lot of money. But, he has nothing that comforts him! He raised four sons. I am certain that he raised them well. Where are they now?" This was a shock to me. She was right -- they were all dead. She continued, "With all his talents -- he raised them only to become cannon fodder. Do you call that survival?" Her point was made. I was satisfied.

I thought about this conversation for a long time on the train. While I did not concur with her completely, I had to agree with her at least partially. I tried to think about other things. About the great conquerors and military leaders. If Uncle Max was wrong on such a fundamental point, then, it was possible that his view of history was wrong also. I started with Alexander the Great.

I thought about Alexander's tiny army which made war against Persia and how Alexander conquered, with his tiny army, this great Empire. Now that was a feat! Was it not?

How did Alexander with his 40,000 Macedonian and Hellenic soldiers destroy an army twenty five times as large? Of course, Alexander invented and used his "phalanx" in this war. This explained it. Did it not? I started to think about the sequence of the war. Was it not in 333 B.C. that he destroyed the huge Persian Army? Did he not lay siege to all the great cities and sacked them one by one? Did he not reach Babylon and crown himself the supreme ruler of Persia and Greece? Did he not go to

India and defeat that army too. What conquests? Oh what a great general, I thought. Uncle Max was right. There was no greater conqueror than Alexander the Great.

Later, only much later, my admiration for Alexander the Great was shattered. I was destroyed when I found out that Alexander the Great only imitated somebody else! -- a virtual nobody in history class -- a man named Xenophon.

It was not that Alexander the Great did not conquer Persia; he did. It was not that he had only 40,000 men to perform this feat; he did. But, an even a greater feat was performed by Xenophon some fifty years before Alexander, and Alexander studied Xenophon's writings, descriptions, and accounts in every detail before he embarked on his conquest. Alexander knew that his mission could not fail with 40,000 hand-picked soldiers.

This knowledge made Alexander embark on the conquest. In a sense, Alexander still deserves a lot of credit. But, the perspective and expectations change. Alexander the Great did not embark on a "Columbian" expedition, to find an unknown. Alexander knew precisely what he was facing and what resources he needed to accomplish his mission. This fact is concealed from us when we are taught history. This fact was devastating to me when I found it out.

The Persian Empire was huge. The Empire could not be ruled from a "central government." It was too large for that. Instead, the Empire was subdivided into "satraps," or regions. Each region had a ruler, a king, who was appointed and approved by the supreme king in Babylon. Each ruler of a satrap swore loyalty and paid tribute to the supreme ruler. Each ruler of a satrap was obliged to provide a fixed number of soldiers, in case of general war, to the supreme ruler. Each ruler of a satrap was permitted to keep a limited army to defend the borders and to maintain law and order in his region. These "standing" troops were highly regulated by the Supreme Ruler in order to prevent insurgency and potential attack from an ambitious king. In other words, each satrap was an independent kingdom, with limited military powers, all paying tribute to the Supreme Ruler in Babylon.

However, one ambitious king decided to overthrow the SupremeRuler in Babylon. This king developed a plan to assemble a large army throughout different parts of his region. He intended to merge the many armies into one large unit. Then he felt strong enough to take Babylon, becoming the supreme ruler himself. His plan called for a multitude of small uprisings which would permit him to assemble the required armies. So, he instigated uprisings throughout his kingdom and was granted permission by the Supreme Ruler in Babylon to expand his armies in order to put down the revolts. In this process, the king hired about 13,000 Greek mercenaries. The Greek mercenaries proved very useful and effective. Slowly but surely, the mercenaries were drawn deeper and deeper towards Babylon. Then, one day, the king revealed his plan and demanded loyalty from his assembled army. The Greek mercenaries agreed and joined the king in his ambition. By now, the Greek mercenaries were only interested in getting their back wages, which had been assured them. By now, they were virtually at the gates of Babylon, deep in the Persian Empire.

The Supreme King had smelled the ruse, however, and assembled a large army which attacked. The usurpers were beaten and fled, leaving only the Greek contingent of mercenaries holding their ground. They had suffered only minor losses. The ambitious king was captured, and the Greek contingent found itself, deep in Persia, surrounded by enemies. The Supreme King felt no urgency to destroy that small contingent. So, he tried "politics." A meeting was agreed to, with the leaders of the Greek mercenaries, to discuss safe conduct and back wages. The Greek "generals" (four of them) accepted the offer and went to the conference. There, they were beheaded; and their heads were then shown to the mercenaries. The situation was now worse than ever. Not only were they deep in Persia, but they had just lost their trusted commanders! The mercenaries quickly got together and elected two leaders -- one of them was Xenophon. The mercenaries vowed to fight their way back to Greece, never surrendering to the Persians under any pretext.

While Xenophon was a commander, he was also a scribe and recorded his retreat in every detail in "The Persian Expedition." This Greek contingent of mercenaries fought their way back from Persia to Greece, a total distance of some 3,000 miles. When they arrived in Greece, more than 10,000 had survived the ordeal.

Aside from the retreat, Xenophon described the Persian Army's methods of warfare. Which was, that not only soldiers went to the battlefield, but also that the entire family of most soldiers was also near the battle scene. This created the appearance that there were many more soldiers than there actually were. That is, a rough ratio of eight to one or ten to one was in order to actually estimate the true size of the enemy's fighting force. This was critical to Alexander. Therefore, when Alexander saw Darius and his great army in 333BC, he knew full well that, they were no match for his legions! That is, in the battle of 333 B.C., Darius had at most 100,000 fighting soldiers. To the well-trained army of Alexander they were no match!

****

By 1944, the Soviet army was unstoppable. Systematically every pocket of German resistance was annihilated. Just as in a chess game, once a material advantage is gained, the opponents minor pieces are annihilated first. The board is cleared of all potential surprises. This tactic does not afford the opponent an opportunity to recover, and the remaining major pieces become exposed. So, 1944 is hailed as the year of "liberation." This is when Leningrad, Estonia, Latvia, Lithuania, Poland, Czechoslovakia, Hungary, Ukraine, Moldova, Bulgaria, Jugoslavia, Albania and Rumania were "liberated" by the "Red Devils."

In fact, this is when the remnants of the German Wehrmacht were systematically destroyed. This is the time when the flower of the German nation was decapitated, and the rest of the German nation doomed to endure whatever the Soviets were prepared to "dish out." By the summer of 1944, this destruction was so complete and so final that Churchill was afraid the Soviet appetite would not end with Germany alone. The defeat of Germany was a forgone conclusion after the Battle of Kursk.

While Churchill, Roosevelt and Stalin agreed to "partition" Germany along the river Elbe, Churchill mistrusted Stalin. Therefore, to save "western" Europe from "Soviet liberation," it became politically important to occupy Western Europe. The combined German western front had fewer than fifty divisions and posed no military threat to the Soviet forces whatsoever. Hitler needed 350 division; just to slow down the Soviet advance.

By May 1944, the "board was cleared," and the pieces were exposed. Only about two hundred and fifty German divisions defending the River Oder had to be dealt with. Then Berlin would be exposed. The first frontal attack along the Oder caused this motley defense to collapse.

By the end of 1944 the fragments of the once-mighty army of the Oder were systematically reduced again. The German Wehrmacht found itself in a "human meat-grinder." The more troops that were sent out, the greater the target. The greater the target, the greater was the destruction, until by the end of 1944, there was nobody left to send out. Only boys and old men remained. So, boys over the age of eleven and old men up to the age of seventy were drafted to defend that last piece -- Berlin.

A whirlwind was destroying Germany. And, we were heading right into the center of this storm.

CHAPTER 5

The Fall of Berlin

We arrived in Berlin, and George met us at the station. He took us to our new quarters. Berlin was now a heap of rubble. Our new quarters were a bombed out building on Claudius Street. The building on Antonauer Street was totally destroyed while we were gone. By now, only a handful of buildings were still standing in our old neighborhood. The stench of death, decay, and destruction embraced Berlin.

Our new building was completely demolished. Only on the ground floor, was one room usable as a "shelter," and another was partially open. Somehow, as the building collapsed, it formed a huge mound around this one room, while the other room was open to the sky. On one side of the room was a gaping hole into the cellar.

George had built a ladder from the lumber in the rubble, so we could easily hide in the cellar when needed. Nails were plentiful, and George had found a hammer. There was no running water. A few houses away, there was still a tap. From there, George would bring two buckets full of water, keeping one near the stove above and the other in the cellar. The stove had an endless number of "elbows" which led eventually to the outside. George insisted, "straight" pieces were nonexistent in all of Berlin. The only way he could direct the fumes to the outside was to use "elbows."

The side room was used as a toilet. George had placed a bathtub there and kept a few bags of lime "handy in order to" kill the stench and keep it "disinfected."

The main room was partitioned into sections with blankets. Each section had a bed or cot, some linens, some clothes, many blankets and a lot of pillows. Grandma and Masha were waiting for us. They had become "lethargic." No enthusiasm, no joy was left in them. They, and the rest of "Berliners," had turned into lethargic moles. They did not even bother to go to the bunkers any more. During an air raid, they would just slip into the cellar. When the raid was over, they would climb out of the cellar and sit by the window.

The window was a huge paneled bay window. Most of the glass was shattered. George had replaced the broken pieces with wood or sheet metal, or whatever else was handy at that time. Now, everybody sat in an area that had some glass left. From there, they watched the street. Right next to us, about two houses away, a flack battery was set up. During the raids, a few boys, not much older than Emma, would fire it.

Even when we opened our luggage, which was half food and half clothes, they still were not too excited. The rationing system still worked. They had plenty of food. It seemed to me that they were saving their energy to dash down into the cellar. No sooner had we "unpacked" when the siren sounded, and - in a flash - they were gone. Only my mother, Emma and I stood there. Almost instantly after the siren, we heard the flack; and shortly thereafter, it went, "Boom, Boom, Boom…"

Our quarters were shaking, and my mother thought this whole contraption would collapse any minute. We dropped everything and dashed down to the cellar. To our amazement, we saw another stove with a similar "elbow" construction. On the stove was George's "Samovar erector set." He was brewing his tea. There was plenty of wood around, so both stoves were kept at a "simmering" level.

The cellar was large and clean. There was plenty of room, and the cellar was "reinforced." So, in every practical sense, the cellar was quite usable as a shelter. Since the entrances were blocked by the debris, nobody else had figured out there was this make-shift entrance into the cellar from our living room. Maybe nobody cared because most Berliners lived under very similar conditions. But my mother did not like the idea of the cellar at all. She insisted that we had to go to the nearest bunker. George told her that this was practically impossible because there was no time from the time of the siren to the actual bombardment.

Finally, a compromise was reached. During the day, we would use our cellar; and at night we would use the bunker. This seemed begrudgingly agreeable to all. The nearest bunker was still the bunker in Tiergarten, but now it was a block further away. That evening, and for the next few evenings to come, we "marched" to the Tiergarten bunker at dusk.

So, our daily routine was again on schedule. In the morning my mother and George would go to work -- the "Reichsministerium" was still functioning -- and we stayed behind with grandma. Schools were closed by then. Emma, Masha and I had to entertain ourselves. And, quite frankly, I don't recall being idle during that time. First, there were many books to be read, and we had a lot of them by then. Second, it was interesting to explore the ruins and to find shortcuts to the stores and to the water supply, and to explore the situation in general.

The stores had moved "underground." The subway was not running any more, at least not on a regular basis. But, the structures below the rails were considered to be fortified, and many stores were set up there. The "trick" became to find out "what" store was in "what" subway sector and how to get there in the most efficient way. So, in a way, our exploring served the purpose of finding the best way to get to and from a particular place.

It was not uncommon, in those days, to get caught "en route" during an air-raid. Then the most prudent thing to do was to find the nearest shelter and wait out the raid. Since my German was the best -- and by now everybody agreed on that – I volunteered most of the time and was allowed to go all by myself. I now felt I was carrying my fair share of the burden for my family.

The mail was no longer delivered to the homes. Everybody was assigned a post office box and had to pick up his or her own mail. My mother would bring the mail when she returned from work. Practically every day, there was a letter from Uncle Max and Aunt Elsee. And, practically every day, I would write a letter back to them.

One evening we went to the Tiergarten bunker in our usual way. Each of us carried a knapsack, a pillow and a flashlight. Of course, I carried the Ranzen Uncle Max had made for me. I am not sure whether it was I or my Ranzen, but I was admired by all bunker dwellers, especially when I would tell an admirer that "this Ranzen" was specially made for me by my Uncle Max.

Well, that evening, the bunker was particularly crowded, so mother let me sit on her lap. We were just sitting there in a sort of "daze" when all of a sudden I saw the stars above. The searchlights were all over the sky, and the sky was "buzzing" with airplanes. The sky was full of them. I didn't know what had happened, but I was obviously outside of the bunker. Yet only a moment ago I had been inside. I had heard no whistling sound of a bomb falling or the noise of an explosion. A quantum jump had taken place: One instant there and the next instant outside.

Within a blink of an eye, there was an adult leaning over me -- then another, and then another, still. I just looked at them and smiled. Then I heard one of them say: "He is all right. Let's look for the others." I was all right. I got up and started to look for my family.

Our bunker had suffered a direct hit. The force tore me off my mother's lap, tore out the entrance door, and I landed in the grass nearby. My mother, Emma, grandma and Masha were "dazed." They actually walked around for a while, without knowing where they were, or what had happened to them. And, George was buried by the debris and had suffered a concussion. George sat on the "other" side of the "zig-zag" in the bunker from the rest of us. The direct hit was in the sector next to George. In that sector everybody was dead.

A crew was at the scene almost instantly. They dug out everybody, administered first aid, and told us what to do with the "dazed people." We had to hold them tight and walk them around gently until they "came too." So, a few hundred people were holding another few hundred people. They were walking them gently around while the bombs continued to rain on Berlin. And, nobody asked whether they were Aryan or not.

George was hospitalized for a short while and released. But George still was unable to work for a while and so was recuperating at home. At last, George had won his argument with the bunker. The bunkers were just as "unsafe" as the cellars. And, from then on we did not bother to go to a bunker.

I had found Emma first. Some elderly woman was walking her gently around, and Emma kept saying: "Son of bitch! What am I doing outside…" I knew Emma was all right. Then, I found my mother. Another woman was walking her around. When I came closer, she recognized me and yelled, "Tola, Tola, Tola!" And, I knew she was all right. Then my mother and I found grandma. She was just sitting on the ground near the former bunker. My mother came up to her and spoke to her, and she was coherent. So, grandma was all right. Then we found Masha and she was all right. By the time we found George, Emma was with us. We found George alive but hurting badly, and my mother went with him to the hospital. The rest of us made our way back to our "home," and we slept in the cellar.

My mother still did not like the "contraption" on Claudius Street. While she was going to work, she looked for a place with a "less bohemian" atmosphere -- one with much thicker walls and a "solid" cellar. Eventually she found such a place.

Only one block from us was the "Reichsgesundheitsamt." The Reich's health ministry building. By the end of 1944, they decided to move underground, and they abandoned the building. That building was built like a fortress. The walls were three feet thick all around, and the cellar bunker was "impregnable." And, wonder of wonders, all the "conveniences" were still operating. Water was abundant, even the electricity worked. It had only one "problem." There was only one toilet on each floor in each section.

The building was massive and built in three sections; a front section along the street, a rear section about two hundred feet recessed, but parallel to the front section, and a section on one side which connected the front and the back. On the fourth side, there was just a high brick wall. The entire structure was shaped like a horseshoe. In the center was a large lawn. Narrow, cement walkways connected the three sections.

Of course as "Volksdeutsche," we could only "take" what we could get. When the building became available for civilian occupancy, many people had the same idea as my mother and applied for occupancy there. The floors were sectioned off, and quarters became available. Of course, the sections with the toilets were assigned to pure Aryans.

The most desirable floors were the first and second, but many Germans took the third, and even the fourth floor. The housing shortage was very acute. The last two floors were burnt out from the many bombs the building had "swallowed." But, after all the sections were assigned, a few marginal sections, which had no toilets, remained. So, my mother applied for one such section on the second floor in the rear section of the building.

That section had four rooms in perfect condition and another four rooms that were ruined but usable. The end wall had collapsed, and a huge mound of rubble sloped to the ground. On the second floor, the end wall was not there, but a sloping mound of rubble led directly to the ground and to the next building, which was also a ruin. The higher floors, above the second floor, had a gaping hole into open space.

George was very reluctant to move. Here he had his "own residence," and he did not have to put up with any racial degradation. But, to my mother, the "safety" of that building was very questionable. She felt that the whole building was standing on "chicken legs." The next good shell or bomb close by would surely "cave in" that contraption. Since wives have it their way in the long run, George eventually agreed that the new residence was safer, especially since my mother was getting on with her pregnancy. George called the new building, "The Fortress."

First we went there and "staked" our claim with papers and all. The superintendent in the building was a woman, a real "Parteigenosse" (a loyal Nazi party member), and very suspicious of all foreigners. She occupied the best part, the first floor of the connecting section. This way she had a full view of the yard and the other two sections. Her relatives and friends occupied about half of the building. Somewhat reluctantly, she agreed to let us in.

We then moved in with all our paraphernalia. The rooms were a definite improvement. The water situation was resolved because almost every room had a faucet and a sink. The building was half the distance to the subway stores. Actually, the building was directly behind our first quarters on Antonauer Street. This street was called "Klopstock-strasse," and the number was eighteen.

As it turned out, from the time we moved in until the fall of Berlin, the toilet problem was not a problem at all. We spent most of our time in the cellar anyhow. In the cellar were superb toilet facilities: a toilet, a bathtub with a shower and sink, and a row of cabinets made out of "Blech," (painted sheet metal). Each family was assigned a section in a cabinet to keep their "supplies," mostly pieces of cut-up newspapers used for toilet paper. My mother's point was that the makeshift toilet George had constructed on Claudius Street was sufficiently sanitary anyway and was a sound alternative for a real toilet. A shower was nice, but not essential. A bucket of water with a large pan accomplished the same thing. Therefore, at least technically, the problem was resolved for the primary functions. However, the "fortifications" in the building rivaled those in the indestructible Zoo-bunker.

Here, my sister Kathy was born on February 22, 1945. In this building we began bracing ourselves for the inevitable fall of Berlin.

By now it was clear to everyone: It was not a matter of IF; it was only a matter of WHEN. And, the WHEN became not postponable. On April 15, 1945, the assault on Berlin started; and on May 8, it was finished. While the surrender was signed on May 7, actual street fighting continued until the 10th of May and even beyond.

This period, from February 1945 to May 7, 1945, made the Berliners introspective. By February, the Red Army was getting ready to assault Berlin. The last glimmer of hope to wage a joint war against the "Reds" with the British and Americans had vanished. The western armies were still hundreds of miles away from Berlin.

Yet, despite the destruction, despite the incessant air attacks, the food supply system was still functioning. In fact, before Kathy was born, my mother's ration card was upgraded. She began getting a larger portion of bread, butter and meat. When Kathy was born, Kathy received a special ration card which included a liter of milk every day. Emma and I would alternate daily to get the milk from the underground store. Each day we would return with the milk and bring a handful of "hot" shrapnel with us. It became a game: to dodge the attack and show evidence of its fury.

Wagner's "Die Gotterdammerung" had turned into reality for the Berliners. Von Clausewitz had advocated the concept of "revanche" or a way to even the score. Every Berliner knew that the "Red Devils" were here to even the score. Stark terror was in their faces as they awaited the "Red Devils."

On April 30, the bombing raids stopped. George knew that the approaching holiday of the "Reds," May 1, would unleash a massive attack. It did. Stalin preferred to start offensives, on major Soviet holidays because, as he said, "The soldiers fight better on a holiday."

As the bombing raids stopped, the shelling intensified. At first, it appeared as though the fortunes of war were turning. The shelling had a much smaller impact. I remember how we even ventured into the courtyard one day. We even inspected the damage to the building. Shells, bombs and shrapnel lay randomly throughout the yard. The super even organized a clean-up crew.

I ran to the front building and decided to watch the street action from a safe place. I found a window on the first floor and sat there and watched. At first there was nothing. Our street was deserted. Then, I saw a German soldier in full battle gear running down our street. The soldier noticed that our street was deserted. He stopped; he turned around a few times; and then, he ran into the ruin directly across from us. A few minutes later, the same man came out, in civilian clothes, without his rifle, and without his gear. He continued to run down our street. He then vanished into one of the ruins. I sat at my look-out point a little longer, and I saw again the same scenario: another soldier in full battle gear. He stopped, made a few turns and vanished in a ruin. In a short while, he returned as a civilian and continued to run down the street. This was very strange I thought. Soldiers were changing into civilians. This was feasible any place in the world, but not in Prussia! Something was very wrong in the state of Prussia. So, I dashed back to my mother. I told her what I had seen. She looked at me and said. "Are you sure!" I nodded vehemently and said, "Go look for yourself." My mother turned around and yelled to everybody, "The Red Devils are here!"

Almost in panic, everybody dropped whatever he or she was doing. Everybody dashed into the cellar. We huddled together in small groups, and my mother and grandma were praying.

CHAPTER 6

Soviet Occupation

The next morning, we were flushed out of the cellar. Actually, it was quite "uneventful:" a knock on our cellar door, a loud Slavic, "Raus," and, we staggered into the bright, clear morning. Then, we heard another Slavic, "Hoch." Obviously, the caller meant for us to raise our arms. We all did.

A very ordinary soldier stood there with a strange looking submachine gun pointed at us. I actually had "visions" of real Red Devils with horns and a tail and a frightening face. I must say I was actually disappointed, but relieved. This fellow in front of us with his submachine gun was not much taller than our super. And, she was very short, I thought to myself.

Here stood a short and stocky man. He wore only a long greenish "shirt," which extended over his pants. The pants were tucked into high leather boots. The shirt was held tightly around his waist by a wide belt. If it were not for his sub-machine gun, he looked more dressed for a picnic than for a battle; -- no battle gear, no grenades, no gasmask only that submachine gun.

He looked at us with contempt, but with anticipation, like a cat ready to pounce on its prey. A few more soldiers provided cover from other strategic places for our captor. Another soldier stepped forward and frisked us one by one. Then, the last soldier who had come forward got closer to the cellar and yelled again in heavy Slavic, "Alle raus!"

Our super turned to him and said, "Da iss Niemand drin." She tried to tell him that nobody was inside. The soldier stepped toward her, shoved his submachine gun in her back indicating for her to go inside. Our super and the soldier went into the cellar. Soon, the super and the soldier emerged from the cellar. "Aha," I told myself, "whatever you do, don't volunteer."

The soldier waved to his comrades and they stepped forward. There were four of them. Then, one of the soldiers yelled again in heavy Slavic, "Forwards." We followed him as he led us from our building into our street. There, groups like ours were moving in one direction. He motioned us to join the procession. Reluctantly, we joined this motley flow of humanity.

My mother was carrying Kathy, and next to her was George. They seemed to whisper something to each other. Then, my mother would fall back and whisper something to grandma, and so on, until she came to me. And, she whispered to me, "Son, this is very important. We are going to be interrogated. From now on, your last name is Grotte, and your first name is Anton. Can you remember this?" I nodded my head. And, she said again," Forget every other name. You are now Anton Grotte, and that's all." So, we became the Grotte family. George, my mother, Emma, and grandma all got to keep their first names. Masha and I had to change ours, because ours were obviously Slavic. So, I was named Anton, and Masha became Maria. Both were good Teutonic names.

We walked like that for about four blocks, to the edge of the Tiergarten. There, in the open, a huge crowd was already waiting. We joined the crowd. We stood together, and my mother kept looking at each of us and mumbling, "Grotte, Grotte, Grotte…"

By noon, the crowd started to thin out. The crowd was now pushing us into the "inferno," into the interrogation center. Pretty soon, the whole setup was in sight.

A long row of makeshift tables was standing right on the grass. At each table sat a Soviet soldier; and behind him, a few paces away, stood another with a submachine gun. Groups of people were motioned to a table. Then, the seated soldier would ask them questions. Then, they were handed papers and left. Occasionally, someone would be led away into another crowd standing nearby. About twenty soldiers or so surrounded that crowd with their submachine gun in a semi-ready position.

My mother kept me near her. Behind her was George and grandma. Behind them was Emma and Maria. A soldier motioned us to step forward. My mother and I were the first at the table. I came up to the table and clicked my heels. The soldier at the table almost perked up. He looked at me and said, "Hm… Hitlerjugend." Then, he asked: "Name?" And, I said, "Grotte."

Then he looked at me again. He was ready to crack up. He was actually smiling at me and said, "Vorname," and I said, "Anton." Then the soldier looked at my mother and asked, "Eine Familie?" ("One family"). She said, "Ja." Then she was asked for our address, and she told him. From that point on, every member of our family was asked for only their first name, and each replied as rehearsed. Only when the soldier came to George did he ask an additional question. Was he a soldier? George replied that he was wounded. The interrogation was over. We got our papers and were motioned to leave.

The first storm was weathered. We returned home. As soon as we arrived home, George lit the stove, and my mother and George burned all their papers: passports, diplomas, correspondence. Anything that had our prior name on it had to be destroyed. My mother and George knew this was only the first of many coming interrogations. Anything with our former name on it was a dead giveaway.

After my mother and George burned their papers, they realized that everybody was hungry. From morning, when we were captured, until now, we had had no food. My mother knew starvation was around the corner, so she and George "requisitioned" all provisions. Our eating habits had to change. Everything perishable had to be eaten first. Anything that would last was stored away. Only after the food was redistributed, and some was "stashed away," did my mother prepare a meal for us. My mother and George were proven right again. Nearly half of the population of Berlin starved to death in the next two years.

Many Berliners realized this, but some did not. To impress my mother's concern, she went to the super and told her that "we," in the collective sense, should do something about it right away. My mother suggested that the lawn within the building area should be partitioned into a garden. That is, to subdivide the yard into small lots so that each family could grow whatever they deemed important for survival. The super thought the idea was absurd and dismissed it.

Meanwhile, food became scarce. Within days, people were literally starving to death. Domestic animals started to disappear: cats, dogs, and many other pets.

I remember one evening very vividly. Our primary mission during the day was to go on "scavenger" hunts for food. Anything would do. Rotten potatoes, acorns, any kind of nut or mushroom was a prime candidate. One day, my mother returned with George from such a scavenger hunt empty handed, and she was sobbing. I tried to comfort her and asked what had happened. She told me her story. They had gone to the Tiergarten looking for food. Everything was picked clean. Even the bark from the young trees was shaved off. After a while, they gave up and decided to return home. On their way home, a truck, ran over a stray dog. The driver got out and heaved the carcass into a ruin nearby. My mother and George returned home, and my mother said:

"I could not get that dead dog out of my mind. The animal was not sick. There were at least ten pounds of meat on it. The liver, the heart, all those pieces could be eaten. That food would have lasted us a long time -- at least a week, maybe more. I decided to go back and fetch the cadaver and bring it home. I went to the place, but it was gone."

I wanted to comfort her, so I said, "Don't cry mama. Tomorrow we will find something else." She looked at me and said, "You understand nothing! I am not crying because I did not find the dog. I am crying because we have turned into animals ourselves!"

Sometime in mid-June of 1945, a German administration was formed to administer Berlin under allied auspices. One of the first appeals of that administration was a call to all Berliners to grow their own food. Every patch of land was to be used. In fact, the administration announced that all the parks in Berlin would be utilized for that purpose. Anyone willing to grow anything would be supported by the administration in whatever way they could. For a starter, they would give away seeds at all local stores.

The next day, the super came to my mother and asked her for ideas. My mother suggested that all families should get together and subdivide the yard into equal plots. Then, each family should cultivate their plot. The next day, a meeting was arranged, and all the families were there. The usable part of the yard was subdivided into equal parts and assigned to each family. A very small "communal" playground area was reserved for the children. Plans were made to put up two swings in the play area.

Meanwhile, the debris from the building was "heaped" into a large pile. This pile of rubbish took up about one quarter of the entire yard, and the pile was not assigned to anyone.

When the meeting was finished and the plot assignments complete, my mother asked everyone to wait. They did. Then, my mother made a proposition: She would trade her parcel for the unassigned pile of rubble. They all laughed and told her unanimously to take that pile and to cultivate it. They wanted no part of it.

By next morning, my mother had a complete agenda. George, Maria and Emma would go on the scavenger hunt as usual. But, my mother and I would stay and cultivate our parcels. Armed with two shovels and two buckets, my mother and I started our work early the next morning. First, the ground had to be "turned over." That took us nearly until noon. Then, while I rested, Mother went to the local store and came back with a host of little "newspaper bags" filled with seeds.

In those days, there were no paper bags. Instead, old newspapers were torn to the proper size, and the piece of paper was rolled into a cone-shaped bag. So, here she was with "hundreds" of these little bags. She had seeds for tomatoes, cucumbers, tobacco, lettuce, radishes, carrots, pumpkins, and much more.

Then we got a rake from the super and raked our plot. Then, every three feet, a row was formed. A little trench was made, about six inches wide, and the soil was heaped on the preceding row. The row was raked again and again, until the soil was nice and "fluffy." My mother then sorted out the bags with seeds, and she kept aside the tomatoes, lettuce, and radishes. Then she proceeded to plant them. She always planted three seeds next to each other. Meanwhile, I was sent to fetch some water. As soon as she planted the seeds, I watered them; and we worked all day and seeded our plot. Ours was the first plot to be seeded. Most neighbors watched us work and smiled.

The next day it was "onto the rubble heap," except now we used three buckets. One we filled with water, and we walked up to the heap and put the water down. Then, my mother walked around the heap. Then, she walked around the heap again. Then, she climbed on top of the heap and looked around again. I had no idea what she was looking for.

Finally, she had it all figured out. We took our shovels and the two empty buckets and went to the neighboring ruin. There, we found a patch of ground, and we dug up the soil and put it in the two buckets. Then I carried the two buckets to the heap of rubble in our yard and stopped. My mother climbed to the top and looked for a spot. Then, she would say, "Here." I would then carry one bucket of soil to the spot.

She would take out a heap of soil and place it firmly between some bricks or mortar or whatever was there to form a small mound. Then, she would place a few seeds into the mound, and I would bring the water. We would water the mound, and we would go on to the next, and the next, and the next... Our neighbors were shaking their heads. Those crazy foreigners had nothing better to do...

By the end of the second day, we had seeded the whole heap of rubble. The once "grayish" mass now looked as if it had the measles. The whole mound was covered with blotches of soil and was all watered to boot!

Each day thereafter, we would water our plots and watch them grow. As soon as the seeds started to sprout, my mother would tear out all the little ones, leaving only the biggest sprout. Soon, we had a regular garden. Our garden was the envy of everyone -- especially the mound. Once our seeds started sprouting, the mound of rubble was transformed into a luscious garden. It had tomatoes, tobacco, pumpkins and cucumbers. Every kind of plant my mother could get seeds for was planted.

The seeds provided to the population were limited. Beans, peas and other high protein seeds were not available, at least not to us. They were eaten as soon as they reached the stores. Instead, another vegetable became popular: "Kohlrabi" (turnip cabbage). I did not like it. It was "stringy," but I ate it anyway.

The scavenger hunts were useless. Too much time and energy was spent on an activity which produced very little. We decided to discontinue them. Maybe the "team" was wrong, but be it as it may -- the results were useless. Emma always took a "good" book with her to read along the way. She would have to trip over something edible before she would bring it home. Maria was disinterested. George was getting to be very irritable. His two most favorite pastimes -- smoking and drinking tea -- had come to an end. Now he was sipping hot water and sucking away on his empty pipe. The fact that we were growing tobacco meant nothing. He had a desperate craving for tobacco now.

So, we began to "experiment" with all kinds of plants and leaves, smoking them in place of tobacco. Nothing worked. We dried the leaves of maple trees, and chestnut trees, and every tree leaf we could find. No leaf, no matter what we did to it, was suitable for George's taste. Then, we tried plants – in particular, stems of plants. We finally found a type of "ragweed" which was quite agreeable to George. From then on, we were on the "lookout" for that ragweed. George tried to "improve" the taste -- he would add dried flower petals to his new blend. But most of the time, it did not work. One time the room smelled like dandelions; another time like wild flowers, and so on. George felt that rose pedals would really enhance the flavor and smell. We looked for roses everywhere; and, low and behold, we found a lonely rosebush in one of the ruins. We stripped the buds off the bush. They were dried and added to his ragweed mix. It proved to be a disaster. The room smelled like roses for weeks, and George smelled like roses for weeks; but, in the end, George complained that the taste was too bitter. His natural ragweed mix was the best after all.

The tea situation was not so simple. My mother and grandmother liked their cup of tea also. So, just before the last tea leaf was used up, we began experimenting with substitutes. Again, we tried leaves, we tried buds from every kind of tree and bush in our neighborhood. The best substitute we found was the acacia tree. We had heard that chicories might be a good substitute also, but we could not find any in our area.

There was another reason why scavenger hunting was a bad idea. The Soviets were patrolling the streets now and would randomly stop passers-by. George in particular was an inviting target. In addition to the patrols, drunken soldiers were now openly molesting young girls. So, the scavenger hunts became a dead issue.

By the end of June, the German administration was ready to count its flock. With Teutonic efficiency, block by block, every individual was scheduled to be interviewed. This served two purposes. The first was to take a "head count" of the survivors and schedule supplies; the second, however, was more sinister. The repatriation of everyone who "qualified" to return to the Soviet Union. While the first interviews had been conducted in haste by soldiers, this interview was much more serious. Now every German interviewer was a Soviet "aparatchik," a skilled and loyal party administrator.

So, we needed a cover, and we needed it fast. Since my German was the best, I was elected to be the "spokesman" for our family. My mother kept on saying, "Click your heels, and speak, but don't overdo it." Meanwhile, George was going to play "deaf and dumb." I was to say, he had suffered a concussion in the war and was still recovering. My mother would "pinch" Kathy to make her cry and hope that not too many questions would be asked of her. Grandma would be "shaking" from old age and look disoriented. Emma and Maria could take care of themselves for mother felt their German was sufficiently good. As for papers, well, we had the papers issued by the soldiers, and all our other papers had been lost during the fall of Berlin.

When our day came, we dressed in shabby, but clean, clothes. In those days, shabby meant with "patched" holes and a bit too short or a bit too long. The homemade look was the best. Clothes could not have holes; that would not be German. All the buttons had to be there, and the clothes had to be clean. Otherwise, they could be near rags.

So, on our appointed day, we went to the administration. This time we were scared. The first time, we had accepted fate just like everybody else. Then we were exhausted both physically and emotionally. We had thought our "ordeal" was over. Now, we were back on our feet, evading the Soviets. Yet we had to tempt the fates one more time.

When we arrived, a small group was waiting their turn just as we were. We waited only a few minutes. We were then motioned by a Soviet soldier into a room. The room was large with a desk near its middle. Behind the desk sat a German bureaucrat. He was obviously German because two very neat stacks of paper were on the desk, and he wore a "monocle."

About five paces behind him, a Soviet soldier was pacing up and down the room, puffing away on a Soviet cigarette. The soldier seemed to be annoyed at something. He appeared completely disinterested. I did my "routine." I walked up to the desk, clicked my heels, and said, "Good morning."

The bureaucrat was not impressed. He just glanced at me. The soldier gave me a quick glance and walked to the window. The soldier was very disinterested. The bureaucrat looked at my mother and said, "Name bitte." At that instant, Kathy started to scream. There was nothing that would stop Kathy. All the "rocking" and all the "shushing" had no effect. Kathy was screaming at the top of her lungs. The bureaucrat looked at me, almost in despair. Then, he asked me almost timidly," Name bitte." And, I replied," Anton Grotte." My mother fumbled in her jacket and pulled a piece of paper out of a pocket. She handed me the paper from our first interrogation. I gave the paper to the bureaucrat.

He looked at the papers and started to match up the list of names with our family members. Apparently, they were in order. He looked at my mother almost apologetically and asked for "real" papers. At this point Kathy let out another scream. George just stood there, rolling his eyes, and rolling his shoulders. It was obvious that George was incoherent. The bureaucrat looked at me. I explained "he" still suffered from a concussion. Then, the bureaucrat looked at grandma. She was "shaking" from old age.

Obviously, this was a "basket" case of a Prussian family. Only a Prussian family member knows how to click his heels and would do so, despite his misfortune. The bureaucrat asked me where the papers were. I told him that we were "completely bombed out" during the war. The bureaucrat looked to the soldier. The soldier just nodded in contempt. It was clear they were fed up with us.

The bureaucrat issued us new papers, new ration cards, and a work order exemption for George. They whisked us out of the office and out of the building. Kathy was still screaming. And we walked home.

As the noose was tightening around Berlin, Germans from East Prussia and other eastern parts of Germany were swarming into the city. Some estimates were that more than six million East German refugees converged on Berlin. This estimate could be high; but nevertheless, the numbers of East Germans was staggering. This was the case because the Germans were scared to death of Soviet retribution. The Germans knew what they had done in Poland, Russia, and the Ukraine. They feared that Soviet vengeance would be merciless. That fear turned out to be unfounded in one way, and well-justified in another.

While there were no mass deportations of Germans and no mass executions, Stalin was determined to transform the Germany in his sphere of influence into an agrarian land. Consequently, on one hand, the Soviets treated the Germans with "kid gloves;" while on the other, because Germany was a highly industrialized nation, these agrarian reforms were dismal failures resulting in chronic food shortages.

Most of the German refugees spoke fluently either Russian or Polish. Therefore, speaking Russian or Polish, in and of itself, was not a "dead giveaway" anymore. But, speaking Russian or Polish attracted attention. If no other proof was available, those Russians and Poles were assumed to be former Soviet citizens; and former Soviet citizens were repatriated on the spot.

As soon as valid papers were available, however, the situation changed. The papers determined "nationality." For Germans, I found that to be understandable -- they were trained to obey documents. But, to this day, I find it strange that the Soviets, by and large, followed the same logic. But, the Soviets did. Our dilemma was, that we had no valid papers. The first papers issued to us were "provisional" papers. The new papers, however, made us "officially" German. While a major hurdle had been overcome, from then on, we still had to be very careful.

Of course, the same administrators which ran the Third Reich were again in power. A few were purged at the very top; but by and large, the same administrators who ran Hitler's Germany also administered Soviet-occupied Germany and later, the Federal Republic, and so on. Our super was now officially the super of our building again. Now, as before, this was official. Many of her family members and relatives were now in the new administration of Berlin just as they were before during the war. So, the "melody had not changed, only the beat of the drummer."

As far as our neighbors were concerned, we were Volksdeutche before, and the "upgrade" to real Germans did not matter anymore. They rationalized that we were from "Eastern Prussia." and this was fine with us. They never asked, and we never contradicted.

On a number of occasions, however, we proved useful to our neighbors. The first time was when my mother suggested the garden idea. They soon realized that as far as survival was concerned, they could learn a few tricks from us. The second case was much more serious.

The super had a daughter. The daughter was about twenty-years old. The daughter was married and had a child. However, her husband was captured by the Americans and was in a POW camp. She had a large "prime" apartment on the third floor in our section of the building. Most of the time, she stayed with her mother, our super. Generally, young girls did not venture into the street anymore for there was a real danger of being raped. Lawlessness and the revenge motive still preoccupied the Soviet soldier's mind at that time. Thus, raping a German woman was considered an almost "normal" event. Certainly, complaining to the Soviet command was like throwing peas at the Zoo-bunker. It had no effect whatsoever. And so, one day, the daughter decided to do the shopping.

On her way home, two drunken Soviet soldiers spotted her and tried to "corral" her. She ran into our building, where one of the soldiers caught her. And, the "three-some" tumbled into our courtyard. My mother was on her rubble heap, weeding the plants. The super was outside too, working on her patch. A few additional residents were in the garden.

When one of the soldiers spotted the people in the courtyard he drew his pistol while the other proceeded to drag the girl into the nearest apartment. Everybody was frozen with fear, everyone except for my mother. She calmly came down off her rubble heap, went up to the soldier who was dragging the girl, and proceeded to slap the girl, yelling at her "how could you insult our liberators in such a way!"

Both soldiers were stunned. They just could not believe that there was actual "support" for them in the "German population." They came over to my mother, thanked her and patted her on her back. My mother told them that she had a bottle of vodka for them. They were more than eager to let my mother take the girl away and bring them the bottle instead. And, my mother did, and they took the bottle and left…

How did my mother have a bottle of vodka handy? Simple. I mentioned earlier that scavenger hunting was a lost cause. The "action" in Berlin, at that time, was the black market. Everybody who wanted to survive participated in that market. Initially, the family jewels were sold there for a piece of bread or a few potatoes. Soon, the market was interested only in watches, nylon stockings, cigarettes and vodka. Primarily vodka.

For vodka, one could buy anything: bread, butter, meat, flour and so on. The black market "valuta," or basis of trade, was one bottle of vodka. So, many private "entrepreneurs" began "brewing" their own. Now they needed a few "risk takers" who actually went to the market and made the trade. Technically, trading on the black market was illegal; but the authorities never tried to stop it and sometimes, actually encouraged it. The market action was in the Tiergarten, between the Brandenburg Gate and the Victory Statue, only a few blocks away from us. And the market was active seven days a week from dawn to dusk.

Living a few blocks away from us was a "brewmaster" who had contacted my mother through an acquaintance. Occasionally, he would bring over a few bottles of vodka. They would agree on the exchange and "commission." Then, my mother would plan her next "excursion" to the black market. So, the bottle came from that "stockpile" which my mother had accrued for her next trip. My mother was certain that the super would "replace" that bottle -- the super was also our primary client for some of the "end-products." In turn, the super had access to stockings and cigarettes. And, the super and our neighbors were buyers of butter, potatoes and so on.

Making vodka is quite simple when the "right" ingredients are available. One can proceed in two ways: The first is from "scratch." Then, one begins with potatoes, and the brewing process and so on. This process was both time-consuming and just not practical. There was an alternative which was quick but very risky. The black market almost exclusively handled this product: pure -- distilled alcohol. It was "cut" with water. Voila, the best vodka in the world!

The danger was that if wood alcohol were used as the base, the user could go blind! Since a good number of Soviet soldiers had gone blind, the seller had to submit to a "risk" test. Any bottle that was sold was opened, and one hundred grams was poured into a glass, about 3.3 liquid ounces. Then, the seller had to drink that one hundred grams. If the seller did not drink the one hundred grams, the seller was shot on the spot. If the seller drank the one hundred grams, the seller would get drunk. After two or three sales, the seller was usually hopelessly drunk and would lose the merchandise. So, in a way, it was a very dangerous way to make a living. Despite all of the risk, my mother would occasionally take this risk, so we could eat.

Since, officially, the black market did not exist, a "pro-forma" check was always made by the military police stationed at the entrance to the Tiergarten Park. Our cover was usually Kathy. We bought a "dilapidated" baby carriage and built a false bottom in it. The false bottom served to hide the merchandise, and Kathy would occupy the top. Then, "this" Berliner family would go into the Tiergarten Park for a stroll, just like any other Berliner family. We would be checked at the entrance for "black market contraband," just like everybody else. Then, we would proceed to the boulevard connecting the Brandenburg Gate and the Victory Statue, and we would walk down this boulevard very slowly. Each passer-by would bow to the other, sort of in a form of a greeting. And each would softly call out the merchandise he or she was selling today. And this walking, greeting and calling would continue until the market "closed" or the sale was consummated. The market closed at dusk. Then, each trader returned home, hoping that the next day would be more fruitful.

Sometimes there were "flashers" in the market. Usually, they were men. Usually, they wore a long, thick overcoat. And, usually they sold watches. Then, as they walked slowly by, they would open their coats and gently call out, "Uri, Uri."

Of course, approximately two-thirds present were Berliners while one-third were Soviet soldiers. The Berliners were the sellers in the market, and the Soviet soldiers were the buyers or market makers. The Soviet soldiers had the foodstuffs, and the Berliners would trade for foodstuffs. Money had no value at all at that time. It was all barter. Now, the Soviet soldiers had an insatiable appetite for vodka.

The secondary item the Soviets were interested in were nylons. By now, many of the Soviet soldiers had "German sweethearts," and nylons were in high demand. Cigarettes were not a "hot" item in the market. Cigarettes were the "valuta" of the population. Apparently, each soldier had a large enough ration of cigarettes, so cigarettes were rarely in demand by the Soviets. Besides, the Soviet cigarettes smelled awful. Of course, the Soviets insisted that it was the natural smell of the finest Turkish tobacco. Their cigarettes, or "papirossy" were mostly a long, hollow paper filter. Only one-third of the cigarette was tobacco. Consequently, the Soviet cigarette was never popular. Maybe the population felt "cheated" with all that paper and only a little tobacco.

The population, however, was "craving" for cigarettes. Berliners would trade food, jewels, and watches for one cigarette. The world had gone mad again. But the world had slipped into a different kind of madness.

For vodka, appetizers were needed: specialty items like sausage, cooked bacon, smoked meat, smoked fish, herring, marinated mushrooms, and so on. These items as a class were the "Zakuska" for the vodka. Zakuska is what you eat while you drink vodka. Drinking vodka without eating was not only "bad" form, but the quickest way to get stone drunk. Herring and marinated mushrooms were valued the most. One salted herring (Schmalz-herring) was worth often two or three bottles of vodka. And marinated mushrooms were worth even more.

Depending on the circumstance, a bottle of vodka was sometimes "worth" a loaf of dark bread and a pound of butter and a twenty-pound sack of potatoes. The standard bottle of vodka was roughly seven hundred and fifty grams (a little less than a quart), the size of a wine bottle. But the bottle had to be clear, labeled, corked, and sealed. A well-labeled bottle with a red banner could fetch twice the valuta.

At the "low" end of the totem pole of specialty items were canned goods. Very likely, the canned foods reminded the Soviet soldiers of their cold and tasteless combat rations, when and if they had any. Among the Soviet soldiers, the canned food was of little value. But Berliners loved canned foods. Soviet soldiers preferred "pickled" foods in jars: cucumbers, tomatoes and beets, just to name a few. Fruits were called, "Damskaja jida" or ladies food.

Since George was afraid to be a "trader," and Grandma was too old, and "we" kids were too young, the burden of trading fell on my mother's shoulders. Of course, vodka was not the only commodity we traded. Vodka was our "last resort" commodity. Most often it was my mother, Kathy and I that went to the market. Occasionally, George would come with us. Our remaining family members were just not cut out to be traders, lookouts, or dependable companions in the market.

Our most effective trading team was my mother, Kathy and I. My mother never lost her cool, nor her nerve. She somehow knew how to extricate herself, Kathy and me from every situation. Sometimes, it was not obvious to me, at the time, but somehow she would find the only right course of action. Kathy was great. She was a plump little thing that sensed the situation and our mission. She would cry at the right time, and she would "blow bubbles" at the right time. Basically, she was a very content baby. She was never a liability. And, her carriage was worth its weight in gold. The carriage was dilapidated and old, so the carriage was a perfect "cover."

Of course, about one quarter of all traders were also using carriages, so we were not very conspicuous. This only proves my point. The market was essential. Everybody knew about it, and nobody stopped it. We were stopped many times. Not once was Kathy removed from her carriage. I am convinced that every carriage on the market had the same false bottom as ours. Yet, nobody would "tear a carriage apart" or try to search one. That is, the rule was to conduct your business in a discrete way. And, we did.

The carriage had one real asset, it was "huge." The wheels were swift, and I always kept them oiled. Despite the fact that we transported sometimes as much as one hundred kilos (220 pounds) of merchandise, the carriage was easy to maneuver and swift as a swallow.

I was a good scout and developed a quick sense for danger. When caught, and this was very seldom, I would stand there and pout.

Eventually, my captors would let me go. A scolding or warning was usually all I was forced to endure.

I used to run ahead of our "trade isle" exploring the market, that is, to look for any danger, and memorize the trades that were being offered. Then, I would get back to my mother and tell her what was ahead. If she had no other directions for me, I would then go out and scout again. This I would do as long the market was active or we were active in the market. George was a sourpuss when he came to the market.

We always started from the Victory Statue and walked slowly to the Brandenburg Gate, then back to the Victory Statue and so on. When George was with us, one pass and he was "petered" out. And this happened regardless of whether or not we had finished our business. I was always disappointed when we left without trying again and again until our business was completed. To me, it was fun and games. But George saw phantoms most of the time. One round trip and the market would unnerve him. In fact, George preferred to wait for us outside, by the market entrance. Then, he would pace up and down the street, some two hundred paces away, waiting for us. I thought that "his" form of support was wasteful and much more dangerous. It was wasteful because, once we came out of the market, the carriage would quickly take our merchandise home. And, it was dangerous because he was the sole individual pacing up and down the street, attracting unnecessary attention. I must say, however, one time George was a godsend.

Sometimes the market was "shortened" not with respect to time but with respect to space. Then, it would start at some distance away from the Victory Statue and end about the same distance away from the Brandenburg Gate. Somehow, the market knew what space was required for its traders to conduct their business in the most efficient way.

The market had two primary entrances, one near the Victory Statue in the Tiergarten and another at the Brandenburg Gate. We used primarily the Tiergarten entrance as it was the closest entrance for us.

I did not like trading in vodka, and for the longest time we did not. But one day we were destitute. Our food had run out. The night before my mother had scraped up all the remaining fragments of flour and made a soup out of it. I remember how my stomach was growling all night long.

My mother had three bottles of vodka, and our most efficient trading team was set into action: my mother, Kathy and me. George stayed away from the market that day. He was pacing up and down the street waiting for us at the entrance.

We went into market action. My instructions were to find a "pair" of soldiers and "pre-announce" the merchandise, so I dashed ahead of my mother, looking for a "receptive" pair of soldiers. Soon, I found two who looked friendly and were obviously "shopping." I "jogged" towards them and called out, "Vodka?" and jogged past them. They turned in a flash towards me.

I jogged about ten paces past them, turned around and jogged back. They stood there grinning and waved for me to come closer. One of them asked: "Gut Vodka?" (is it any good) and I said, "Prima" (the best) as I jogged by them again. This time, I passed them only by a few paces and stopped. They looked at each other and said to me, "Chorosho." This meant that a potential deal was in the making. I put my hand to my head and "saluted" acceptance.

Then, I turned around and ran as fast as I could toward my mother, all the way watching her intensely. My mother was only thirty or so paces away and had watched the "prologue" of the trade. She nodded to me, and I knew that she approved of the buyers. First, I ran past her, turned around and came back to her. This matched up buyer and seller. Together we approached the two soldiers.

One of the soldiers looked at my mother and repeated again, "Gut Vodka?" And, my mother said, "Prima." The soldier said to her, "Komm." And, this meant, "Let's go and do the trade."

The soldiers turned toward the Brandenburg Gate and started to walk in that direction. About ten paces behind them was my mother, Kathy and I. The soldiers knew we were following them. We kept pace with them every step of the way. They passed the Brandenburg Gate and the market entrance. Then, they proceeded to a "makeshift" trailer, or small barracks, which was set up on a grassy patch. One of the soldiers opened the door and said, "Komm."

My mother picked up Kathy, and I pulled out one bottle of vodka. My mother put Kathy back into the carriage. She took the bottle and went inside. After a little while, she came out with a large slice of dark bread and a hefty piece of cooked bacon for me and a small end piece of bread for Kathy. I started "tearing" into the food. That piece of cooked bacon was out of this world! And the bread was divine. I just kept munching away. Kathy held that end piece and licked it. I could see how

Kathy enjoyed her meal, also. She had no teeth, but she loved to put things in her mouth -- especially a hard piece of bread or a cracker.

My mother went back inside again and came out with a knapsack in one hand and all kinds of goodies in the other: butter, two loaves of bread, cans, and much more. I don't know how she managed to get everything to the carriage, but she did. I gulped my last few morsels of food. I picked up Kathy and put her on the ground. Then, I opened the lid so she could put the merchandise inside.

First, she told me to take out the other two bottles, and I did. Then, she put the knapsack into the carriage and turned it over. I could see potatoes tumbling to the bottom. Then, she dumped the other items on top of the potatoes. She closed the compartment, straightened out the carriage, and put Kathy back into it. Then, she took the two bottles and went back inside.

After a while, she came back out again. This time, I could see she was tipsy. She came "swaying" out of the door, both arms loaded with more goodies: two loaves of bread, a small sack of flour, another small sack with dried milk, butter, and more goodies. Quickly, I picked up Kathy and put her on the ground. Then, I opened the lid for the merchandise. My mother swayed to the carriage and dumped her goodies into the carriage. The compartment was full to the top. I had to push and shove all this wonderful food around so we could close the compartment. Finally I was able to close the lid. My mother was standing there and "swaying." She felt no pain at all. She kept giggling and swaying and giggling and swaying. I put Kathy into the carriage, and she tried to straighten out the blankets. Finally, we were all done.

Getting back home was not a simple matter. The shortest road home was actually through the market; but since we were loaded with foodstuffs, this was very risky. Too many hungry wolves were lurking in the market, and the state my mother was in was very dangerous. She was attracting too much attention with her giggling and swaying. So, I decided to take a small detour around the market. I knew the way alright, but my mother could not walk a straight line. She would lean on me, then on the carriage, and sometimes she would sway toward a ruin nearby or towards the curb. I had a heck of a time trying to keep her on the sidewalk, keep the carriage in motion, and make sure we were going home. I prayed that George would spot us and come to my rescue. The way home seemed to last forever.

Finally, George spotted us. I could see that he could not believe his eyes. My mother never drinks -- not in company and not by herself. Yet, here was this "threesome" swaying down the street, and that "threesome" looked just like the traders he was waiting for. I could see how he took another look, recognized us from afar, and marched quickly towards us. He arrived not a moment too soon. My mother's condition was "deteriorating" swiftly. She was swaying more and more, and her forward progress was less and less. George came and put his arm around her. She started giggling and bubbling away, trying to describe the good deal she had struck.

The deal she had stuck was fabulous. We ended up keeping nearly half of the food after the "brewmaster" was paid. But, I still thought that this vodka trade was bad "business." It was bad because my mother was incapacitated after a trade and her self-preservation defenses were at their lowest. The risk was not worth the reward.

The Slavic nations have survived not only because they defeated the intruder or conqueror time after time, but they also have had to survive the internal terror of tyrants. In fact, it is easier to cope with external terror then an internal terror. The external terror is known and can be dealt with, but internal terror is of a different form. It requires different defenses.

Suppose for a moment you meet a friend and wish to tell your friend that he or she is in grave danger, but you can not tell him or her outright because a spy is watching. Your message would only make the situation worse and could also place you in grave danger. Yet somehow, in the most "innocent" way, you must convey your message, emphasizing its urgency. This "secondary" form of communication was highly developed by the Slavs out of necessity.

This form of communication is both "written" and "verbal" in form. They were developed during the Czarist regime and are still in use today. Writers and poets who criticized the government overtly were banished for a long time. This caused the evolution of the written form. The written form was easy. The "animal kingdom" was used to characterize the position, the person, and the action (George Orwell and Franz Kafka introduced this in the West much later). That is, it was often written as a children's story, whereas in fact it was a "political" condemnation, a "manifesto," or a call for rebellion. Taras Schevchenko was such a writer and nationalist in the Ukraine. The verbal form was much more subtle.

The most "innocent" statement out of context signifies the danger and the type of danger. For example, "The guests have arrived," or any such variation, signifies that the "Police have arrived," and so on. Of course, these statements are a warning when they are "out of context." The kinder the reference, the greater the danger. Thus, "Uncle Vasja" meant the greatest danger of all -- Stalin, and so on.

Western culture never developed this covert form of communication to guard against its own government. Thus, it was always difficult to express a warning to a Berliner. We, however, were in "tune" with this communication technique and used it often. The "nice" part of it was that once you were in tune, other signals were interpreted easily. This is why the "unexpected" was used often as the norm for our behavior.

Sometime in July of 1945, the long-awaited American, English and French occupation forces arrived. Now, the military police had four members acting as a unit: An American, an Englishman, a Frenchman, and a Russian soldier. Even though the western allies had arrived, there was no "political" relief for the families in our predicament. This was true because the Soviets had the right to repatriate anyone forcibly to the Soviet Union if they had ever been a Soviet national. (Keelhaul agreement in Yalta accord.)

Before, the patrols had four Soviet soldiers in a jeep with a blown up rubber dangling from the antenna. Now, four allied soldiers were making the rounds in a jeep with a blown up rubber dangling from the antenna. In other words, the streets were still unsafe. Only in a dire emergency was it prudent to go out on the street.

As soon as the western allies arrived, the Soviets built a monument to the "Unknown Soviet Soldier" in the Tiergarten right between the Brandenburg Gate and the Victory Statue. The monument was of marble, about fifty paces long and forty paces wide. In the background, towards one side of the Tiergarten, was a row of open columns. In front of the columns was a huge statue of a Soviet soldier with a rifle. On both ends was a tank. The front of the monument faced the boulevard which connected the Brandenburg Gate and the Victory Statue. That is, the monument was in the very center of the black market.

As soon as the monument was finished, the provisional government in Berlin doled out the parcels of land to all families who wanted them, in accordance with their earlier agrarian reform for Berliners to "become farmers." It appeared as though the Soviets wanted the "prime" lots first, to erect their symbols of victory.

When our turn came, we wanted ours; and we got a plot right behind the newly built Soviet monument. My mother organized our family to go there and prepare the plot. Each day, we would go and dig and rake until the plot was ready to be planted.

Planting the plot was a bit of a problem. We were encouraged to plant vegetables. My mother, however, was determined to plant potatoes on that lot. But, there were no potatoes to be planted because everything edible had been eaten and nothing was left to plant. Beans, peas and potatoes were just not available. At least not for us. So, my mother went to the "agrarian" center, which was set up to assist the Berliners in their farming effort, and asked for "rotten potatoes." Now rotten potatoes were plentiful! The next day, a truck full of rotten potatoes was delivered to our lot in the Tiergarten. We were all there when the "mush" was "dumped" on our plot. My mother tipped the driver -- two cigarettes. The driver was very pleased. As soon as he left, we went to work.

Of course, before we went to work my mother explained to us what we had to do. Her explanation went as follows: We were to look for fresh growth or tiny potato growths that were just budding. They had to be white. Not brown, not black, but white. "They look white," she kept on saying, "… and can be easily found in that heap of mush." Four or five mushy potatoes with buds on them were then planted in the prepared ground. We planted them about four to five inches deep. We all took turns. Two would dig the hole in the ground, and the others would slush in the potato paste in search of the elusive potato buds. But, as strange as it sounds, by the end of the day our plot was seeded and we even used the slush as fertilizer.

Of course, the last item was water. The "Berliner agrarian committee" was prepared for that also. A water truck was parked nearby on the boulevard. We took our buckets, fetched some water and watered our crop. Utterly exhausted, we made our way home.

Western occupation brought a "novelty." Orthodox churches were opened, and the "Slavic" community was invited to attend. This was advertised by radio and newspaper. I remember how one Saturday evening we went to the first Mass I ever attended. Maybe it was not the first Mass, but it was the first Mass I remember. Now there is a practical reason why there is a Saturday evening Mass. Every Mass provides the opportunity for "confession." "Absolution" is normally given the next day on Sunday morning. Technically, one is supposed to fast, from confession to absolution. To most, fasting from Saturday night to Sunday morning was not a big deal.

By then, the "subway" was operating, and we took the subway to a "Sabor," a cathedral. I was very impressed but very tired. Orthodox churches have no seats and the full service is very long -- two hours. I remember how my mother was crying throughout the service. At the end, the priest announced that the Russian library was also open, and everyone was welcome to go there to sign up and to take books out. George was very excited. He went there the next day, signed up and took a few books out.

George would go to the library during the week and bring new books home. Then, every Saturday evening we would go to the cathedral and pray. One day, George went to the library and did not come back. He was gone all night, and he was gone the next day. There was no sign of George anywhere. My mother went to our few Russian and Ukrainian friends who were in the same predicament as we -- hiding from the Soviets, but nobody seemed to know. Then, one day we got the message from someone we trusted. We were told that George had been arrested at the library and was deported to the Soviet Union. We were struck with shock and total disbelief. From then on, we avoided both the church and the library in Berlin.

As soon as we got the message, we dropped everything and went to Elvira's parents. We knew that we had to leave right away. There was a good chance that a Soviet truck would pull up and repatriate us all. We also knew that some of our friends would give us a temporary hideout. We just got dressed, took only the essentials and locked up our rooms. We told our super that we would be gone for a little while. We were still stunned and in shock. Grandma and Masha were crying and sobbing all night long.

A few days passed by, and each day my mother went back to our former place and would ask the super if we had had visitors. The super told her that there had been none. In a way, this was reassuring because there was a glimmer of hope that the message could be false. But, by the fourth day, when neither my mother or Emma or Kathy or I were at home, grandma had taken Masha and disappeared. When we came home there was a letter from her and all it said was, "I have taken Masha, and I am going to find my son. I am returning to Russia. God bless you, Emma, Tola and Kathy."

Grandma had taken Masha and voluntarily returned to the Soviet Union to find her son. She knew full well that, if his identity became known, he would be hanged in the public square.

Yet, there was also the chance, no matter how small, that he would be exiled to Siberia. In that case, she was prepared to join him there. At that time, Grandma was seventy-two years old and Masha going on nine.

With Grandma and Masha gone, we had to leave our place of refuge again. Elvira's parents were not afraid of repatriation, they were from the "first" emigration and were never Soviet citizens. They had an international status of "displaced persons," however, we did not. We were subject to forced repatriation as soon as we were found out. For the next ten days or so, we moved from friend to friend like gypsies. We were afraid to return to our home. Then, one day my mother said," We are going home." We returned to our garden, to our "heap of rubble," to our home, and started anew.

By now it was early August, and our gardens were in full bloom. Our "heap of rubble" was a lush green hill full of vegetables, pumpkins, tomatoes, cucumbers, and many other wonderful plants. Our potatoes in the Tiergarten were thriving, and the garden needed a lot of attention; weeding, watering, fertilizing and so on. The food shortage was not acute, but we still did not have enough to eat. Money was still worthless. Money was good only to redeem the ration-card coupons.

One late afternoon, I was sent out to buy some food. The stores were underneath the subway, just as they were before the fall of Berlin. The lines were always very long, and it would take a long time to get served. But, I had developed a way to sneak through the queue. I developed two methods. The first was just to sneak around the adults. Many thought I was such a "cute" and needy boy, they would actually encourage me to do it. The other way, was to start a conversation and then, nonchalantly, move in front of them. Again, most of the time, they would encourage me. Very seldom would I hit a "pedagogue," who would grab me firmly by my hair and pull me back to my place. Usually, I could do the shopping in half the time my mother or Emma could. This was important because the stores would always run out of foodstuff early.

This one particular day, I had just finished the shopping and was returning home. I noticed a very curious thing. There was a truck standing on the other side of our street, directly opposite our building. I was generally not permitted to cross to the other side of the street. This was so because the military patrol was always driving at full speed down our block, and there had been a number of accidents when they hit someone or ran someone over. But, trucks were very rare in those days, and this truck was very unusual. This truck was completely covered, like an armored vehicle. This truck warranted investigation. I crossed the street and approached the truck. There was no driver. In fact, there was nobody near the truck. I walked around it and noticed the back door was slightly ajar. I looked inside and saw no one. Then, I decided to walk around again, and I did. Again, not a sign of anybody, so I decided to walk into the rear door.

I walked in and I could see racks on all sides. The racks were full of money. There were stacks and stacks of money. From floor to ceiling were stacks of money. I have never seen such stacks of money. This demanded a quick explanation, I thought. I took a pile of money and stuffed it into one pocket, then into the next, and the next, and the next. Until my coat and pants were bulging. Then, I got out, left the door slightly ajar and dashed to our apartment and my mother. There, breathlessly, I told her my story. She was not at all impressed. She looked at me and said, "First of all, I want you to take that money back immediately. Second, that money is not worth the paper it is printed on." Then, she pulled out a "wad" of money and said, "Do you see this money? Go try and buy a loaf of bread with it!"

Sadly, I went back to the truck. Very sadly, I put all the money back. Then I went back home. By next morning, the truck was gone. That same weekend, we had the first "currency" reform in Berlin. The "old" money was exchanged at ten to one for the "new" money. But, each family was allowed to exchange only ten thousand Reichsmarks per person. The "wad" of money my mother was showing to me was less than five thousand Reichsmarks.

The currency reform instantly created a new black market. On one hand, there were people who had a lot of "old" money; and on the other hand there were some, like us, who had very little. The new black market consisted of selling one's "conversion" rights. That is, someone with a lot of money found someone who would act as a nominee and convert his or her allotted share. The standard conversion commission varied from five to twenty-five percent, depending on the astuteness of the nominee. I have no idea if my mother "converted" her rights or at what rate. All I know is that initially the new money had very little effect on the primary economy. Most products were still rationed. But, the new money had an instant effect on the "black" market. Exotic items were now offered on the "black" market: furs, coats, shoes and so on. Many trades could now be conducted with the new money. Actually, this first reform took the currency with the picture of Hitler out of circulation, replacing it with a new "Reichsmark," without the picture of Hitler.

Slowly but surely, Berlin was digging herself out of the ashes. Work-crews were operating throughout the city. They would start with a ruin, clean off every brick, and stack them into piles. They separated the different metals and placed them in different piles. Everything was systematically "recycled," wood, steel, copper, brass, nails, keys, bricks, glass bottles and jars. Soon, there were "drop-off" points, which bought these items at a fixed price. Let us say: copper at two Marks per kilo (2.2 pounds), brass at one Mark per kilo, cast iron at 25 Pfennig per kilo and so on. The population was encouraged to bring in these "commodities" for redemption.

Our building, in fact our whole block, was not scheduled for a work-crew for a long time. The rubble behind and around us was a "gold mine" for these materials. There was, however, one problem, how to get that material to the drop-off points? What I needed was a cart. I built myself a frame, found four wheels and built myself a cart. I loaded the cart with one commodity and would wheel it to the redemption center. There, my merchandise was weighed, and I was paid.

Pretty soon, I became our family "banker." I would finance Emma. I also would offer to share with my mother, but she always refused. But, on occasion, if I did lend her money, she would always return it promptly even though I never asked for it and I never wanted it back.

Systematically, I started to strip our adjacent ruins of all their raw materials, converting them into currency. Of course, my "bankroll" hardly ever exceeded one hundred Marks, but to me that was a "fortune." My mother allowed me to do this for two reasons. First, the city asked its citizens to clean up the city; second, I had to promise that jars, bottles and pots would not be sold, but given to her. This posed no hardship at all. After a "day's work," I would bring a jar or two to my mother, and she was always very happy. She would wash them and put them away. In no time at all, we had one spare room practically filled with jars. I could see her plan, I was building up something for her next phase, but she would not tell us what it was.

Then, one day -- out of the blue -- George showed up! George was arrested at the library, interrogated and put into a prison by the Soviets. Then, he was put on a transport to the "homeland." En route, he was able to escape and make his way back to Berlin. We were very happy that he was alive and well. But, we were also very sad to tell him that his mother and Masha had repatriated voluntarily to look for him in the Soviet Union. George took it "stoically," but I know, he never got over it.

The next order of business for my mother was to find a job. With all her documents burned, this was not a small matter. First, we were thinking of writing to Uncle Max and Aunt Elsee. My mother dismissed that idea because she did not know how Uncle Max would react to our new name and identity. But, most importantly, we had to stay inconspicuous; and mail is the "first" thing that gives one away. So, the idea of Uncle Max and Aunt Elsee was "dismissed," or put on ice. Next, came the major from Proskurov and the addresses he had given us. One of the names we still had. He was a medical doctor right by us, at the largest hospital in our area.

The next day, my mother made an appointment to see him and he hired her as a nurse. In fact, little by little, my mother started to get her credentials back. Even though they were far inferior then before, they were sufficient to keep her employed. She always received the highest marks and recommendations on her job. George also needed a job because, otherwise, he would be assigned to a work-crew. So, George found himself a job as a secretary-typist. His employer was Schneider, a free-lance writer. Later, George worked as a journalist and, much later, as editor-in-chief again.

Meanwhile, the relations between the Soviets and their allies began to deteriorate. Germany and Austria were divided into four zones; and the two capitals, Berlin and Vienna, were also divided into four sectors. We ended up in the British sector of Berlin as did our plot in the Tiergarten. In fact, the black market ended up in the British sector, also. Our building, our garden, and the black market were all in the British sector.

By the end of August, many could see the new storm forming over Berlin. Some refused to prepare for it, and most of those who did not perished. But those that saw the new signs and prepared for it survived. A new battle for Berlin began to shape up. This new battle was eventually called "The Blockade of Berlin."

АВТОРСКОЕ СВИДЕТЕЛЬСТВО

НА ИЗОБРЕТЕНИЕ

№ 39091

Настоящее авторское свидетельство выдано на основании Положения об изобретениях и технических усовершенствованиях от 9 апреля 1931 г. (С. З. СССР 1931 г. № 21, ст. 181) _____

на _____

всем согласно с приложенным описанием и указанными в заключительной его части отличительными признаками изобретения, по заявке

от 20 - января 1931 г. № 4092.

Действительн___ изобретател___

Реализация изобретения, указанного в настоящем авторском свидетельстве, производится согласно ст. ст. 20—29 и 33—36 Положения об изобретениях и технических усовершенствованиях (С. З. СССР 1931 г. № 21, ст. 181).

Действие авторского свидетельства распространяется

1 of 107 patents of Ivan

Ivan founds the Ukranian Chemical Society

Ivan's work papers

Emelia and her mother vacationing in Crimea

Ivan and Emelia

Tony in Grunewald

George at his desk

Emma

Cathy

CHAPTER 7

The Mushrooms

Very slowly my mother's jar mystery began to unravel. By now, there were stores that sold used books and used clothing. One day, my mother and I went shopping. We went to the largest bookstore we could find. My mother went straight to the reference section and started looking for a specific book. She looked over everything in that section, but could not find it. She called me over and said, "Go to the owner and ask for the encyclopedia on mushrooms."

I thought this was a very strange request. But, I went to the owner anyhow and asked. The owner was very kind and explained that he had one encyclopedia which was complete, but very dilapidated. He also explained that he kept it separately in the back. He was embarrassed to mix it with his other fine books. I went back to my mother and told her what the owner had said. My mother was very excited. She exclaimed, "Wonderful. That's just what I need."

We went back to the owner and asked to see the book. He went to the back of the store and came back with a book about five inches wide, eight inches tall, and two inches thick. The cover was missing, and some pages were loose. The owner placed the book in front of my mother on the counter top. She opened the book, and I could see beautiful colored pictures of mushrooms. On one page was a picture, and on the other page was a complete description. Above the picture was the name of the mushroom in bold letters. Then came the colored picture. Below the picture were the dominant characteristics: Whether or not the mushroom

119

was edible, the season it was most abundant, and much other useful information.

My mother opened the book and quickly turned the pages. It looked as though she was counting them. My first reaction was that she was going to make an offer based on the number of pages in the book. Actually, she was scanning the pages for familiar mushrooms and "completeness." Patiently, I waited. When she finished, she turned to the owner and said: "How much?" The owner said, "Two Marks." My mother reached into her pocket book and paid the owner. The book was ours! Normally, my mother loves to bargain. She would start with a ridiculous price and gradually move up in her offer. This time it was different, no haggling and no counteroffer. The price the dealer asked for was so ridiculously low that bargaining made no sense. I must say I was still surprised.

I could see that my mother was genuinely excited. We walked out of the store, and she looked around. She was looking for a place to celebrate our victory. I could see it. It was all written on her face. But, there was no such place at that time. So, we walked home.

George thought my mother's plan was insane. Obviously, my mother wanted to go into the "mushroom business." George insisted that with the first batch of mushroom we would not only poison ourselves, but also all our customers. My mother was un-deterred. She sat all day studying the characteristics and the descriptions.

Now my mother was not a novice to mushrooms. In the Ukraine, she and my grandmother, on my father's side, picked and ate mushrooms. They used only a few varieties. But, my mother argued that the mushrooms in the Ukraine were different because the terrain was different. Here, we had to adapt to the new environment. Besides, she insisted that she had a very detailed course in mushrooms in her biology curriculum, and only certain details had been forgotten.

The plan was laid. Now it required execution. That was to be. The next Sunday, George, my mother, and I would go to "Grunewald," while Emma would stay with Kathy. This was fine with everybody.

Grunewald is a large forest at the southwest tip of Berlin. Berlin is surrounded by forests, but Grunewald is the largest and the best.

Saturday, my mother prepared food for everybody. Sunday, at daybreak, George, my mother, and I left for our first mushroom expedition. We went to the subway and took the train to Grunewald.

We arrived at Grunewald; and by the time that we got out of the train, there was a mob. My first reaction was that. With all these people how could there possibly be a blade of grass left, never mind mushrooms. We got out and the mob practically pushed us in the direction of the forest. We walked with the crowd for a while. As we walked deeper and deeper into the forest, the crowd started to thin out. Now it was almost bearable, but still very crowded. My mother pressed on. We walked for about an hour. Now there were only a few stragglers left. My mother stopped and started to look at the trees. She was looking for a particular type of tree. I was completely mystified. George started to look at the trees also, and George started to get a "kick" out of the excursion. He would look at the odd shapes of the trees and make comments. Then my mother spotted a cluster of trees and called out, "There!"

But, "there" was off the path we were on. We had to actually go through some underbrush to get "there." To George, this was just not civilized. Why would anybody ever want to get off the path and maybe get lost in this vast forest? George literally refused to go "there," and he refused for my mother to go "there" also. Undauntedly, my mother called me over, pulled out her mushroom encyclopedia, flipped to a page, and pointed at a picture. Then she said, "Do you see this mushroom?" I nodded. Then, she continued, "Go see, if you can find these mushrooms there."

This was great. I dashed to the cluster of trees. Through the underbrush, through a patch of ferns, and arrived at the trees. Then, I slowed down and started to look. At first, I did not see any. But then I spotted one, then another, and then many more. I picked them and soon had a whole arm full.

Meanwhile, I could hear my mother shout: "Are there any?" And, I shouted back, "A lot. A whole lot!"

As I kept on picking mushrooms, my mother was by my side. She "whipped" out a tight "netted" bag, and I dumped the mushrooms into it. Then, for the next hour or so we kept on looking and picking mushrooms. Soon, the net was full and bulging with mushrooms. George had not joined us. When we got back to the path, there was George puffing away on his pipe, pacing up and down. George was in a different world.

My mother showed the bag to him, "Here, did you ever see such nice mushrooms?" George came closer. He inspected the mushrooms and mumbled, "Hm… they are nice." My mother "shoved" the net full of mushrooms to George. He took the net, took mother by the arm and we proceeded further down the path. A little while later, we stopped again. Again, my mother scanned the trees, and again she would spot the trees she was looking for. And, the scenario would repeat itself. By midday, we had four bulging nets full of mushrooms. Then we found a nice clearing and had a picnic. Afterwards, we spent the whole afternoon continuing our search. By about five o'clock, we had ten nets bulging with mushrooms. George carried four, my mother carried four, and I carried two. Our mission was completed, simply because my mother had run out of nets. Very proud and content, we made our way back to the subway.

As we approached the subway, more and more people were returning. They were looking at us with disbelief. They could not believe that we had gathered so many edible mushrooms in the forest. People came up to us wanting to buy some. But we would not sell any. When we got home, Emma was overjoyed. All she would utter was "Menscheskind…dass ist ja 'ne Wucht," a typical Berliner expression for ultimate success.

Our job was not over. A huge pail was brought out, and the mushrooms were dumped into it. We then cleaned, sorted and washed them. Then, some were cut up and strung on a thin line to dry. Then some were set aside, and some we used ourselves. That night, we had the most delicious mushroom soup I had ever eaten. It was much more delicious than the mushroom soup we had had at Uncle Max's house.

Still, with all this success, there was one ingredient missing. There was no way to "marinate" the mushrooms. While vinegar was plentiful, and a few kernels of pepper and other spices could be bought, one ingredient was not available at all: laurel or bay leaves.

It so happened that the next day, the newly built Soviet monument was to be inaugurated. The inauguration of the monument of the "Unknown Soviet Soldier" was pre-announced with great pomp and fanfare. To my surprise, my mother asked me to go with her to the parade. Since this was such a "great" event, it was made into a holiday. I was all excited, but she kept saying not to say a word to anyone. And, I did not.

Since our potato garden was right behind the monument, my mother just told everybody that she and I would go to our potato garden and weed. She assembled all the tools, and by late morning we were off. We came to our potato garden and weeded for a while. As we were weeding, a crowd started to assemble on the boulevard. The crowd got larger and larger. At some point, my mother stopped. We cleaned up and went to the boulevard right next to the monument. The parade was already in progress.

I watched as the Soviet soldiers marched by, as tanks rolled by, and as large trucks rolled by. While I was watching the display, my mother kept her eyes peeled on something else. She was constantly looking for something. Then, her hour came. A truck rolled up close to the monument. It was loaded with wreaths. A line of soldiers unloaded the wreaths and passed them on, in a "human-chain" fashion, to a specific point. Then, one wreath was handed to a soldier who would carry it to the monument. The soldier would make a salute, and a speech, and then place it on a stand. Stands were specially prepared for that purpose. Some stands were near the columns, others near the statue, and still others at the far corners, near and beyond the tanks. My mother took me by the hand and slowly we approached one end of the monument near the tank. We came to a "barrier," and civilians were not allowed past that point. Now, my mother was looking intensely at the wreaths. I could see it. She was satisfied, and we went home.

On the way home, I asked her what she was looking for and she explained, "Those wreaths came from Italy. They're real laurel wreaths!" I only looked at her and said, "So, even if they came from Italy. What good are they?" She looked at me and continued, "We need those laurel leaves to marinate our mushrooms." Aha, I thought, this is why she took me to the parade. I looked at her in disbelief, "But, the monument is guarded. How do we get to them?" She looked at me very calmly and continued, "Tonight, when everybody is asleep, I will go to the monument and sneak up to the corner stand. Then, when the patrol is walking back, I will pick a few leaves. I will pick them gently from the wreaths without a sound. And, I will pick as many as I need." "Can I come?" I blurted right away. She looked at me, "No, this is too dangerous. You stay at home and watch the others."

This was too exciting. There was no way I was going to let her do this job alone. I kept begging, rationalizing, and insisting that I had to be part of this mission. Finally, she agreed, and we made plans for the night. The key to the plan was to sneak up very quietly to the furthest edge of the monument, and then, very gently and quietly, to pick off one leaf at a time, but only when the guard was walking away. The key to picking the leaf was not to pull on the wreath, but, to twist gently or roll one leaf at a time until it fell off. All she kept telling me was, "Whatever you do, do not pull."

That night we sneaked out very quietly. We were dressed all in black. We even covered our faces with ashes from the stove. We went to our potato patch. From there, we inched our way to the corner of the monument. My mother went to one side, and I went to the other. I was on the Brandenburg Gate side; she was at the Victory Statue side of the monument. I inched right up to a wreath. I could see the guard marching from one tank to the other, and then back again. I waited until the guard turned. I felt for one leaf. I turned the leaf, and it came off right away. I kept on picking until my netted bag was full. Then, I inched my way back to our potato patch. My mother was already there. I showed her my bag, and quietly we went home. We washed up and went to bed.

Next morning when I got up, my mother was drying the leaves. Some were literally "roasting" on our stove. Others were baking in our oven. Others she had strung up on a line to dry. Still others she placed on a large metal sheet which she used normally for cookies. Every available room was cluttered with the leaves. By evening, we had all the leaves we would ever need.

That evening, my mother started to marinate the mushrooms. A huge pot was used to boil the water, and the cleaned jars were lined up. As soon as the water boiled, the mushrooms were dumped into the pot. Then, vinegar, spices and the laurel leaves were added. This concoction was then cooked for a short while. Then, the huge pot was taken off the stove and cooled. With a large ladle the jars were then filled. Into each jar one Laurel leaf was placed; a few pepper corns were added, and the jar was sealed. The sealed jars were then placed in a special area in the kitchen to cool.

Next day we were in the "mushroom business." My mother gave one jar of mushrooms to the super as a gift. She took her encyclopedia with her and showed the super the picture of the mushroom and the description. The following day, we had a horde of customers. Her neighbors and their friends were knocking on our door to buy or to barter for our mushrooms. My mother knew what the going rate was, and she got the top price.

From that day on, Sunday was reserved for mushroom hunting. It was mostly my mother and I, however, who would go on the hunt. Only in "peak" season would we take others with us. George and Emma were just not cut out to hunt for mushrooms.

Every season produces different mushrooms. Actually, during the summer, the worst varieties are abundant. By worst, I mean they were the worst tasting. The worst does not imply they were not edible. In fact, most mushrooms are edible if certain parts are removed while they are still fresh and crisp. However, we concentrated on only the major edible varieties.

The "king" of mushrooms is the "Steinpilz." It grows abundantly only in the fall and usually among oak trees. Of course, because of the many leaves, the mushrooms are usually not visible at all, as they grow beneath the leaves. There, it grows "in colonies." A colony could be as many as twenty mushrooms, the largest of which could weigh as much as two kilos (about 4.5 pounds)! So, one good size colony could easily yield twenty pounds of mushrooms or more. The "Steinpilz" has the texture of meat, a robust aroma and, therefore, is valued the most. During the season of the Steinpilz, we would on occasion bring home one hundred pounds of mushrooms, or the "equivalent" of one hundred pounds of meat! Once they were marinated, they could yield slightly more in merchandise! The season was not long. As soon as the frost sets in, the mushroom dies and wilts away. Consequently, it was critical for us to harvest as many Steinpilzes as we could during their short growing season. We had to work fast and efficiently. My mother would spot the oak trees. I would then "dash" over, kicking up and scattering the oak leaves in all directions until I had a "hit." Or I "decapitated" one mushroom. Then, we would gently clear that area searching for the colony. The rest was easy.

The first frost would bring out new varieties in abundance. We called them "Opoenky." They are edible, but look mangy, almost poisonous. They always grow right at the root of a tree or tree stump. Again, they grow in colonies, in the open. But, because of their poisonous and mangy look nobody picks them. Yet they were considered the "greatest" delicacy when marinated. They then take on a slightly different appearance. So, while everybody drooled for them, hardly anyone knew what they looked like in "real life." The Soviet soldier would pay "anything" to get a jar of these mushrooms.

This particular mushroom is about two inches tall, with a "sagging" brown cap and a thin, almost fragile stem. The cap is brown or light brown. On the cap there are white dots. Below the cap, the mushroom is "ribbed." The white dots on the cap make the mushroom appear poisonous -- sort of, "Aren't all dotted mushrooms poisonous?" The cap looks mangy and the stem looks mangy, while the mushroom looks poisonous. But, neither the stem nor the cap are poisonous. Once the mushroom is marinated, it takes on a deep dark-brown color and becomes "plump and juicy," and the mushroom becomes a little bit "slimy" or "slippery." So, the end product does not resemble in any way the original mushroom. Again, the season is very short -- from about the middle of October to the end of November or mid-December. Again, one hundred pounds of mushrooms would yield about one hundred pounds of marinated merchandise. So, during this short season, we worked feverishly to harvest the abundant crop. These were the last mushrooms until the following spring. Once they were harvested, we concentrated on other things.

One early October day Emma, and I had to meet our mother at Grunewald. It was the season for Steinpilze. My mother had some errands to do and left earlier by herself. George stayed with Kathy, so Emma and I ran to our subway station: Belevieu. As we ran up the stairs, Emma got ahead of me. When she reached the platform, "our" train was just pulling out. Someone kept the door open for her to jump on, which she did. When I reached the top of the platform, the train was already in motion. Emma looked back. and I waved to her to go on with the train she was on, but Emma jumped off the train at the end of the platform. She fell down and tumbled on the floor. I ran up to her and asked her if she was alright. Emma assured me that she was. She was vehement with me not to say anything to mother.

We caught our next train, arrived at Grunewald and met my mother. We then went into the forest and did our routine. By the end of the day, my mother, Emma and I were carrying all the Steinpilze we could manage back to the station. We arrived home and proceeded to marinate our "crop."

Next morning, Emma complained of a "backache." By the end of the day, she only could move with great pain. My mother took her to the doctor that evening. The doctor scheduled another appointment for the next day. The next day, Emma and my mother went to the appointment. Only late in the evening did my mother come back, all by herself. Emma was very sick. She had broken her spine in three places and was hospitalized in the "Oskar-Helene Heim," a hospital specializing in spinal injuries. Emma was diagnosed with a full-fledged case of "spondylitis," a form of TB. For the next seven years, Emma went from one hospital to another until she was completely cured. While she was in the hospital, she completed her Abitur, learned a multitude of languages -- ranging from Sanskrit to English, and became an ardent Ukrainian writer.

Later, when she was cured, she attended the University in Munich and got her degree. But, from then on, the focus of our survival activity centered more on Emma than anybody else. She needed butter, milk, meat and many other foods that were not readily available at that time. Had it not been for our "mushroom business," we could not have provided for her as we did.

To this day, Emma insists the subway fall had nothing to do with her sickness. I contend, the fall was a direct cause of her sickness. True, TB is a disease all by itself. Its root cause is malnutrition. But, at that time, half of the population of Berlin would have qualified for hospitalization, and in half of them TB would have been found. So, I believe that the direct and primary cause which triggered her illness was her fall from the subway.

We normally think that grand events determine the future of our lives. This is not so. Sometimes background events are longer lasting and more significant. In war, we think that battles decide the future of humanity. Again, it is not so. At least, it is not entirely so.

I remember seeing a cartoon. The cartoon was allegedly dropped by German planes over the Western Allied armies, that is, in France, Italy, Belgium and so on. Germany's purpose was to alert the Allies to the dangers of Stalin and was Hitler's last ditch overture to the West to make war on Stalin. I do not know if the cartoon was actually dropped or not, or if it was just another phantom of Hitler's. The cartoon was created at the very end of the war. The cartoon was a series of caricatures depicting the two prior conferences at Teheran and Yalta. George had brought a few copies home from the office.

The purpose of the cartoon was to illustrate to the West how Stalin was "shortchanging" his partners, Churchill and Roosevelt.

The cartoon begins with Churchill, Roosevelt and Stalin sitting together, and Churchill is addressing Stalin: "Tell us Uncle Vasja -- which parts of the world would you like?"

The next frame showed Stalin standing in front of the map of the world. He had just marked "his" territory with a broad red crayon. He had outlined the contours of his domain. Stalin started at Murmansk (near the northern end of the Soviet-Finnish border) and drew a bold circle around Norway. From there, through the English Channel and straight to Spain. From there, straight through the Straights of Gibraltar and to Cyprus. From there, through the Suez Canal, through the Red Sea and straight through the Straits of Aden. From there, a few bold circles around Saudi Arabia, India and the Cambodian peninsula. Then, up the China coast embracing Japan and ending at the Soviet tip of the Sakhalin Island.

The next frame is Stalin turning to Churchill and saying, "Comrade Churchill, this is what I want!"

The next frame is Churchill and Roosevelt looking at each other in amazement, with their hair on ends

The next frame is Churchill saying to Stalin, "Uncle Vasja, this leaves nothing for us."

The last frame is Stalin responding, "You comrade Roosevelt, take the American continent. You comrade Churchill, take the African continent… and all the islands that are left."

This cartoon was made before the end of World War II. How close was it to the truth? The fact was that Stalin's pattern of conquest was already apparent, but everyone refused to acknowledge it.

When Hitler made a pact to partition Poland, England declared war on Germany -- but not on the Soviet Union.

When Hitler raided England, Stalin stood by and "laughed" at both Hitler and Churchill. Then, England was alone and isolated. Only Roosevelt saw the urgency and provided supplies.

When Hitler invaded the Soviet Union, Churchill breathed a sigh of relief. But, after the first few months he found the German success "frightening." Surely, Stalin could not last another year sustaining those losses! So, Churchill scurried to Canada, and a conference was held with Roosevelt. Again, it was Roosevelt who recognized the full danger and sent supplies to the Soviet Union. When compared with the total supplies used during the entire war, the American supplies were only a tiny fraction of the whole. That first year of supplies, however, was critical to hold Moscow and to launch the later Moscow counteroffensive. That year, Stalin "held" no trump cards, so he was not going to flex his muscles. He stayed away from all conferences with the West.

The following year, 1942, the picture looked a little better. Leningrad was holding. Moscow was holding, and Stalingrad was holding on by its "fingernails." At least Stalin had a front. There were no overwhelming victories, but there was a real front. The victory at Moscow had to be downplayed because Vlasov, the highest decorated general, was now a traitor. A very embarrassing situation for Stalin had developed. He needed a new victory, one not marred by controversy. Yet, Stalin was invited for a conference. He declined. Why? It was simple. Stalin knew he was not the dominant player, yet!

The next year, 1943, was different. Churchill, Roosevelt, and Chiang Kai-Shek met first in Cairo and decided on a "Pacific" strategy. But, after the conference in Cairo, Stalin called for a conference in Teheran (Nov 28 to Dec 1). Stalin knew he held the real "trump" cards. In Stalingrad, the Germans lost a quarter of their armies! In Kursk, the Germans lost half of their armor and half of their armies. Stalin could now prove that he could win the war all by himself. Now, Stalin had to be courted!

Both Churchill and Roosevelt knew that Stalin held real trump cards. How could they be defused? Simple. Find an allied victory which would take the sting out of every trump card Stalin held. So, to counter Stalingrad -- El Alamein was used. For Kursk -- well, there is no historical parallel. No battle in the history of humanity ever had a front of nearly one thousand miles long! Therefore, defuse that one massive victory, into a series of smaller skirmishes! The fact that Stalingrad dwarfs El Alamein by a factor of approximately forty to one is irrelevant. The fact that El Alamein involved only one German division was also made to be unimportant. So, our history books record that El Alamein was the first Allied victory over the Axis powers! A mosquito was crushed, yet we are led to believe it was an elephant herd.

What happened to our victory against the Vichy-French when we landed in North Africa? Quiet please -- please don't mention it -- don't you know that they will be our allies sometime in the near future!

Of course, Churchill and Roosevelt are willing to concede almost anything Stalin wanted in order to keep him in the war, that is, not to make a separate peace with Hitler. So, Stalin makes demands:

1) Stalin wants the South Sakhalin Island.
2) Stalin wants the Kuril Islands.
3) Stalin wants East Prussia.
4) Stalin wants the Baltic Coast (Estonia, Latvia and Lithuania)

5) Stalin wants the Finnish-Soviet border of 1940.
6) Stalin wants the Polish-Soviet border of 1940.
7) Stalin wants all former citizens of the Soviet Union, no matter where they live or what nationality they have.
8) Stalin refuses to declare war on Japan.
9) Stalin "discusses" the invasion of Western Europe, and some time in 1944 is targeted.
10) Stalin refuses to discuss the "Polish" question.

Point nine is interesting for two views prevail. The official view in our history books is scarred with controversy. Western history suggests Stalin requested an invasion of France by 1944. Why the urgency and why Normandy?

There is another view. A view more consistent with Stalin's character. Suppose Stalin put forward the following scenario:

> If you do not invade France by 1944, then I will liberate France and whip the Vichy government, too. Then, I will liberate Italy and fascist Spain. But, if you do, we will divide Germany at the Elbe. This must have sent chills down Churchill's spine. This would create a new colossus, a new monster, at the doorsteps of England. What was the next intention of Stalin? Was it to "liberate" England next? One gulp and the Empire was gone. There was no time to waste and the "soft underbelly" theory had to be scratched. The urgency was real. It was now imperative to invade France at Normandy. The urgency was to save England from Stalin, not from Hitler. English geopolitics needed to be resurrected really fast! This is why Churchill mistrusted Stalin to the very end.

When Churchill mentioned the Polish government in exile in London, Stalin replied that he too had a Polish government in exile -- he just did not know exactly where it was at this moment. And, Stalin promised to enter the war against Japan as soon as Germany was defeated. Both Churchill and Roosevelt agreed -- to Stalin's terms! Only on one point did Stalin concede: Each of the sixteen Soviet republics needed not be a member of the Security Council of the United Nations. Belarus and the Ukraine would do.

In Stalin's view, the United Nations was controlled by England. Every conceivable country had a government in exile in London: France, Poland, Czechoslovakia, Hungary and many more. This meant that as soon as peace was established, the Soviet Union would be outvoted. Therefore, Stalin needed a veto power in the Security Council, and he got it.

As soon as Churchill agreed to invade Normandy in 1944, Stalin had bought himself a year to "liberate" all those other countries: Albania, Bulgaria, Czechoslovakia, Hungary, Jugoslavia, Poland and Rumania. Clearly, if Stalin liberated them then, who could possibly lay a claim to them? So, 1944 was spent "liberating" these countries and at the same time annihilating all remnants of German armor in the area.

Of course, the prior agreement with Chiang Kai-Shek was scuttled. All promises made in Cairo were revoked. Besides, Stalin preferred the Mao movement anyway. (Stalin supported both against Japan).

By the end of 1944, Stalin was in complete control. To make his point, the next conference was held in Yalta (Feb 11, 1945).(See comrades, no enemies in sight!). Now, all the promises made in Teheran were formalized. Without firing one shot, Stalin annihilated the Vlasov movement!

As far as Germany was concerned, it should be made into an agrarian state and, all its industry removed. Of course, the factories would be relocated to the Soviet Union in lieu of reparations. Then Germany could feed the victors! And, to make sure that at least most of the German questions were handled properly, an imaginary line was drawn along the River Elbe. To the west of the Elbe, was the English and American administration, and to the east of the Elbe, was under Soviet administration. "Let's call them ZONES my comrades." (Austria was divided along similar lines). You rule yours, and I rule mine. Then, Churchill made the suggestion to partition the capitals (Berlin and Vienna) into sectors which would be jointly administered but individually run. Stalin agreed.

As far as Poland was concerned, Stalin now remembered. That the government in exile -- was in Lublin. But, let the Poles decide their fate. Is that not the democratic way? Churchill and Roosevelt agreed. When

Stalin was asked about the western Polish border, Stalin replied, "What border? The Germans were gone and the Poles moved in."

On the question of war criminals, Stalin's answer was simple: "Line them up and shoot them."

Of course, the next meeting was to be held in Potsdam as soon as the war ended. The war ended officially May 7, 1945. The Potsdam Conference was held shortly thereafter, July 17 to August 2, 1945. By that time, Roosevelt had died, and Harry Truman now represented the American interests. Churchill was in the midst of a bitter election campaign at home in England. While Churchill came to Potsdam, Clement Attlee was elected and replaced Churchill at the meetings. So, of the "original" big three, only Stalin remained in power. Stalin insisted on the document of Yalta being followed to the letter. And, it was. When France (De Gaulle) was introduced as a new member of the Allies, Stalin only said, "Who is he? Where did he come from? You divide your part as you like!" So, the Americans and English carved out from their "share" a part for France.

While the Conference was in session, the Soviet armies were feverishly moved to the border of Manchuria. They were prepared to attack as soon as word was received from Stalin.

Meanwhile, for three years, the Japanese had fortified Manchuria. Under German supervision, massive, "impregnable" fortifications were built to defend Japan from the mainland. Over two million Japanese soldiers defended these fortifications.

But, Stalin kept his promise. As soon as the meeting was concluded and Stalin was satisfied, he declared war on Japan. On August 9, 1945, he invaded Manchuria. The Soviets crushed the Japanese defenses on their first assault. Stalin was ready to "liberate" Manchuria and Korea.

The picture was clear to Harry Truman. The war needed to be finished before the Soviets completed their conquest in Asia. At this point Truman made the decision to use the Atom Bomb, not only to end the hostilities, but more importantly to send a "message" to Stalin.

At one point, General Mc Arthur was asked what the expected casualties would be to establish a beachhead in Japan. General Mc Arthur replied, "One million." Now one million casualties to defeat Japan was unthinkable to Harry Truman. Besides, an invasion and subsequent defeat of Japan would play right into the hands of Stalin. Manchuria and Korea would be lost! So, on August 6, the first atomic bomb was dropped on Hiroshima. On August 9, a second atomic bomb was dropped on Nagasaki.

On August 10, Japan surrendered. For the first time Stalin was outflanked by an ally. Harry Truman snatched the victory and the impending annexation of Manchuria and Korea from under Stalin's nose! All Stalin got from his "Manchurian adventure" was to accept the Japanese surrender down to the 37th parallel in Korea.

On September 2 1945, Japan formally signed the surrender agreement aboard the U.S. battleship "Missouri." Finally the war was over. (Soviets were present but not shown in the news clips.)

Stalin was said to be raging with fury. Manchuria and Korea had slipped through his fingers. Stalin had not counted on the power of the atomic bomb. Stalin knew that an invasion of Japan with ground troops was "insanity." In a democracy, it would be certain political suicide. Stalin knew this. The West would not engage in a ground war with Japan. And, Stalin lost his gamble.

The three conferences shaped the future spheres of influence. They shaped the borders of Europe and Asia. These three conferences are still with us. It is most unfortunate that Churchill, the most ardent opponent of Hitler, could not complete the conference at Potsdam. Maybe -- just maybe – if Churchill had attended, the Korean War and maybe even the War in Vietnam could have been avoided.

When the war ended, Stalin openly supported Mao. Chiang Kai Shek, our staunchest ally against Japan, had to be satisfied with Taiwan. France lived under the delusion that it was still the Great Empire that it was before the war. But, that Great Empire was an ardent supporter of Hitler. The Vichy government of France was an ally of Germany! France was the "vacationland" for battle weary German troops from the Eastern front. When Allied troops landed in North Africa, the only enemy they encountered there were the Vichy-French, who fought for Germany! Rommel and his "expeditionary force" of twenty thousand Germans, was on the other side of North Africa, causing havoc to the British army.

Rommel himself was surprised how his tiny contingent was running circles around the British. Rommel even had thoughts, at least for a brief moment, that he could take Cairo. Of course, that was hubris all over again.

Meanwhile, the great French colony of Indochina had fought the Japanese. But, the fighting was divided. The Vichy-French were allies of

Germany. Germany was allied with Japan. So, the Vichy-French were allies of the Japanese. The "natives" fought Japan, nobody else. And the "natives" fought the Vichy-French. Their leader was Ho Chi Minh. Ho was promised independence if he continued his war against Japan. The new country would be called Vietnam. After the war, Ho asked for the fulfillment of that promise. Ho was told he had to deal with the new France – the former administrator of that colony. Ho went to Paris, but could not get an audience. When he got his audience, he was dismissed and told that the new France had no intentions of abandoning its former colonies. Ho returned and waged war against the French. France had no more soldiers to send to Indochina, so they sent mercenaries: The French Foreign Legion. This French Foreign Legion was defeated at Dien Bien Phu. There were no more mercenaries to send. France was tired. The rest is history.

When World War II started, many countries declared neutrality in the war. However, to Hitler, the declaration of neutrality was viewed as a repeat of World War I when neutral nations overtly supported the allied war effort. Therefore, to Hitler, the declaration of neutrality was meaningless when the country posed a potential military threat or advantage. Thus, Hitler made war against many neutral countries and occupied them. While it was wrong of Hitler to seize the neutral countries, strategically they were important to Hitler in the war. In particular, let us look at Belgium, Denmark, Netherlands and Norway.

In the Netherlands and Norway, the monarchs fled to England and established governments in exile in London. These leaders valued their personal fortunes and safety more than the fate of their country. Consequently, once these nations were stripped of their leadership, they became allies of Germany in World War II. On the other hand, King Leopold of Belgium and King Christian of Denmark remained with their nation during these dark hours for humanity. Notice the consequences: First, neither country became an ally of Germany. Secondly, and most importantly, when minorities were persecuted by the Germans, both Kings found ways to save and to protect those minorities in some way.

King Christian was not imprisoned by the Germans and staged many acts of civil disobedience against them with much success. In particular, when Jews were forced to wear the Star of David publicly, the King urged all his subjects to publicly wear the same sign. In fact, King Christian wore the Star of David himself. This act must be applauded by all nations. A tiny country found a way to defy Hitler's edicts.

King Leopold of Belgium did not fare as well with the Germans. When he refused to collaborate, he was imprisoned. But, while imprisoned, his nation refused to collaborate. Consequently, no Belgian legions were given to the Germans in their war effort, and Belgians actively resisted the German occupation during the war.

What happened with the other two nations? As soon as the leadership abandoned them, they became allies of Germany. They provided actual legions who fought with the Germans or with their allies against the Soviets. They persecuted the Jews and other minorities as vigorously as the Germans themselves. The Norwegians fought with the Finns, and the Dutch fought with the Germans. In fact, both nations issued stamps commemorating the exploits of their legions and their support for the German war effort. Soldier mail is plentiful for this period confirming these facts. These were not isolated cases of Fascist individuals seeking glory, but a national commitment to support the new world order.

Of course, the situation in France was slightly different. When France was defeated in 1940, Hitler proposed a treaty with the defeated government of France. The French leader was Marshal Petain, a hero of World War I. Hitler permitted a French government in southern France, with its seat in Vichy. The northern part of France was occupied by the Germans and was used mostly as "vacationland" for battle-worn soldiers of the Eastern front.

According to that agreement, the Vichy government was autonomous. It governed the French colonies and maintained the French Navy for German military use. In addition, a number of French legions were given to Hitler, and countless volunteers went to Germany to support the war effort. (In fact, the French Charlemagne division defended Berlin to the end!) Again, stamps were issued in the colonies and in France, flaunting the French alliance with Germany. Some catalogues nowadays do not list these issues because they are viewed with national shame. However, most standard catalogues do list these stamps, and again, soldier mail is plentiful for that period.

Marshal Petain remained a German ally until he was arrested by the Germans on August 20, 1944. By then, he was of no use to them or their war effort.

When Marshal Petain agreed to collaborate with the Germans, General De Gaulle fled to England. In London, De Gaulle became the "self-appointed" leader of the French government in exile.

Oh, how easy it is to encourage a nation to resist when personal safety and security are assured! This act by De Gaulle was viewed by the French as treason. De Gaulle, in fact, was found guilty of treason by a French court and was sentenced to death in absentia. Of course, once the fortunes of war changed, so did the glory of De Gaulle particularly when he became the de facto "liberator" of Paris. Despite this glory, his rule of France was short.

Neither Churchill, nor Roosevelt trusted De Gaulle, even after France was liberated. He ended up "retiring" shortly after the war's end in 1946. He made a political "come back" during the Algerian uprising in 1958 when the military was in control. De Gaulle wanted to be the "dictator" of France's Empire, yet the people gave him that mandate only in time of total chaos when the military threatened a "take-over." Thus, the people of France did not trust him either.

After the war, Petain was brought to trial in Paris. He was found guilty of collaboration, treason, and crimes against humanity. He was sentenced to death. But, De Gaulle, then still in power in 1946, quickly commuted the sentence. He died in 1951.

This clearly underscored the earlier mistrust for De Gaulle by the Allied leaders for, it became clear that he and Petain, tried to manipulate Hitler and the Allies to save France. Petain made an alliance with Hitler, and De Gaulle made an alliance with Churchill and Roosevelt. Sort of a win-win situation. Should Hitler be victorious, France was saved by Petain, and Petain would save De Gaulle. Should Roosevelt, Churchill and Stalin be victorious, De Gaulle would save France. Germany was defeated. France was saved by De Gaulle, and De Gaulle saved Petain.

How did the rest of Western Europe fare after Germany's defeat? What happened to Hitler's supporters in Western Europe?

In Norway, Quisling was tried, found guilty and executed. Sweden was neutral, thus no action was necessary. In Denmark, King Christian was an ardent antagonist of Hitler's regime; he was left alone. In the Netherlands, the self-exiled monarchy from London was restored, and the Netherlands' involvement was "white-washed." King Leopold of Belgium was an ardent antagonist of Hitler. He suffered personally, yet his citizenry did not let him down. But, Belgium's thunder of resistance was grabbed by France, and the Allies lost track of Belgium's courage, promoting France. In France, De Gaulle saved Petain and all we heard was the brutality of "Barbie" and the courage of the French resistance fighters. The blame was shifted, and the shame was "white-washed." In Austria, the Allies blamed Hitler, not the Hapsburg's. Austria was sufficiently punished in her partition after WW I by England and France. In Italy, King Emmanuel's III monarchy was confirmed by England. The blame was squarely placed on Mussolini, not on the head-of-state. But, in 1946, the citizenry of Italy banished their King and established a Republic! In Greece, England restored a monarchy, in order to prevent Stalin's expansion into the Mediterranean. In 1973, the Greeks deposed their monarch and became a Republic. By then, it was safe -- Jugoslavia and Albania had left Soviet's sphere of influence. Jugoslavia was wooed into the "United Europe," and she became a member in 1969. Turkey was neutral in the war. So, no action was necessary.

Portugal was neutral in the war, hence she could be left alone. But, in Spain, we had an ardent Fascist -- Franco. He was not only Hitler's ally who provided troops and arms, he decimated his citizenry -- see Pablo Picasso and his painting "Guernica" -- but he also committed countless atrocities against humanity. Franco, posed a definite dilemma. Because, if "we" punished him like Quisling, then the opposition would take over. The opposition, however, were Communists. If "we" punished him like Petain, then there was no "groomed" savior for Spain like De Gaulle. Thus, "we" had no alternative for "our" geopolitics. England resigned to accept Franco and allowed him to outlive his rule, simply because he was a better alternative than a lackey of Stalin potentially threatening the British Empire. When Franco died, England restored a monarchy -- Carlos I.

Thus, English geopolitics is alive and well. How can we identify the primary allies of England's geopolitics today? Actually, it is quite simple. All we need to do is to follow the trail of "good" monarchs. Good means monarchs cooperating with the English monarch, and "evil" means competing for the same economic markets. Thus, the "Kaiser" was evil because he competed for the same markets. The "Czar" was evil because he infringed on England's empire in Europe and Asia. The "Sultan" was evil because he denied England's exploitation of the Arab world. Yet, the Emperor of Japan was "good" because he was policing the Pacific rim for England! Since the Emperor abdicated, he was not tried, not banished, but merely lived out his life as a free man. His "indiscretion" was made into an example for the new age monarchs. So, how do we follow the alliance of geopolitics? We just follow the trail of ruling monarchs. England was cast in the role of the new Emperor (still German, Hanoverian), while all other monarchs were her obedient vassals. Thus, the new age monarchs rule by the "grace of England," not by the "grace of God."

CHAPTER 8

The Winter of 1946

By the end of August, we began to harvest our garden, and the harvest was bountiful: tomatoes, cucumbers, tobacco, radishes, beets and dill. All the vegetables were in abundance. My mother would pickle them and dill them, and we still had an abundance of fresh vegetables left. Borscht was again our staple food. We had a "warehouse" of homemade produce. Times seemed to improve. Even our ration cards were upgraded.

Our small world was changing. We now had to interact with the outside world. My mother had a steady job. George had at least a "part-time" job working most of the time from our home. The schools were opening. The life at our fortress was turning outward -- George called our building the fortress. One day I was told to go to a specific place and sign up for school. The place was not too far away, but I had not been in that area for a long time. To get there, I had to cross the Spree River.

So, one morning, I put on my best clothes and went to that "place." I put on my clothes, strapped on my Ranzen, and waved good-by to everybody. I was off to school. At that time, Emma was still with us; but she had to go to a different school, so we each walked our way alone.

I started to walk to the designated place -- the Bochumer School. I walked from our fortress to the "Hansa Platz" and then up to the Spree River. I arrived at the river, but there was no bridge! How convenient I thought, maybe after all, I did not have to go to school. As I stood there, I was debating with myself, if I had a strong enough reason to return home. School was going to ruin my metal business and so on. However, my verdict was that I had not a good reason, at least not at that moment. Simply because this bridge was not there did not mean there were no other crossings. So, I decided to walk towards the Belevieu subway stop, but this time along the river.

Along the Spree River was a walkway with many trees. Next to the walkway wound a street with buildings. Of course all the buildings were ruins, and the trees were singed from the war. The Spree River, on my left, was about twenty feet below me. A stone wall held the river in its path. At periodic intervals, there were stairways leading to a cement platform on the river.

I walked a short distance along the Spree and watched how people walked down to one of these platforms, that is, down the steps and to the platform. There, they stood waiting for something. I looked across the river and I saw what they were waiting for: A small "dingy" was floating across the river and approaching the platform. Well, I thought, there was a crossing after all. "Charon" was ferrying a few souls back and forth.

This was not to be missed. So, I followed the small crowd down to the small platform. There, Charon was unloading a few souls. When I reached the platform, the adults were already seated but Charon waited for me, and I got to sit right across from him at the end of the dingy. The adults were very helpful. They held me by my hand and guided me to my seat.

Meanwhile, as Charon pushed off, he announced, "I work here every day from seven in the morning, to six at night. The fare is fifty Pfennig for adults and ten Pfennig for children. No credit please. Just put your fare into the bucket." And, he stretched his neck into the direction of the bucket. Then, he proceeded, "No rocking, no moving about, and we will all get across. Otherwise, you will have to swim to the shore."

I was not prepared for this. I had no money on me to begin with, and I did not know how to swim. I was almost ready to jump into the Spree right there because the landing was still only a few feet away. Instead, I heard myself say calmly, "I did not know. I have no money with me."

I must have said the magic word. Every adult started to fumble in their pockets and out came a handful of change. They insisted that I take the change, "Just in case," each would say. I was embarrassed. I did not know what to do. I did not need the money. I had my own "bankroll." I was just not prepared to pay a "toll" in order to cross the Spree. I ended up taking about one mark in ten Pfennig coins, and I was determined to pay everybody back. The next day I did. The same people "travelled" at the same time every day. Berliners are very punctual. I knew then that it was my Ranzen which confirmed the truth of what I said.

On the other side, we disembarked and went our ways. I went straight to the school. An adult stood at the doorway and directed me to go to the yard. In the yard, I could see a few adults, each with a child. I was the only one without an adult. Soon, the yard filled up with more adults and more children. Soon we were packed like sardines. The yard was humming with noise.

Apparently, the principal had come out from a side entrance at the far side of the yard because total quiet set in. Apparently, the principal stepped on a stool because I could see how the heads shifted. Then I heard a loud scream, "Can you all see me?" And, the mob yelled back in one voice, "Ja!"

I could not see a darn thing. In front of me were all these adults. I felt like a midget surrounded by Cyclops. The next thing I heard was, "Age seven, over here!" The mob started to tremble and vibrate. People were pushing and shoving to get "over here." When the wrestling subsided, I heard another loud scream, "Age eight, over here." Again, people were shoving and pushing in every direction.

Since, I did not know where "over here" was, I decided just to stay put. This went on in the same manner until all ages were called out. When all was finished, I stood there all by myself. Now I could see the principal clearly. He looked at me and yelled, "How old are you?" I yelled back, "S-e-v-e-n!" He yelled at me back, "Can't you hear? Your group is over there!" and he pointed a finger at a mob. I trotted over to my assigned mob.

The principal then started again in a loud voice," I can see we are going to be overcrowded. Therefore, we will work in two shifts. The first shift will be from eight in the morning to one o'clock in the afternoon. The second shift will be from one o'clock in the afternoon until six o'clock. All ages from six to ten will be in the first shift. All other ages will be in the second shift. A teacher is assigned to each class, so please complete your registration with your teacher. Thank you." He got off his stool and vanished into a side door.

Sure enough, as soon as the principal got off the stool, a middle-aged female stepped forward from our group. I thought she was our classroom teacher. First, she looked us over and walked back and forth a few times.

She was waiting for something, I thought. Then, I heard someone call out in a loud voice, "Follow me!" One of the other groups marched into the school building.

As soon as that group disappeared, our teacher came almost to attention in front of our group. Then, she called out in a loud voice, "Follow me!" Our group marched out after her.

She led us into a classroom. The classroom was much too small for our group. About half of us had to wait in the hallway. The others tried to move into the aisles of three rows of fixed benches. This time I was right in front following the teacher. She went directly to her desk. I planted myself right in front of the desk.

The desk was standing on a one step platform. The platform spanned from one side of the room to the other. On the wall behind her was a blackboard. The blackboard took up the whole side of the wall behind her. It was about three feet off the platform and reached almost the ceiling. The blackboard and the room had seen better days. At one end, a large hole gaped in the wall going right through the blackboard at one end. But the room was clean and freshly painted.

Behind her desk was a chair. She sat on the chair and for a moment wiggled back and forth. Aha, I said to myself, she is getting comfortable. On her desk was a pile of papers, all neatly stacked on the left corner. In front of her on the desk were her glasses and a few sharpened pencils. Once she was comfortable, she took one sheet of paper and placed it in front of her. She put on her glasses, pushed the pencils aside and took one pencil. Then she looked at me and said, "Name bitte" (name please).

For some reason, her question to me was a total surprise. Be it that the day had so many new experiences, or be it that I was not reminded of it, I spurted out my real name: "Anatoly Korniev." I did not even realize, that I had done it. She just filled out the form and continued her questioning. When she finished, she put my form on the other side of the table and said, "You are finished for today. Be here in this room tomorrow at eight."

I was dismissed, and I was very happy. I pushed my way out of the classroom, ran into the street and strolled back to the Spree. I was home by ten o'clock and was more than glad to be back.

The next few days were very uneventful. I would go to school in the morning and come back in the afternoon. But, one day our classroom teacher came to class and handed us forms to take home. The forms had to be verified and signed by our parents. So, I took my form -- I did not even look at it -- and put it in my Ranzen. I came home and handed it to my mother.

The next thing I know "all hell" broke loose. My mother was screaming and yelling at me. She was slapping me and yelling at me, "You have ruined us. Now we all will end up in Siberia!" And, this went on and on. I had no idea what I had done to get her so upset. I had never seen her like this before or since. She was raging, and I was the cause of it all. After her rage, I was punished. She took me into an empty room. Facing the corner of two walls, I had to kneel there and face the wall. I still had no idea what I had done. Kneeling and facing the wall was usually the ultimate punishment my mother would dish out.

Finally, Emma came home. Now I heard wailing and crying in the next room. Emma came into the room I was in. She just looked at me and said, "Why did you do this?" I just turned my head towards her and said, "I don't know what this commotion is all about." Emma came closer and said, "How did that name get on your paper, Bruderherz?" Now I understood my crime.

By evening, a solution was found. Elvira would be recruited and sent with me to the school. She would take me to the principal and tell him that I made up that name. That I was a prankster and my parents had a hard time with me. Since both of my parents were working, she was sent. To prove that she was authorized by my parents they gave her a "Vollmacht," or note of authorization, to make the name change. My name was Anton Grotte, and I would confirm that. She would "erase" all records with the other name.

Sending Elvira was actually the best solution. This played down the gravity of the situation. Thus, it was degraded into a common prank of mine. This prank did not even warrant my parents going to the principal.

Next morning, Elvira arrived and together we went to school. Elvira did not think much of the fuss. She was confident that she could straighten out the situation. We went straight to the principal's office. There, she told him the story.

The principal was very upset. He looked at me sternly and asked me, "Is this true?" I said firmly: "Ja." Then, I got "ten lashes" on my rear end with a short stick.

The documents were changed on the spot. The old document was given back to Elvira, and I was given the new papers. Next day I had to bring them back, signed by my parents. That day, class was very uncomfortable for me. I kept saying to myself, 'Next time I am going into the principal's office, I will have a nice padding on my rear.'

The class I was assigned to was very boring. Within a few weeks, this was also apparent to my teacher. I was reading fluently, my math was much better and in other subjects I was even more advanced.

One day, she took me by my hand, and we went to the principal's office. Again, I had no idea what was happening. All I knew was that I was not prepared for another lashing. But, my teacher was very friendly, and I thought maybe I was taken there to make peace with the "pharaoh" (principal). I was hoping my stigma as a prankster was about to be lifted.

We walked into his office. To my surprise, the teacher was praising me. I was doing so well that by all standards I should be in the next higher class. The principal recognized me rightaway. He looked at me sternly and said, "We met before, did we not?" I looked at him and said, "Jawohl." He looked at me again and said, "I am glad that my discipline put some sense in your head." Then, he continued, "Tomorrow you will go to class 3B."

The teacher left me in his office. The principal wrote out some forms. He gave one to me and told me, "Have this form signed by your parents. Return it tomorrow." I took the form and went back to my class. I was very happy when I returned home. I gave the new form to my mother, and she was very happy also. I felt I had redeemed myself from my former crime.

While school became a major factor in my life, the other activities could not be slighted. The garden needed constant attention for now it was harvesting season. The garden was safe from intruders as each family guarded not only their plot but each other's. So, the garden could be harvested last. We kept some vegetables almost until frost. The last ones to go were the pumpkins.

Our pumpkins on the "rubble heap" were not large. They were enormous. By the time we harvested the pumpkins, they were so large that a blanket and four adults were needed to carry them away. We had a virtual feast. We shared with all our neighbors. Everything from pumpkin pie to "pumpkin kasha" (a pumpkin puree) was made. And, everybody loved it!

The plot in the Tiergarten was a different story. The lot was looted repeatedly. Not only our lot, but all the lots in the Tiergarten. Special police were assigned, even "vigilante" groups were formed. All efforts were in vain. They did not stop the looting, they only slowed it down. Still, we harvested many sacks of potatoes that year and stored them so they would not freeze during the winter.

Our main setback was Emma's illness. But we had gained the strength to deal with that also. My mother tried very hard to store and save as much produce as was possible. My mother had visions of the Soviet winter to come.

Winter came early. Somehow the forces of nature tend to unite with a calamity to come. Snow fell early that year. While we were storing food, we forgot another major item -- fuel for our stove. Technically, wood was plentiful. The ruins were full of it. But, when the frost came and was followed by snow, it became nearly impossible to find a day's supply. The stove was just devouring the dry wood. There was no coal, no briquettes, no "lasting" fuels. The stove had to be burning, or we would freeze, regardless of whether meals were cooked or not and regardless whether George kept his tea brewing or not. We concentrated our efforts on finding wood first. We would locate it, dig it out, carry it home and prepare it for use. No matter how big a pile we prepared, by morning the pile was gone.

So, George came up with an "alternative" source of fuel supply -- the rubber tiles used for flooring. First, we scoured the neighborhood and found a few floors that had badly burnt tiles. We chiseled them off the floor and brought them home. They did have a "funny" smell, but they lasted longer than the bone dry wood from the ruins. By February, our neighborhood was essentially exhausted of tiles. Then, we collected anything that would burn and was not edible.

For example, a horse was a welcome sight. Not that there were many horses in Berlin, and especially in February of 1946. Most had been eaten a long time ago. But some were still in use for transportation. Then, one could see a procession of energy collectors, picking up the droppings of the horse. They would walk behind the horse and beg it to unload enough to satisfy all followers. A few times I followed such a procession myself.

By the end of the winter, the situation became desperate. George scrounged around our fortress. At night, he would sneak up to a bombed out floor -- a floor without residents -- and there he would gently chisel away a few tiles. Of course, the noise, no matter how small, was overheard by the resident below. Next morning, that resident would report the strange noise to our super. Our super was an elderly lady, and her husband was very old. It was customary in Europe (and during the classical Greek period) to have a large age difference between husband and wife -- at least twenty years. The average ran about twenty-two years or so. Again, with soldiering as a major occupation, a soldier would "retire" at age forty-five or older. Then, he would raise a family.

The same situation was true with our super and her husband. I was very friendly with her husband on account of my "commodity" business and later my "stamp" business. In any event, our super would ask her husband to go and investigate. He would. Then, he would come back and give her a "damage" report. Very often I went with him to the scene. Then, he would say, "I am going to lay a trap here and catch the scoundrel."

I would come back and tell George of my collaboration with the super's husband. George was always very interested. He would ask, "Are you sure? What scoundrel would do such a thing to our fortress?"

Then, on the next night, the damage was in another section of the building, and it would repeat itself time and again. The scoundrel seemed to know were the traps were. The scoundrel was never caught. I found out much later that George was that scoundrel.

In George's mind, he was performing a service. He used only burnt out tiles which were of no use anyhow. But, on the other side of the coin, the super viewed it as a damage to the building. I was shocked that George played that game with me. I assured him I would not have told on him. Yet he replied, "You don't understand. You actually helped me by being on his side. At least we were not too cold that winter, were we?"

There was one bright side to that winter. I discovered a new toy. I got my own radio -- not a radio that is covered on all sides, oh no, but a piece of wood with a crystal and a small screw with a needle which acted as a selector and tuner. A pair of ear-phones was attached to a socket in the wood base. Then, I would move the needle very gently on the crystal and tune into my favorite station. I thought this was magic, real magic!

That first winter was the cruelest of all. There was practically no food, only starvation rations-more over, it was one of the coldest winters in Berlin. Nature and misery combined to punish the Berliners.

That winter, many died from starvation. That winter, many died from the cold. Many couples, mostly elderly who could not cope any longer with that misery just turned the stove exhaust inward and suffocated from the fumes.

CHAPTER 9

The Ruins

In early July 1945, work crews started to clean up Berlin. Their progress was slow. The Government first utilized POW's and volunteers. Then, the workload shifted to the civilian population. But, the civilian population tried almost anything to get out of this work. The primary reason was that the work was very hard and the money and wages would not buy anything. Even the upgrade of ration cards had virtually no effect. (Workers engaged in hard labor were issued special ration cards).

Berlin was still a barter town. In one day on the black market, one could earn more than in a year of hard labor. The crop from a garden was more valuable than a year's wages, and a systematic utilization of the forest resources was much more productive. Besides, profits in the metal recovery business were at an all time high. It made no sense whatsoever to join a work crew. Our history books, of course, say,"…Due to a shortage of capital investment, the reconstruction was slow."

Once I left the safety of our fortress and went to school, I met new kids. At first, they were mostly my age. But, some had older brothers. Soon that circle began to expand. Before I went to school, kids on the street were just other kids. I paid very little attention to them because my focus was on our fortress and its constant activity. Once I went to school, kids on the street became peers. They went to the same school, they lived in the same neighborhood, and they played on the same street. Since school ended relatively early, I had practically all day to do other things. Then, the most common thing to do was to "hang out" on the street.

Since most parents did not want their kids to hang out on the street, the kids moved into the ruins.

My mother was adamant with me. I was not to hang out on the street. Each time I was caught, or someone squealed on me, I was punished. The kids, however, began to move from the streets into the ruins. This was not happening just on our street; it was taking place throughout the city. Of course, once we moved into the ruins, our loyalties became more closely knit. Very soon, each street had its own gang.

Again, be it from boredom, or be it a natural phenomenon, the gangs began to compete with each other -- not for "turf," but for recognition. This recognition was expressed in terms of strength. Strength meant war. That is, gangs played war with each other. At first, a show of members was sufficient. Then, a small fight was in order. Then actual wars began to be staged.

Many ruins still had plenty of live ammunition: unexploded bombs, discarded shells, antitank guns (Panzerfaust), rifles, revolvers, and so on. These stray weapons were gathered and stashed away in a well-hidden cellar. Then, when they were needed, the weapons were distributed among the gang members who knew how to use them.

Naturally, the older boys controlled the gangs, and school- age gang members were recruited. The older boys, at fifteen or sixteen years of age, had actual war experience. Many had participated in the defense of Berlin and knew how to use the weapons. The oldest became automatically the "general." At least on our block. The general then appointed his staff. The staff members were called "Oberst" or colonel. Each Oberst picked his recruits. Depending on the street size, other ranks were also assigned.

Our street had one general, Jurgen, and five Obersts. EachOberst had about five to six recruits, so our street was relatively strong. I was a recruit and my Oberst was Dietrich. I don't remember the names of the others. Of course, each member had to swear to total secrecy and total allegiance to the general.

Nonmembers were called cowards, or other choice names, and were usually harassed by the gang members. We had two kids on our street, about my age, who would not join our gang. I remember how, at every opportunity, we used to laugh and ridicule them. We would do that, not only on our street, but also in school. They were treated as lepers.

Girls were not regular members. Girls were not recruited. Only the most obliging ones were reluctantly accepted into the auxiliary.

Assembly was relayed by recruits. The standard message was "Come out and play 'now.'" Then, if someone else was to be notified, his name was appended to the message. For example, "Come out and play 'now' with 'Dietrich and me'" meant that, it was my job to notify Dietrich if I could get away. The only valid excuse not to show up at the assembly area was when a parent would specifically forbid us to go out and play. When my mother was around that was a given -- I could not go out. But, when anyone else was around, then I had to obey the orders. At least, that is how I felt at that time. The assembly area was usually a designated ruin.

One day, I was called to the assembly area. By the time I showed up, almost everyone else was there. When we were all assembled, our general explained that another street had challenged us to a war. They were much larger and much stronger. Therefore, we would use our weapons. Accordingly, weapons from our cache were assigned to specific individuals. The plan was as follows:

We would meet the opposing army at a predetermined location without weapons. Then, a street would be selected where the war would be fought. We would then get weapons from our cache and bring them secretly to the war area. Then, we would "blast" them from their assigned territory and win the war.

During a "normal war," a desolate street was picked, and opposing armies would occupy the opposite ruins across the street. We would then bombard each other with rocks until someone was "wounded," that is, when blood was flowing. Then, a cease- fire was called. The loser was whoever called the cease-fire. Of course, if an army left its assigned territory, it also lost the war.   After the briefing, we marched to the designated meeting area. When we arrived, the opposing army was already there. They were indeed much larger. There were at least twice as many of them as of us.

We stopped about fifty paces away from them. We looked each other over. Then, the two opposing generals met in the neutral zone between our two armies. They stood there and talked to each other. After a while, our general came back and called his Obersts.

They talked for a while. Then, two of the Obersts got one recruit each and took off. Their remaining "division" was assigned to another Oberst for the march to the war zone. Once our leaders agreed on our strategy, they stepped in front of us, raised their hands and waved us on. At that point we shouted obscenities at the opposing army. As soon as we started shouting, the opposing army shouted obscenities back at us. After a while, our general lowered his hand and said, "Let's go." Then, our general started to jog, and his army jogged behind him to the war zone.

We arrived at a small street which was all bombed out. Only two or three ruins were standing on the whole street. Our general led us to our territory, to a ruin. In our ruin, the larger part of the front wall was still there. The ruin had no floors, only the staircase was still standing and led to two windows. All the windows were blown out, and a huge heap of rubble covered the first floor.

The older kids took up positions at the windows on the first floor and at the two windows on the staircase. The younger kids were told to stay behind the next wall, or wall section, and collect ammunition. Ammunition were "good throwing rocks." These were rocks slightly larger than a golf ball. I ended up about twenty feet behind my Oberst, who was at a first floor window. There, I feverishly collected good throwing rocks for my Oberst. Each time I had a good bunch, I would bring them up to him. He would take a look at them and point to the ones he preferred. We were ready to make war.

All of a sudden, a barrage of rocks came our way. Most of them fell short of our ruin. The majority of the other rocks hit our front wall. A few rocks, however, whizzed though the windows or opening and landed on the rubble heap.

At that moment our other two Obersts arrived. Each carried a Panzerfaust, an antitank gun. One of them crouched at a window and aimed at the opposing ruin. The next thing I heard was a loud -- boom. I could see how a section from the other ruin collapsed. Then, I heard obscenities from the other building across the street; and then, there was silence. They had fled the battlefield. Therefore, we were the victors.

We waited a while and then went over to the other ruin. It was deserted. I had visions of wounded kids, and I was already thinking what explanation I could possibly give to my mother. I must say that I was genuinely relieved when I found out that nobody got hurt. From then on, I knew that I would never join another gang again, no matter what the consequences would be to me.

Our general assembled his army, and triumphantly we marched back to our street. Most were excited -- we had just defeated a much stronger enemy.

I must say that, after this incident, our army got smaller. I was not the only one with my sentiments and feelings. I never participated in another war. Nobody had to forbid me anymore. I started to evade and to avoid the gang altogether. I was desperately trying to be accepted yet I was determined not to participate in their wars.

Eventually, one of the Obersts lost his arm. Another member lost his eye, and many kids were maimed. Most of these accidents were attributed, in the newspapers and radio, to "playing" with live ammunition. The newspapers and radio were full of incidents of inadvertent accidents. If playing war is considered to be an accident, then they were accidents. But, in many instances these were actual casualties of gang warfare.

The general later on became a scoutmaster, and many of the recruits became Boy-Scouts. In fact, I became a Boy-Scout myself. When I was a Rover (older and independent Boy-Scout), I met many former gang members later on at Rovermoots and at Jamborees (World-wide assemblies).

The ruins were a haven for illegal, subversive and criminal activity. This was a known fact. Yet, Berlin did not have the manpower or the resources to clean the ruins up quickly. Only little by little and block by block were they cleaned. By 1954, Berlin was completely clean. But, until then, the life in the ruins and from the ruins continued.

****

When the German invasion into the Soviet Union started in 1941, the situation was not much different then our street war tactics. The initial invasion carried with it the element of surprise. This element of surprise lasted about six months. During that time, however, many Soviet citizens saw an opportunity to escape Stalin's reign of terror. So, many Soviet army units surrendered to the Germans in the hope of fighting with them, in the hope of fighting Stalin and his terror. Many German victories in the first six months were of dubious nature. They ranged from victory to voluntary surrender. Hitler preferred to call them victories because that only accentuated the invincibility of the German

Wehrmacht. Stalin called them defeats because, otherwise, Stalin would have to admit that there was a large sector of the population who was prepared to fight him. Therefore, history was reconciled: Both opponents agreed that they were victories or defeats, depending on the respective side. Thus, voluntary surrenders became a "nonexistent" entity in our official history books.

The fact that there was a third alternative was dismissed. This third alternative is essentially still dismissed today.

After 1941, Germany made no real progress in the war, but Stalin could not show a clear victory once Vlasov was dethroned as a hero. So, Hitler rested on his glory of the prior year while Stalin searched for a decisive victory.

This situation came to a head at Stalingrad. While Hitler was convinced of the invincibility of the German army, Stalin was determined to inflict a mortal wound. Hitler committed hubris and split his forces. Paulus was sent into Stalingrad, and the panzers were sent towards Baku. While Hitler waged war with propaganda, Stalin brought all the forces he could muster into the Stalingrad sector. Paulus was doomed. These forces were used again at Kursk and in the second Battle for Kiev. Stalin brought even more armor into the Battle of Kursk; Von Manstein was doomed. The very teeth of the German Wehrmacht were now shattered. From then on, the war was irreversibly determined. The ultimate direction of the war was now cast.

We hear so much about the superiority of German armor. Was that a fact or was it also a myth? Tank for tank, the Soviet T34 was a better tank for the terrain than even the latest German tanks, the Tiger and the Leopard. A T34 required from six to twenty direct hits before it was put out of action. One hit from the T34 and a Tiger or a Leopard changed into a heap of scrap metal.

However, the tactical use of the T34 was archaic. The T34 was used as a single fortress. The German tactic was much better -- they attacked in a pack. Just like a wolf pack attacks a much larger prey. However, once that tactic was exposed, the remedy was simple: Use T34's in counterpacks. This tactic was used at Kursk, and the result was that the German panzers were decimated while the T34's survived the battle. It was also the first battle when the Soviets had a slight superiority of men and armor.

No ground war can be won without the artillery, at least not then. While Hitler preferred long guns, Stalin preferred shorter range mobile rockets. The Katjusha was the marvel of the war. It was a light and mobile rocket system. It could be easily transported by a truck, deliver its cargo, and move on to another place. A large gun was fixed. Once it was spotted, it was doomed. Let us say for a moment that there is an advantage with a large gun. Let us say a large gun fires one shot at a time. That is, sequentially. The cost of one large gun was more than five mobile rocket systems. Let us say for a moment that the early rocket systems had twelve barrels. Then, the cost effectiveness of a Katjusha was sixty times that of one large gun! That is, the firepower and devastation of the Katjushas was sixty times as large. In a barrage, what matters is the density of firepower and very little else. As far as density was concerned, the advantage was clearly with the mobile rocket launchers.

Hitler captured a number of the rocket systems and tried to duplicate them for his own use, but he could not. The "inherent technology" of the rocket system was beyond German engineering. How could that be?

What everybody forgot was that Euler had trained the best mathematicians in St. Petersburg in Russia. Yet, Euler's work was virtually unknown in the West. Euler was a Swiss. How could this man's work be of such significance? Euler had died 150 years before the war. The fact that Euler's work was virtually unknown in the West was the other part of the hubris committed by Hitler. He felt that anything of value originated in Germany.

Finally, let us examine Fermi and his exodus from Italy. In 1939 Fermi, whose wife was Jewish, decided to leave his home, his country, and give up all the titles bestowed on him, and escape the bigotry of Mussolini and Hitler. He went to Stockholm to accept his Nobel Prize. Fermi was the founder and originator of a new field in physics: Quantum Mechanics. Fermi accepted his prize. Instead of returning to his beloved Italy, however, he asked for and received sanctuary in the United States.

For the next three years, he worked feverishly to demonstrate the possibility of a nuclear bomb. In 1942, Fermi demonstrated in Chicago the feasibility of a chain reaction. Los Alamos became a reality, and Fermi built the first nuclear bomb there.

In Rome, in 1938, Fermi wrote the first text book on quantum mechanics. It served as the basis for the new science of quantum mechanics. The book is still on display at the University of Chicago.

He was the first to demonstrate a chain reaction. He was the first to build an atom bomb, and he was the first to establish a school for quantum mechanics in Chicago. For his contributions, Fermi received this country's highest honor -- the Congressional Medal of Honor and a prize was established in his name -- the Fermi Prize. He died from overexposure to radiation in 1954. Yet, how much do we hear of Fermi when "authorities in the field" squabble about antimatter, or other tangential topics of quantum mechanics? The truth is we hear very little. The Royal Society of England sees to that, and we oblige! How come?

****

I started to turn my energy inward, toward our fortress and the adjacent ruins. Metals were now much harder to find. The surface had been picked clean of saleable metals. One needed to conduct "digs."

To conduct a dig, all one needed was a shovel and a lot of "elbow grease." Then, one would stake out a pile of rubble and dig. Of course, digging meant to turn the debris over and move it to another site. The object of a dig was to find anything salvageable: Metals, pots, jars, bottles and so on.

One day, I staked out an adjacent rubble heap and started to dig. The first few hours were sort of useless. I found practically nothing of value. Then, I came to a new layer, and the results started to improve. Copper, brass, and cast iron were plentiful. I recovered it and piled it into a heap. When the heap was large enough, I carried it to my stockpile in the apartment and sorted it out. I actually had a burnt-out room on our floor which I used as my storage area.

Larger pieces I would load up on my cart and take directly to the redemption center. Periodically, I would sell my smaller inventory in my room. As soon as I had enough in my room of a particular commodity to sell, I would load up my cart and take it to the redemption center.

Most commodities were sold by weight. This included keys. George always got a kick out of it when I sold keys by the pound. It made no sense to him. It was illogical. He would say, "It was like buying sausage by the yard." To me it did not matter: The market was the market. If the market bought keys by the pound, then that is what needed to be sold.

I worked away on this rubble heap for weeks. One day I reached bottom, and there was a very curious thing. There were a number of large books. I pulled one book out to investigate and it said in large letters: "Album." When I opened the book it contained even stranger things: Stamps.

The book contained stamps I had never seen before. Large, small, some very pretty and some very ordinary looking. They were all attached in a strange way to the page. A small "glassine" like piece of paper was attached to the stamp, and at the same time, to the page (a hinge). This needed to be investigated.

I pulled out all the books and cleaned up that area thoroughly. The books were not uniform. Some were "albums" with stamps mounted in them, and some were books with cellophane strips. There, stamps were loosely clustered between the strip and the page. I took all the books to my "warehouse" and stashed them away -- out of sight. Then, I took one book into our living room for Emma to tell me what it was. I pulled Emma away. and went with her to a table. Then, I placed the book on the table and said, "Here, do you know what this is?" and I opened the book to one page. I could see how Emma's eyes were popping. Emma had started stamp collecting and had many stamps. But, her stamps were loose. She had made little, flat envelopes from discarded newspapers and kept them there.

The first words out of her mouth were, "Where did you get this?" I told her that I had just dug them up from a ruin. She closed the album, put her hand on my shoulder, and said, "Let's go. You show me where you dug them up."

I took her to my work-site. She could easily see I had been busily working there. She started to look for more evidence. I told her that the heap was very large, and if it was not properly worked on, it could collapse. Then, I would lose at least one day to get it in the shape I wanted it. I wanted to be able to see the layers of debris, so I could easily recover the metals. I also knew that Emma was not going to dig. She preferred intellectual activities. So, Emma just looked around, scratched her head, and she seemed satisfied. We went back home.

We arrived home and went back to the album. Then, Emma declared, "You know, this is not for you. You don't understand these things. So, why don't you give the book to me."

I protested. I had labored for a long time on that pile to get those books, and all I wanted to find out was, what they were worth. Now, my product was about to be confiscated, and by my own sister. My mother was drawn into the argument. My mother agreed with Emma. But, my mother also said that I should be paid for my work. The album was much too valuable for me. So, reluctantly, I agreed to sell the album to Emma. She paid me two Marks.

This did not sit well with me. I did not like the transaction, because I was still in the dark about the value of the stamps. The next morning, I took one of the smaller books with me to school. I put it in my Ranzen, and I was off.

Our school had one break. At about eleven o'clock, we ran into the yard and ate our "lunch." That is, if we had anything to eat. That was when I asked the other kids if they knew anything about stamps. To my amazement, almost everybody collected stamps. So, I told them that I was a collector myself, and had many stamps. Invariably they would ask, "How many stamps do you have?" When I replied, "Thousands," I got a lot of respect and admiration, and they all wanted to trade with me. During the remainder of my class, I kept thinking, "How come I was not exposed to stamps before? How come stamp collecting was so popular?" This needed to be investigated further.

After school, I was determined to make another try. I found one of the kids I had spoken to during the recess and went up to him. "So, you have a lot of stamps too," I started. He was very eager to talk to me. He said, "Yes, a whole lot. Do you want to trade someday?" Then, I asked him, "How do you get your stamps?" He looked at me, as if I fell off the moon and said, "I buy them." I nodded with great understanding, and I said, "Me too."

Then, I thought for a while and asked, "Who do you buy them from?" Again, he looked at me strangely and said, "From a dealer, of course." Now I was getting closer, and I explained, "You know, I am new in this area, and I don't know where there is a dealer near our school." He grinned and said, "Come on, I will take you to one. He is a real nice guy," he added.

Sure enough, right on my way to school was a stamp dealer. I never noticed the store because he had nothing in his store window. In fact, the shade was drawn about half way most of the time. My new friend took me to him. We walked in and my friend introduced me, "This is Helmut," nodding to the dealer; and then he turned to me and said, "And, this is my friend. What's your name?" I answered, "Anton." My friend turned to me and said, "I am going to leave you two alone. I am in a hurry to get home," and he was out the door.

156

The dealer was very friendly. He stood behind a long counter top. In back of him were shelves with albums and smaller books, similar to the one I had with me. He pulled up an old wooden cigar box. It was loaded with many different stamps. Then he said, "Every stamp in this box is five Pfennig." I looked at him and asked, "Do you buy stamps?" The dealer looked at me in amazement and said, "Of course I buy stamps. I have to buy stamps all the time, to stay in business." I took off my Ranzen, pulled out the book with the stamps, and put it on the counter. The dealer flipped through the book and said, "Where did you get these? There are some nice stamps in here." I said: "They are mine."

He looked at me firmly. I could sense that he knew a great deal from the book. I could see that he knew that the book and its owner did not match up. I said, "I dug it up in a ruin and I want to know the value."

He looked at me again, but now his look was gentle, almost kind. And, he started, "You see, many of the stamps in this book are worth very little. But, there are a few stamps that are nice. They are worth a few Marks each. Do you know these stamps?" I knew I was cornered, "No, but I want to find out."

He started to grin, "That's going to take you a very long time. You see, there are many different countries. They all issue stamps, and they all have a different value." Then, I looked at him and said, "How does one learn fast,… really fast?" I added.

He thought for a while and continued, "The first thing you need to do is to get a catalogue. In a good catalogue, there is a picture of the stamp and its value for mint or used. A stamp is mint if it is not cancelled and has the gum on the back. A used stamp is one that's cancelled. Real collectors collect used stamps. Although, there are many mint collectors, they misuse the hobby -- they invest," he paused. Then, he continued:

"Good catalogues are expensive. I have only a few that are old." Then, he looked at me and said, "If you want, I will give you an old catalogue. You browse around and see if you find the stamps you have. But, remember the value in the catalogue is a trade value and not the cash value. The cash value is much less. It is only a fraction of the catalogue value."

He turned around and pulled out a book. He gave it to me and said, "Here,… here is one from 1940. Take a look at it and when you finish, come back and we will talk some more." Then, he thought for a moment and said, "This catalogue is arranged by country and the date a stamp was issued." Then he said: "You want to learn really fast? Well, observe the catalogue value and the face value. In most cases there will be a direct relationship in value... But then, of course, you will have to know the many different currencies," he mumbled.

I took the catalogue and my book of stamps. I put them into my Ranzen. Then he looked at me and asked, "Do you have more of these books?" I said, "Yes... and I have others too. They are inscribed album." I could see he was interested.

I went back home that day and spent the rest of the afternoon with the catalogue. To my amazement, I saw "astronomical" values in the catalogue. Some stamps were worth twenty thousand Marks and some even more. But the majority were below one Mark. I was fascinated, and I found many of the stamps in my book. He was right. Most were below ten pfennig, but I found one that was ten Marks. Wow! I thought to myself, I am rich.

From then on, I spent some time with Helmut practically every day. I eventually brought all my stamps to him and he helped me build my first real stamp collection. Within two months or so, I knew "every" stamp in that catalogue. Now, the world was very small. While my catalogue had about 20,000 different stamps listed, they were not that difficult to remember because most came in sets. In terms of sets, there were fewer than 3,000 that needed to be remembered. Generally, within a set, the highest face value stamp was also the most expensive.

This was the time I learned how to use the paraphernalia associated with stamps: the stock books, and how to use them most effectively, and about hinges, tongues, glassine envelopes, and the mounting and stripping of stamps on pages. I learned how to take stamps off properly, how to steam them, how to get creases out and many other "tricks of the trade." Then, one day, Helmut made me an offer to sell for him at the school. I rejected his offer at first. Later, I came to him with my counteroffer and he accepted. We became good friends and reliable "businessmen."

Our school had a small stamp club. We would meet there once a week and swap stamps. But, the swapping was done "in the dark." We had no catalogue to consult, and there were no catalogues in our school. Besides, the use of catalogues at that time would have slowed down the trade action. We swapped for size or for the picture on the stamps. Having a catalogue would take away from the skill and knowledge, would it not?

Since everybody was thought to be an expert, it was "fair game" to swap for whatever one considered to be most valuable. I found the swap session to be very informative and exciting. By and large, I usually made out very well. But, selling at the club would have been counterproductive. In fact, it may have been prohibited by the school officials. But, I must say, I never bothered to find out, and nobody ever sold at our club. We only swapped.

CHAPTER 10

The Blockade and Airlift

The political situation was rapidly deteriorating between the western allies and the Soviets. Stalin was determined to exercise his reparation concessions from his western allies. Most important on his mind was territory as a means of reparation.

The new borders with Finland, Poland, and the Baltic coast were firmly integrated into to Soviet Union. East Prussia was his main prize for German reparations. For his declaration of war on Japan and the conquest of Manchuria, he was free to grab the south of Sakhalin Island and the Kuril islands. This he did, and parts of China were conveniently integrated into the Soviet Union.

The puppet governments in Albania, Bulgaria, Czechoslovakia, Hungary, Jugoslavia, Poland and Rumania were firmly in Stalin's hands. Then he extricated additional pieces from Italy, Germany and Austria. East Germany was an obedient slave to Stalin. Only one isolated spot remained free within East Germany: Berlin.

The other aspect of war reparation included the dismantling of entire factories and industrial complexes. So, East Germany and Berlin were systematically raped of their remaining industries for war reparations. Finally, there was the human toll: All former Soviet citizens were subject to forced repatriation.

Berlin was fighting a bottomless "black hole." As soon as an industry was created or repaired, it was dismantled and shipped to the Soviet Union. Starvation rations kept the population chronically undernourished and unfit for hard labor. Stalin's attempt to convert the Berliners to farmers was essentially a dismal failure. The small patches of land were plundered before the crop was ready. Berlin needed food. That food had to come from West Germany.

While Berlin has many canals, most of them lead to East Germany; and East Germany was essentially in the same predicament as Berlin -- no factories, no work and no food. The only main arteries from Berlin to West Germany were roads. In fact, three main roads connect Berlin to West Germany: One to Hamburg, the other to Hannover, and the last to 'Frankfurt am Main.' This was the 'Autobahn;' which Hitler had built.

Stalin saw an opportunity to strangle Berlin, to cut off all supplies from the West. This, he hoped, would force the western allies to abandon Berlin. Then, East Germany would be "homogeneous." The corrupt western influence would be eliminated.

First, Stalin tried political means to win over the Berliners. They were promised larger rations and better working conditions if they voted for the SED in the combined Berlin election of 1946. The SED was soundly defeated. To the Berliners, the Americans, the English, and the French were their last glimmer of hope. There was no way Berliners would vote away their presence. Each Soviet attempt to front another Communist party was defeated. What remained was an annexation by force.

Of course, a pretext needed to be found. That pretext was right at hand. West Germany had just instituted its final currency reform. The "Deutsche Mark (D-Mark)" was created and the provisional currency was replaced. This pretext was used by Stalin to begin the blockade in June 1948. His explanation to the allied powers was simple: The new currency reform undermined the currency in East Germany.

Fortunately for Berlin, the Allies did not see it that way. They recognized the act for what it was, another way for Stalin to wrestle more territory from the West. The Allies responded swiftly. An airlift was created to supply Berlin with much needed food and fuel.

When the blockade began, the Berliners trembled at the possibility of another war. Was Hitler's assumption right? Could Communism and Capitalism not coexist? Was war the only inevitable solution?

At any rate, it can be said that the cold war between East and West began with the blockade of Berlin on June 1948.

The situation in Berlin now deteriorated quickly. No more joint patrols. No more collaboration with the Soviets for forceful repatriation.

An actual border was established between East and West Berlin. Barbed wire was strung between East and West Berlin. (Only much later, during President Kennedy's term, was the infamous wall erected). Berliners took to the streets and demonstrated, and "Checkpoint Charlie" was created at the Brandenburg Gate.

I remember how, on the first day of the airlift, I listened to my radio all day long. The tension continued for the next few days as I listened intently. Allegedly, the first few flights were "buzzed" by MIG's. But, no incidents occurred to provoke a war. Within a few weeks, the airlift became routine. Just another inconvenience for the Berliners to deal with. Special taxes were imposed to pay for the airlift. The tax was paid not only in Berlin, but also in West Germany.

With the airlift, the rations improved. Many products could now be bought in the stores. The black market began to disappear. The airlift lasted until September 1949. It is said that the airlift cost nearly two hundred million dollars. In 1949, that was a tidy sum.

Because of the airlift, approximately two million West Berliners were saved. Also because of the airlift, Berlin became the refuge for most refugees from East Berlin, East Germany and Eastern Europe. Berlin became the showcase of the West and a nagging eyesore for the East.

While exact figures are not available, the following estimates can be made:

In 1941, Berlin had a population in excess of 4.5 million inhabitants. As the Soviets came closer to Berlin, more than 2 million refugees flooded into the city. Let us say that 6.5 million people were in Berlin at the end of the war in 1945. Of these, fewer than 1 million were killed during the bombings and the subsequent battle for Berlin. This left 5.5 million inhabitants at the end of the war in Berlin.

A 1959 census revealed 2.2 million West Berliners and 1.1 million East Berliners were left, or a total of 3.3 million Berliners. Let us say that the "exodus" from Berlin, which was a trickle until 1949, and the natural birthrate cancelled each other out. Then, the starvation of Berlin killed approximately 3.2 million people. This starvation was deliberate and planned. This starvation was masterminded by Stalin.

Trading with the western allies was impossible. They were called Joe, Tom or Pierre, and we were called Fritz. I do not know how they came up with Fritz, but they did.

I personally met few Fritz's. But, there are many Russian songs which specifically use "Fritz." They originated in the Seven-year War with Prussia. Then, Frederick was at war with Elizabeth and Berlin was captured by the Ukrainians. Many Soviets knew that song because I heard it then often. So, most likely this was the origin.

As a matter of fact, in every major war between Russia and Germany, the German capital was taken by the Russians. Not once did the Germans capture the capital of Russia. This is why the defense of Moscow in 1941 was psychologically so important to Stalin. He refused to give Germany the satisfaction to equalize history -- von Clausewitz's "revanche" motive was never equalized. Yet, the distance from the Niemen to Moscow and from the Niemen to Berlin is nearly the same. Conversely, since Napoleon captured Moscow in 1812, the Russians occupied Paris in 1814. Thus, "their revanche" motif was equalized.

The new soldiers did not like the vodka, and they did not like the cigarettes we normally traded with the Soviets. Papirossy were out, and real cigarettes were in. They still liked the nylons and the "services," however.

The prevailing service they liked was to have their shoes shined. To most Germans this was the "most demeaning job imaginable" -- manual work on the lowest extremity of the body. Yet overnight, a service industry was created. Kids swarmed to the subway station and set up shop. I went there to investigate. Our station already had too many kids shining shoes. I debated for a long time about entering the shoe shining business, but my other activities were just too profitable. So, I did not.

The new soldiers were very generous. When they were approached for a trade, they would laugh and often give things away without accepting merchandise. I felt frustrated because I wanted to trade. I had become accustomed to trading. But, they seemed to have everything we could possibly offer. From then on, I concentrated on stamps as my primary trade item.

Trading in stamps was a very uneven business. Only one in ten, or even fewer, of the soldiers cared for the merchandise. But, on occasion, somebody could be found who was interested. Then I would bring out additional merchandise. At that time, I had only a limited idea what the value of a stamp was -- the idea I had formed from Helmut's catalogue. Of course, I believed I was a real expert. But, I could easily observe that Americans clearly preferred American stamps while the English preferred

English stamps, and so on. That is, there was a direct relationship of preference. There was one exception. Many wanted stamps with Hitler on them. So, I would go back to my dealer friend Helmut and stock up on only the items in demand.

What was nice about that business was that the buyers would set another date to view more merchandise. This, I found to be intriguing because my "traditional" business was to deal with different buyers all the time. Therefore, while only a few were interested, those few were coming back very often.

So, one day, a plan was clear to me. I had to set up four books -- with American, English, French and Hitler stamps. The Russians were no longer coming to the western sectors, so I did not bother with them. Only one book for each "nationality" and one with Hitler stamps was needed. Then I would find buyers and sell the stamps to them. Helmut would supply me with the stamps. I would get my commission and restock my inventory. In this way, the cycle was endless.

What I found amazing was that the "prettiest" and "cheapest" stamps came from France and the French colonies. They were large, triangular, colorful and were definite "eye catchers." They flaunted "naked" women and men. They depicted many beautiful landscapes, historical events and persons. They were the "honey" to catch the unsuspecting "bear." The American stamps were mostly large (commemoratives). Their paper and print quality were not nearly as good as the French, and they were very low priced. As a matter of fact, all the American commemorative stamps I carried were priced at one value -- 5 Pfennig each (about one cent), while for "French" stamps I had ranged from 5 to 50 Pfennig. The least pretty stamps were the English, and they were the most highly priced, from 5 Pfennig to 1 Mark each. (I did not carry anything over 1 Mark in my inventory). They were small in size and very "monotone" to look at, mostly George V. But, there was an "endless" array of them, from the many British colonies. Of course, the most "monotone" were the stamps with Hitler. They were issued either in Germany, Bohemia and Moravia, Czechoslovakia or Poland (General Gouvernement).

The next day, I went to Helmut. I asked him if his offer to sell stamps was still good. He told me it was. Then, I told him that I had a "lot of buyers, adult buyers" for specific categories, and I explained my plan to him. I could see he did not fully trust me at that time, but he agreed and stocked my four stockbooks with stamps. In effect, I got my first stamp "consignment." Helmut would tell me the price I had to charge for each stamp, on each page, in my stockbook. Helmut showed me how to mark the value on each stockbook page. That is, a secret code was used to indicate the value, but only Helmut and I knew what that code was.

I was told to keep the merchandise in a safe, dry place, at home until I had a buyer. Only after I found a buyer was I to take the merchandise out. Helmut tallied up the merchandise and I was in business. From then on, the sale was easy once I had a buyer. Each stamp on each page was multiplied by the unit amount. The total was tallied, and that was the amount of the sale.

The accounting of the transactions was also easy. I would bring back each book to Helmut, he would count the stamps left, tally the sales, and deduct the sale from his prior total. I would pay him in full for the outstanding balance, and he would pay me my commission. Then, he would restock my books. Each time I came to Helmut, we started out with a clean slate. Occasionally, he would ask me if I wanted to keep the unsold merchandise. Usually, I did -- I kept the unsold merchandise.

The rest was easy. I would take the merchandise home and put it away in a safe place. Then, I would go out and find buyers. This was not easy at first, but soon I had a regular clientele. In fact, often they were looking for me.

Sometimes, I would really "score." That happened when a buyer bought everything in the book. Then, I was "itching" to get back to Helmut right away. I never did. Even though I had a hard time containing myself in those instances, my emotion needed to be contained to conduct "business." The next day, however, after school, I would go to Helmut and we would "celebrate." Then, I would get a bonus: Either stamps for myself or additional money. My commission was a standard twenty percent of the sale. Pretty soon my stamp trading became my most profitable business. Sometimes, I was embarrassed to show all that money to my mother. At the same time, I started to build up my own inventory and collection. True, most of the business was "nickel and dime," but to me that was a lot of money.

On September 3, 1948, Berlin issued its own stamps. At that time, to the rest of the world, this meant very little; but to the Berliners, this was the first time they were recognized all over the world as free "spirits." This was sort of like an "independent" country for, according to the UPU (Universal Postal Union), only free and independent countries were authorized to issue stamps. This is the case because, there is an inherent "currency parity" in stamps. A new industry had been created by the West for West Berlin in its struggle for survival. Those who recognized the significance of the event got paid handsome dividends. An original set sold at face value at the post office, in the old currency. The value of the entire set sold for approximately 17 Reichsmarks.

The currency exchange was at ten to one. The adjusted face value became approximately 1.70 D-Mark. A mint (never hinged) set today commands about 400 D-Mark. Now, the same set on covers not even first day covers -- commands in excess of 6,000 D-Mark!

As it turned out, the first set was not even the "best" price performance set issued by Berlin. Some items achieved a price performance ratio as high as 20,000 to 1. That is, a one thousand D-Mark investment would yield twenty million D-Marks today.

At that time, when the D-Mark was first introduced, the dollar was officially pegged at ten to one to the new D-Mark. (Later, it became four to one). Thus, a one thousand dollar investment at that time would be worth approximately one hundred million dollars today!

****

By the time the allied occupation forces started to administer their Berlin sectors, most of the wargangs disappeared. The energy was channeled into two major new directions: Scouting and sports.

Scouting became very popular and many former Hitler Youths (HJ) joined the scouting movement. Of course, as the new generation came of age, they joined the movement also. But, the scouting leadership, by and large, were former members of the HJ. I joined the scouting movement at that time but found it to be overly regimented. Instead, I was fascinated by a new sport that had evolved in Berlin.

Many team sports revolve around a ball. Depending on the game, the ball differs in size -- for example, a soccer ball, a volleyball, a handball, and a tennis ball. Basketball, football, softball, and baseball were not known in Berlin at that time; and a soccer ball was very expensive. Consequently, soccer was initially not played. The same applied for volleyball and handball. But, the new soldiers had tennis balls. That tennis ball was the key for the new game. The game was called "Koeppen" or "headball."

Both Europe and America have a game called handball. Except for the name, the two games have very little in common.

In Europe, handball is a team sport while in America it is an individual sport. European handball is played outdoors and indoors. When it is played outdoors, a soccer field is used and the team consists of eleven players -- five forwards, five defenders and one goalie. When it is played indoors, a basketball court is used and the team consists of three forwards, three defenders and one goalie.

The goal is a regular soccer goal when the game is played outdoors, and it is a hockey goal when played indoors. In front of the goal is a "goalie safety zone" and a "defensive zone." The goalie safety zone is a semicircle from the center of the goal. Outdoors, the semicircle has an eleven meter radius (about 12.2 yards); indoors, the radius is six meters (about 6.7 yards).

The goalie safety zone cannot be entered by the attackers or the defenders while the "action" is in the vicinity of the goal. Otherwise, a violation results. That violation is called a foul. The defensive zone is sixteen meters outdoors (about 17.8 yards) and ten meters indoors (about 11.1 yards).

Defenders have a slight advantage between the two zones as far as physical contact and "positioning" is concerned. For example, a defender can "position" himself, and the attacker may not run into him.

A handball is smaller than a soccer ball, about six inches in diameter, and has to be passed by hand. Kicking the ball results in a foul. For this reason, it is called handball.

Dribbling is permitted, provided the ball is bounced on the ground within three seconds. Unlike basketball, one can hold the ball for only up to three seconds. Therefore, one must either dribble or pass the ball very often.

One can pass the ball for any desired distance, provided the pass does not result in an "offside." An offside occurs when the ball is passed into the opponent's half of the playing field and there is no other defender between the attacker and the goalie at the time of the pass. This rule is used to prevent attackers from "lounging" around at the opponent's goal. Thus, when the defense advances to support its attackers, the opponent's attackers are forced to retreat towards their goal.

A point is scored when the attacker throws the ball from outside the goalie safety zone, and it enters the goal. Limited physical contact is permitted, similar to basketball. The game was developed by Hitler, as a "women's sport" -- an alternative to soccer -- and became very popular. By 1950, the sport became very popular in Europe as a men's sport, and the "indoor" variety is now an Olympic sport.

Koeppen was an individual game. The rules of the game and the playing field were simple. First, for the playing field, the two goals were about ten meters apart (about thirty three feet). Each goal was about six meters wide (about 20 feet) and two meters high (about 6.6 feet).

In the center, between the two goals, was a line parallel to the goals. The center line separated the opponents territory. The end lines were "infinite," and the center line was "infinite" also. The game was ideally suited to be played on a street.

One goal was set up on the curb; the other was set up in the middle of a four-lane street. Since posts were not available, the corner posts were marked off with chalk; and the center line was drawn with chalk also -- only a three -- or four -- foot dash was marked off.

Second, the rules of the game were the following. The game lasted for twenty-one points, similar to Ping-Pong. The ball was a tennis ball or a ball which resembled a tennis ball in size. Each contestant took turns to score a point in an alternate manner. The server was the contestant whose turn it was to serve the ball. Only the server could score a point. When the server served, his opponent guarded his own goal.

As for serving the ball, the server stayed on his line, threw the ball into the air above his head, and gave the ball a "whack" with his head towards the direction of the opponent's goal. If the ball passed the opponents goal a point was scored by the server.

In effect, the opponent was a goalkeeper at that time. If the ball was caught, the play terminated and the opponent began to serve. When the ball missed the goal it was "out" and became the opponent's ball. However, when the ball was slapped away or got away from the opponent, it could be kicked into the opponent's goal. This was called the after-kick. The game incorporated many aspects from other games, soccer in particular.

The purpose of the center line was to limit the goalie's position at the time of the serve when the goalie had to be behind the center line. Once, the "after-kick" started, it was permissible to dribble and to use as much of the playing field as was necessary.

When this sport came to our block, it took our block by storm. At first, I was very bad, and practically everybody would beat me. I decided to get my "own" tennis ball. I went to Helmut and sold enough stamps to buy one. Soon, I found a ball for sale in our local market, and I bought it. Then I practiced and practiced until I was pretty good.

First, I practiced the goaltending part. I would use a wall as an imaginary server. I would throw the ball at the wall and attempt to catch it without dropping the ball. Then, to make the return less predictable, I would use our staircase in the building.

When I felt pretty good about my goaltending, I would practice the "whacking" part. The trick in whacking the ball was to throw the ball up only six to ten inches above the head. You would then jerk your head at the right moment, and the ball would fly away like a bullet. Naturally, placing the ball into the corners of the opponents goal with sufficient force was "the name of the game."

I was addicted to this sport and played it at every opportunity I could. To my surprise, this game is not played anywhere else, not even in West Germany. During our last year in Berlin, I was the one to beat on our street. The new street challenge became to beat the champion of each street. Then, we had "huge" crowds of kids, who watched the game and cheered on their favorite player.

Sports and excellence in a sport disarms potential antagonism. Sports permit the individual to demonstrate excellence. This excellence is usually universally accepted by peers. Thus, the pursuit of sports is an excellent deterrent to combat prejudice and bigotry.

Once this game caught on in our street, all war game activity ended. All our excess energies were channeled into this new game.

CHAPTER 11

Life in Confinement

After Emma was hospitalized, we felt the ultimate calamity had overcome us. At least my mother felt that way. She expressed it openly. All her energies were now focused on Emma. Foremost on her mind was how to save and cure her.

At that time, there was no cure for spinal spondylitis. In fact, there is no cure today. Only much improved techniques exist, which sometimes work. Other times, they do not. Her case was particularly bad because her spine was fractured in a number of places. That is, after curing the TB part, her spine needed to be fused or healed. At that time, this treatment was new and experimental.

Oskar-Helene Heim was the best hospital in Berlin, specializing in bone disorders. Emma's doctor felt that the only place which could offer help was this hospital. My mother took Emma to the hospital, and she was immediately admitted. Since my mother was employed, Emma was covered by mother's medical insurance.

As soon as the diagnosis came in, the treatment was recommended. The treatment was to put Emma in a cast and cure the TB first. The prognosis was devastating to my mother. Permanent confinement to a cast. A cast was made, and Emma now faced the prospect of being permanently confined to it.

In order to cure TB, it was necessary to consume rich foods -- butter, milk, meat and so on. The hospital did not have this kind of food. That kind of food was available only on the black market. Even standard medicine was not available in the hospital. The burden to provide the food and certain medicines now rested with my mother.

By now, we had a small stockpile of marinated mushrooms and vegetables, so my mother began trading that stockpile for the supplies and food needed for Emma. My mother was determined to save and cure her regardless of the prognosis. My mother would always say, "I have seen too many cases where the prognosis was false. I have seen too many patients that were given up by their doctors and then recovered despite the prognosis. I know this is such a case."

Be it my mother's determination, or be it an independent determination on Emma's part, I don't know, but Emma was not broken, or fatalistic about her confinement. She always insisted she would be cured. All Emma would say was that, "That cast, it means nothing. I will walk again, and I will be well again."

I would come to the hospital often. Each time I came with the intent of cheering her up. Yet it was Emma that cheered me up. I felt bad. I seemed not to be able to contribute anything to her comfort. I was not able to uplift her morale. In fact, she always improved mine.

I came one day, and my stomach was growling. Meanwhile, Emma was served her meal, not the food my mother would bring her, but the hospital food. First, she was served a soup. I think Emma heard my stomach growling. She turned to me and said, "Bruderherz... eat this soup." I refused. Emma insisted and said, "If you don't eat this soup, I will send it back." That did it. That was the magic word. Then, I agreed to eat the soup. In those days, you sent nothing back. You ate everything that was edible.

I pulled the plate, over to my side. Then, I looked at the soup, and it was water -- boiled water with a few tiny cut slivers of something floating in it. I took one spoonful, and I knew what these tiny slivers were. They were "half-cooked" onion slivers. They tasted sweet while the broth tasted salty. Disgusting, I thought to myself. How could anybody eat this? Even though I was starved, I had to force myself to eat this soup. From that day on, I developed an aversion for cooked onions.

Days turned into weeks, and weeks turned into months. Emma was still in the hospital in the cast. Her condition was not improving, but it was also not deteriorating. Her principal doctor was Dr. Heim, the leading orthopedic doctor in Berlin. Dr. Heim performed an operation to take out the puss which developed on her spine. This relieved a lot of pressure and pain for Emma. According to Dr. Heim, the only cure left was to stay in the cast from then on and let the bones heal by themselves.

Meanwhile, my mother was arranging for tutors. Emma's home became the hospital. Tutors and visitors would walk in and out all the time. The hospital actually developed a schedule, to suit Emma's needs. A time was set for tutors, and another time was set for visitors. Meanwhile, practically each day, my mother would come and bring her nutritious food which she had prepared. Each day mother would check Emma's diet and schedule. Soon, my mother became a "standard fixture" in the hospital. She would even help out on occasion -- as mother was a nurse herself.

Months turned into years. Again, her condition was not deteriorating, but it was not improving either. She was still in the cast. One day, a new doctor arrived at the hospital. This young doctor had an idea how to proceed with Emma's cure. His idea was new and unconventional. One day he came to my mother and said, "Frau Grotte, we are academicians at this hospital. What you need is a practical doctor who handles many bone injuries daily, one who must cure his patients every day." My mother was stunned. Was this hospital not the place that specialized in bone diseases? Was this not the best hospital in Berlin for Emma's ailment? My mother turned to him and said, "Where do I find this doctor?" He looked at my mother and said, "Don't get me wrong. We are the finest hospital, but look for a doctor who specializes in "sports medicine," one who has a responsibility for a team. That kind of doctor may have other forms of treatment." After this conversation, my mother had new hope, a new focus.

Sports medicine was not highly developed at that time. Her search in Berlin yielded nothing. Little did my mother know at that time, that our days in Berlin were numbered. But, when we left Berlin she did not forget this conversation and looked for a doctor in Sports Medicine.

When we left Berlin in 1949, Emma and my mother ended up in Wiesbaden, and George, Kathy and I in Cornberg. Emma was still in the cast, and my mother worked as a nurse at the hospital in Wiesbaden. My mother was trying to locate us through the IRO-DP Network, which proved useless at first. We were not DP's, and we did not qualify for any assistance. On top of that, there were no records on us anywhere within the IRO-DP Network. Meanwhile, all this relocating and boarding came out of my mother's salary. That is, while we could not be located, the number of dependents was known and my mother was charged for our daily upkeep. George was not allowed a work permit, so he became the official baby sitter. My mother ended up working two shifts to make ends meet, to make the required monthly payments.

Finally, she located us, and we were assigned to Fulda for screenings and interrogations. Our new objective was to obtain the DP status (Displaced Persons). This DP status would enable us to leave for America or Canada. It would also make us eligible for food aid and Care packages, but we did not qualify at that time. The closest orthopedic hospital to Fulda was in Hanau, so Emma was moved to Hanau and we moved to Fulda. Again, my mother worked in the hospital, and we stayed in Fulda. During that time, I saw very little of my mother.

The screenings in Fulda were incomplete because the new IRO (International Relief Organization) administration was in Mittenwald. So, we moved to Mittenwald, and Emma was moved to Gauting. Again, my mother worked in Gauting while we were screened, interrogated and debriefed.

In Gauting, my mother was the head nurse in the maternity ward. One day, they had a very difficult delivery. A woman was scheduled to deliver twins.

The first baby was delivered stillborn, and the next one was "stuck." The feet were coming out first. While another nurse tended to the woman in labor, my mother dashed to the doctor in charge to help in the delivery. My mother anticipated a difficult delivery. The doctor came to the scene and looked at the situation. Then, the doctor started to pull the baby out by its legs.

While the doctor pulled, my mother rolled up a pillow and pushed the baby from the woman's stomach. Finally, the baby was delivered. My mother looked up, and the baby was three feet long!

My mother got scared. Surely this baby was dead from this ordeal! But, she could not see one sign of anxiety in the doctor's face. The doctor placed the baby calmly on the table next to them, and proceeded to "reattach" the baby's bones!

Meticulously, he pressed each limb back into its former place! To my mother, this was nothing but a miracle. She could not believe her eyes. When the doctor finished, he said calmly, "Bundle him up very tight. In ten days he will be completely normal."

After the baby was bundled up, my mother went straight to the doctor. She was anxious to find out where and how he had learned this technique. She came up and said, "I am the nurse from the maternity ward. I have never seen anything like that!"

The doctor turned to her and said, "Glad to meet you, nurse. My name is Kulish. This is nothing," he continued, "I had much worse cases at Dynamo."

There was only one "Dynamo" he could be taking about. The soccer team from Moscow. Click, click, click went her mind. "Doctor, my daughter is in this hospital. Will you please take a look at her," she blurted out. "Be glad too," he replied.

Doctor Kulish took Emma as his patient. After all the preliminaries were completed, he came to my mother and said, "We will have your daughter up in no time at all. I want you to make a corset for her." This was music to my mother's ears. Finally, after all these tribulations, she had found someone who actually offered the prospect of a cure.

The special corset was made, and Dr. Kulish continued to work on Emma. Emma was given daily injections so the bones would heal. Actually, Doctor Kulish performed the first injection and explained every detail to my mother.

Thereafter, my mother performed the injections while Emma was still in the doctor's care. Within a few short months, Emma was ready to get up for the first time in almost six years. She was ready to take her first steps again. But, Emma could not walk. Her muscles had nearly atrophied. Emma had to learn how to walk all over again. Her muscles required extensive therapy.

As it turned out, the baby was fine. He was named Paul for two reasons: the first was that the birth date was on St. Peter and St. Paul's day, and the second was that my mother had an uncle she loved dearly whose name was Paul. When the woman did not have a name ready for the child, my mother suggested naming him Paul. The woman was very happy to do so.

That day, the woman's husband came and heard of the difficult delivery. He was elated and jubilant about his son. He went out and came back with all kinds of gifts and presents for everyone. Of course, neither the nurses nor the doctor would accept any gifts. Instead, they agreed to "throw a party" as soon as the baby was completely healed. About ten days later, they had a party, and the hero of the party was Paul. By then he was completely healed!

My mother loved to give injections. She was very good at it. She administered injections at every opportunity. Every time someone had a bad case of the "flu" or another ailment, she would give an injection. I did not like the injections, and I would always run away from her. Then, she would chase me with her "huge needle" and give it to me anyway whenever she could catch me. In a sense, Emma's cure was tailor-made for my mother's specialty, and it was followed to the letter.

In Gauting, the tutoring was also coming to an end. Emma was ready to take her Abitur, the graduation exam. The nearestGymnasium was in Oberammergau, about twelve miles away. The school was asked for special permission to give Emma the Abitur. The permission was granted. Emma went to Oberammergau in her corset, took the exam, and passed it.

****

Many thinkers, philosophers, scientists and military leaders were confined at one time or another, most against their will but some voluntarily. Descartes went into voluntary confinement to "think out" the implications of the number zero. When he came back, the implications were clear to him: An equation could be changed into a function, and the function could be characterized completely by its roots. Thus, a "revolution" began in mathematics. Modern mathematics was created. Mathematics was functionalized! Surely, many steps still had to be completed. Many great mathematicians were still to follow, but Descartes broke the gridlock which bound mathematics for 1700 years, from Archimedes to Descartes.

Enrico Fermi and his family were quarantined by Mussolini just before he was to receive his Nobel Prize. This period allowed Fermi to become introspective. He understood the madness which had overcome humanity, and he fully realized the danger his family was in. During this quarantine, Fermi found the determination to leave his beloved Italy and to collaborate with the enemy. He planned his escape in every detail, and he made good on his escape.

The capture of Vlasov is shrouded in mystery. Officially, he was captured by the Germans at Volkhov. Some of his followers say that he turned himself in, that he surrendered to the Germans voluntarily.

But, during his imprisonment, he was able to assess the methods of Stalin's rule. His conclusion was irreversible and final. Stalin had to go. A pact with the devil himself could not be worse. Most of his family had been exterminated by Stalin. His victorious soldiers from the stunning Moscow-Offensive were starving. Humanity meant nothing to Stalin. Humanity was used as convenient cannon fodder for personal worship and glorification.

Was Vlasov a traitor? Do we call Fermi a traitor? What do these men have in common?

Both men collaborated with the enemy in order to defeat their government. Both men were decorated with the highest honors their government could bestow. Yet, they changed their loyalty.

Vlasov received the Order of the Red Banner for his success against the Germans at Moscow. Fermi was promoted to the highest rank in the Italian Royal Academy for his contribution in quantum mechanics. Both men were citizens of their country when they changed their allegiance. Both men followed their conscience to combat tyranny, or bigotry, or both. Both men rose to the occasion and accepted the dictates of their conscience.

Fermi left for the United States to complete his mission. But, Fermi had many alternatives. Fermi could have gone to Brazil, to England, or to Switzerland, or to many other places. Vlasov had only two choices: to stay loyal to the Soviet Union and Stalin, or to lead the millions who were prepared to fight Stalin and Stalin's tyranny. Vlasov decided to be the voice of these millions. These millions had no opportunity to go to the Western Allies and fight with them. The only opportunity they had was to join the Germans and fight Stalin, but they wanted to be partners, not servants of the Germans. Many other nations were partners: Italy, France (Vichy), Finland, Hungary and so on. But, Hitler did not want to share in the glory of victory. Hitler believed that he could destroy Stalin with the allies he already had. An alliance with Vlasov was against his "Ostpolitik." The subjugation of the Slavs was foremost in Hitler's mind. Hitler created "Die Herrenrasse," (master race) -- the Slavs were an "Untermensch," (subhuman). For that reason, Hitler did not use this resource until the bitter end. Not until there was no hope of defeating Stalin. Vlasov's ally lost; therefore, we call Vlasov a traitor.

Fermi came to the United States and, once his loyalty was unquestionable, helped millions of Italian-Americans with his example.

Italian-Americans were relieved of curfews and travel restrictions. Italian-Americans were even drafted for the war. Italian-Americans were proud of the contributions Fermi had made to win the war for his new country. Fermi's ally won, and this country bestowed on him its highest honors. In addition, Fermi set the "brain drain" in motion, which depleted Europe of their finest minds both during and after the war. Most came to America.

Does this mean the winner takes all? Does this mean the end justifies the means? I hope I am not alone when I don't agree with this thesis.

Both men were guided by deep moral convictions. Vlasov saw how his victorious soldiers were fed starvation rations and sent out to be killed without a chance of defending themselves. Vlasov and his men had seen countless members of their families destroyed by Stalin for no reason whatsoever. Vlasov had a change of heart because his new family were his soldiers. He refused to have them slaughtered senselessly by Stalin.

By the end of the war, Hitler accepted Vlasov's terms. By then, Hitler had nothing to lose. Vlasov raised an army 900,000 strong and engaged the Soviets on the Oder. His soldiers fought in German uniform as regular German units. Yet, the Allies would not accept their surrender! Instead, the Allies allowed the Soviets to hunt them down, to kill them on the spot, and to repatriate them to forced labor.

Fermi saw how Mussolini became a puppet of Hitler's whims. He watched how humanity was cast overnight into racial classes, how his family, for no reason whatsoever, was about to be purged. His family were loyal Italians. Overnight, bigotry took over, and he found himself in a position where his family was in jeopardy. Fermi did what any family man is supposed to do in order to save his family from senseless persecution. Fermi protected his family; and his family became larger: it became humanity.

Both men saw their mission change, and both men accepted their new responsibility and their new mission. Both men became collaborators.

Germany also worked on a "doomsday" weapon. Heisenberg was the leading German physicist, but Heisenberg's staff was hopelessly depleted, mostly purged by Hitler. Some of his colleagues were dehumanized overnight. Heisenberg lacked the depth of Fermi's understanding, and Heisenberg lacked actual experimentation, which Fermi had conducted from 1936 to 1939. So, Heisenberg embarked on his own theory -- but his theory was wrong and did not produce results.

Suppose that for one moment that Heisenberg had been right, and he had succeeded in building that "doomsday" weapon, for how long would the war have continued? My guess is that we would all be speaking German now.

While we may say today that the forces Fermi unleashed should have stayed hidden from humanity, we tend to stress the wrong applications. Fermi showed us only what the new physics was capable of doing. The applications were up to us. The urgency and the direction of the application was not mandated by Fermi. There were countless other uses. We chose one path, one direction which was urgent at that time.

CHAPTER 12

Freedom and Liberty

Here we were, all together again. We were sitting in the Tempelhof Airport terminal in Berlin waiting for our plane. Our baggage had been sent out a few days earlier, and all we had was carryon baggage. Scheduled flights hardly existed in those days. Cargo flights brought the food, fuel, and supplies to Berlin, and we were scheduled to leave Berlin on one of those cargo flights. But, there was only one hitch: Emma.

Emma was with us. Emma was strapped to a stretcher and wrapped in a huge down blanket. She was in a cast, and the huge down blanket was wrapped about three times around the cast and Emma. Five straps held Emma, her cast, and her down blanket in place. She looked just like a mummy. Only her nose was sticking out from the down blanket.

It was cold. It was January 6, 1949. We were sitting on our baggage waiting for a plane. From time to time, an airport official would come over and say, "Frau Grotte, you have to wait some more. All I am getting now is coal and cargo -- I cannot let your daughter on those planes. Soon, very soon, I expect a hospital plane." Then, he would leave us.

I was very excited. This was my first flight! I had visions of flying next to the pilot, guiding a "big bird" to our destination. Instead, I cuddled up to my mother and asked, "How did you manage to get us a plane? A whole plane?" She looked at me sadly and said, "Do you really want to know?" I nodded very intensely and said, "Please, tell me the whole story and leave nothing out. You hear? Nothing." And, she began: "When the market in the Tiergarten disappeared, I still had to trade with the Soviets so we could eat. Except now, I had to travel to 'them' because they were not coming to the market. I had to find a Soviet settlement, and I found one at Wustermark, near Potsdam."

"One day I filled my knapsack with three large pieces of fabric: You know, the kind they really like -- English wool. Then I took the train to Wustermark."

"Berlin was full of East Prussians, and many speak perfect Russian. So, I decided to act as an East Prussian and talk to them in Russian."

"I arrived at Wustermark and spotted their settlement right away. You know they build these prefabricated buildings in rows and rows. And, I walked into the settlement. I had walked about fifty paces into the settlement when I saw a car pull up. Out of the car came a real general. He had this cap and stripes and every conceivable medal on his uniform. He spotted me and yelled out to me, "You there, who are you? What are you doing here?" I answered him, 'I am a German. I am trying to sell some fine English fabric for three suits,' and I went closer to him."

"He looked at me and my knapsack and said, 'This area is off limits to civilians. This is a soldier town. Take your knapsack and get out of here.' I was sad and started to turn when he called out again, 'Go down a stretch, that way,' and he pointed a finger, '...the families live there, and I am sure someone can use good English fabric.' I thanked him and walked in the direction he had pointed."

"After a short walk, I could see the settlement he was referring too. I walked into the settlement and was determined to knock on every door until I had sold the fabric. But, when I arrived at the very first door, I heard a child crying and a woman screaming. So, I just ran inside."

"There was a woman and a little boy at a sewing machine. The boy had one finger pierced by the needle and could not get his finger out. The boy was crying, his mother was screaming, and a maid stood there with her hand over her face. Nobody was doing anything to help the boy. So, I walked up and gently rolled back the wheel, and the needle came out. As soon as the needle came out, the boy pulled out his hand and started jumping, but he was also crying at the same time. I asked his mother for some iodine and bandages. She yelled at the maid to get her husband and the medicine. The maid ran out and came right back with the iodine and bandages. Meanwhile, I had washed out the wound. Then, I put on some iodine and bandaged the boy's finger."

"No sooner had I finished, when the woman's husband arrived. He was elated and thankful that his son was taken care of. Then, he turned to me and said, 'Who are you and what are you doing here?' And I replied, 'I am a German and I am trying to sell some good English fabric for a suit.' And he said, 'Show me.'"

"I pulled out the fabric, and I knew that he liked it. He looked at me and asked, 'How much?' I told him, and he bought all the fabric I had in my knapsack. Then, he handed me another two hundred Marks and filled my knapsack with bread, cooked bacon, flour, and dried milk until the knapsack was bulging. Then, he said, 'Whenever you have something to sell, you come to me first. My name is Senzov.' I thanked him, took my knapsack, and left."

"From then on, every time I had something to sell, I would go to Senzov first; and he would either buy it or find a buyer for me. One day, after I made a sale, he asked me if I knew how to cook. He meant if I knew how to cook Russian food. I understood right away, and I said, 'Of course: Pirogy, Piroshky, Borscht, Kasha, Kapusta and much more.' He was excited and asked me if I would come and cook for him one weekend for he was having a party. I agreed, but only on the condition that I would stay in the kitchen and be the cook and that I would not have to mingle with his guests. I felt it was too dangerous for me to be seen by his guests. He agreed. Then, he asked me, 'I have someone who wants to buy two Silver Foxes. Can you get them?' And, I said, 'Maybe, I'll try. But, Silver Foxes are very expensive at least 10,000 Marks.' He smiled and said, 'Price is no object here. Just get the best quality if you can.' We said good-by, and I left for home."

"As soon as I came home, I went to the furrier -- you know, the one we always deal with when we have such a request. He showed me two of the finest Silver Foxes I have ever seen. He wanted only 4,000 Marks for each. I took the silver foxes home -- you know, he always trusted me."

"That weekend, I went to the Senzov's early and took the Silver Foxes with me. I cooked and baked all day. Senzov was very happy, and he filled my knapsack with bread, butter, cooked bacon, dried milk and other things until it was full and bursting. In the late afternoon, he came with a couple. He introduced them as Mr. and Mrs. Shutenko. She was the buyer for the silver foxes. She looked at the silver foxes, and she was excited. All she said was, 'I take them, how much?' I said, 'Ten thousand Marks for both.' She looked at me and said, 'I don't have the cash, but

I will give you four large suitcases packed to the brim with "papirossy" (Russian cigarettes).' I was aghast. Only a little while ago "papirossy" were still popular, and four suitcases, were worth twice as much but now that English and American cigarettes were on the market, the bottom had dropped out. Nobody wanted them anymore. Western cigarettes were ten marks a piece, yet there was virtually no market for her "papirossy. So, I had to decline the offer. But, the question was how?"

"I racked my brain for a good answer. Then I told her, 'I can't take four suitcases of merchandise. There are checkpoints on the way. I will be searched, and the merchandise will be confiscated for sure. The foxes are not mine. The seller expects cash. I am sorry, but I cannot make the deal.' I could see that she was upset. She and her husband left. In the evening, I went home and returned the silver foxes to the furrier."

"For my next trip to the Senzov's, I got a beautiful leather coat. You know how they like leather coats -- it was bought on the spot. Again, Senzov loaded me up with food in addition to the money for the coat. We parted and I walked to the train station. Then, I heard footsteps behind me. I turned, and there was Shutenko with two soldiers behind him. He passed me, turned around and faced me. Then, he called out loud:

'You are arrested! You are an English spy!'

"The two soldiers grabbed me under the arm. Shutenko led the way, and the two soldiers dragged me behind him. They took me to a building and into a cellar. There, they took my money, my identification card, and my knapsack. Then, I was thrown into a cell and fell down."

"The cell was empty, but freshly painted. Only a small stool stood in the middle of the cellar room. I got up and sat on the stool. I don't know how long I sat there, but I kept praying to be strong enough not to give any of our friends away. You know, the other Russians we know, because surely they would be deported right away."

"Sometime the next morning, two guards came to my cell and took me upstairs into a large room. There was a giant table in the middle of the room, and in front of the table stood a stool. Behind the table sat Shutenko. The guards plopped me on the stool. Shutenko stood up, came toward me and, called out loud, 'Confess you English spy!'

"And I replied, 'I am a German. I sell merchandise and if you want to arrest me for that, then go ahead. But, I have no idea of what you are talking about.'" "The next thing I know, I saw stars and was on the floor. He hit me with his fist, with all his might, on my right ear. I could feel how the blood was flowing down my cheek. And, he yelled again, 'Confess you English spy! Confess! I want to know the names of your leader. The names of your fellow spies!'

"The soldiers picked me up and put me back on the stool, and I just repeated what I had told him before. I was praying now because I was afraid that I would never see any of you again."

"Shutenko just motioned to the soldiers, and they led me away. Back to the cellar. Then, a guard brought me a slice of bread and a cup of water. Even though I was hungry, thirsty and hurting, I decided not to touch anything. I cleaned off the blood and prayed to God to let me die in peace."

"I sat on that stool for a long time. Then, a guard came and took the bread and water away. I sat there all day. In the evening, I slept on the cement floor. It was cold, but I was so tired that I slept a few hours anyway. The next morning, a guard brought me, again, a slice of bread and a cup of water. And again, I touched nothing. Then, in the afternoon a guard came and led me to a toilet. Then, it was back to my cell. The bread and water were gone. Just the stool was there. I just sat on that stool and prayed."

"The third day passed the same way. But, at night two guards came and dragged me out again into Shutenko's office. Again they seated me on the stool. And again Shutenko yelled at me, and again, I gave him my reply. Then, a general entered the room. The general pulled up a chair and started questioning:

'Who are you?' and I told him: 'I am German.'
'What are you doing here?' and I told him, 'Selling goods.'
'Where do you live?' and I told him, 'Klopstockstrasse 18'
'Who are your neighbors?' and I told him, 'Germans.'
'Who lives below you?' and I told him, 'A sculptor.'
'Who lives next to you? and I told him, 'Dr. Derz.'

"At that point the general stopped. Dr. Derz was the leader of the liberal party in Berlin. He knew it. Then, he turned to me and said:

'I am going to let you go. I am going to return all your things. But, remember this: One word of this incident to anyone, and we are going to get you! Do you understand?' "Then he continued:

'I am going to give you two escorts to take you to the station. Just remember, not a word to anyone!'

"A guard stepped forward and put my knapsack next to me. Then, the guard put my things on the table, on Shutenko's table. Even the money for the leather coat was there."

"I understood too well. But, I still had my doubts. I could see the clock on the wall. It was two o'clock in the morning. I knew they were going to shoot me on the way to the station. I could see the headline in the newspapers: Soviets Kill Spy as Spy Makes an Escape."

"I turned to the general and said, 'Please let me stay in the cell until the morning. The trains start running at six o'clock, and it is bitter cold outside.' I could see how the general and Shutenko exchanged looks. Then, the general turned to me and said:

'That's fine. Go back into the cellar and I will send an escort in the morning.'

"Of course, they had my papers. The information I gave them was in my papers. The only thing they did not know about was Dr. Derz, that he was my neighbor. Maybe, I thought, just maybe, they might let me go. I took my things, and the guard took me to the cellar."

"All I kept saying to myself was, 'Stay calm. Stay calm. Maybe the ordeal is really over.' And, I walked to the stool and sat down."

"A few hours later, a Kalmuck soldier came into my cell. He looked at me and said, 'Who are you that they let you go? Do you know this is the headquarters for "Smersh"? Not too many people leave this place alive!' I only put on my knapsack and followed him out of the building."

"We walked a short distance, and I could see how many people were hurrying to the station. It was cold outside, and I was still alive. Maybe, they were letting me go, I thought."

"We came to the station, and the Kalmuck soldier turned around and left without a word. I went inside the station. Now I was trembling, not from the cold but from the fear. I think I was trembling the whole ride home. When I got home, George fell on his knees and prayed, 'Thank God you are back.' He had to say no more.

I told the incident to George, in all its detail. We thought about it and decided that on the next occasion we would go to the English commandant of our sector. We would tell the truth about our past and ask for political asylum. With things being as they were, there was a better chance now to be freed. We were getting our things ready when there was a knock on our door. I opened it, and there stood a well-dressed gentleman. I looked at him and said, "Who are you?" He told me his name and then he said, "Are you Frau Grotte?" And, I said, "I am. What do you want?" And, he said it was an emergency and could he come in. So, I let him in.

He came in and said, "Can you lend me one hundred Marks? I have to go to Hamburg, and I am short on cash. I will make this inconvenience worth your while." I looked at him and said, "I have no money. I have only three starving children. Who sent you to me?"

He looked at me and said, "Herr Schneider," as he pulled out a silver cigarette case. He opened it, and it was full of English cigarettes -- at least twenty. I could see them. If this man needed one hundred Marks, all he had to do was to sell ten cigarettes!

While I talked with the stranger, George excused himself to go shopping. Actually, George went directly to Schneider and inquired about this man. Schneider denied having sent anybody over. George knew that sending this man to our home was just a ploy to get us all! That man worked for the KGB.

When George arrived, we knew we did not have a moment to waste. We took Kathy, and we went directly to the English commandant. We told our whole story. The commandant gave us political asylum and told us to be ready to leave in three days. Meanwhile, he promised that during that time, we would not be repatriated. Not from his sector!

I asked if I could have ten days because Emma would need three days all by herself. He granted us ten days. We packed and sold whatever we could not take with us.

Three days ago we sent our baggage, and now we are waiting for the plane to take us to freedom and liberty.

The airport attendant came over to us again, "Frau Grotte, I am sorry, but I can not place your daughter on a plane today. I promise you that in three days, I will have a plane for your daughter. I promise," he said. Then he continued, "I can put everybody else on board right now." "What are we to do? We have no place to go!" my mother replied. Then, she continued, "I can not leave Emma by herself! George, why don't you leave with the kids right now, and I'll stay with Emma and join you in three days," my mother said.

George just stood there. Then, he stuttered, "Where are you going to sleep for two nights? You cannot go back. 'They' will be waiting for you!"

My mother just turned to the airport attendant and asked, "Can I have an ambulance to take Emma to the hospital?"

"Of course," he said.

"Well, then it is all done. You go with the kids, and I will stay with Emma," my mother's decision was final.

The attendant directed us to the plane. We left my mother and Emma in the Tempelhof Airport. Only much later, was I told what happened in those three days.

As soon as the ambulance came, my mother went back with Emma to the hospital. Once they were there, my mother worked at the hospital for the three days. This took care of the food she and Emma needed.

The first night, she decided to spend with a friend, Lala. But, when my mother arrived, Lala was not at home. Neighbors let my mother in. Lala had a huge bed with two or three fluffy down blankets. My mother was very tired and fell asleep. When she fell asleep, she rolled herself into one of the down blankets. Lala came home late that night. When she went to bed, she discovered that there was another "body" in her bed. Lala raised a ruckus and stopped only when she discovered it was my mother. By then, all the neighbors were out and banging on Lala's door. Eventually, Lala calmed them down. My mother and Lala ended up staying up all night talking.

The next day, my mother went to work. After work, she decided to go over to our fortress and say farewell to our super. As she walked up the street, the super came "jogging" down the street. As the super approached my mother, she told her to turn around and "jog" with her. My mother did. While they were "jogging" along, the super told her that the "Reds" were at the house and searching for us in every apartment. They had the truck outside and were determined to find us. My mother went straight to Lala and stayed under the covers all night. The next day, she worked half a day. When the ambulance came, Emma and my mother went to the airport. The airport attendant had a plane for them as promised. But their plane flew back to Wiesbaden; whereas, our plane had taken us to Cornberg.

In any event, our family reached freedom and liberty at last.

Printed in the United States
By Bookmasters